A Labor of Love:
AL & JOANNA LACY'S

HANNAH of FORT BRIDGER SERIES

OTHER BOOKS BY AL LACY

Angel of Mercy series:
A Promise for Breanna (Book One)
Faithful Heart (Book Two)
Captive Set Free (Book Three)
A Dream Fulfilled (Book Four)
Suffer the Little Children (Book Five)
Whither Thou Goest (Book Six)
Final Justice (Book Seven)
Things Not Seen (Book Eight)
Not by Might (Book Nine)
Far Above Rubies (Book Ten)

Journeys of the Stranger series:
Legacy (Book One)
Silent Abduction (Book Two)
Blizzard (Book Three)
Tears of the Sun (Book Four)
Circle of Fire (Book Five)
Quiet Thunder (Book Six)
Snow Ghost (Book Seven)

Battles of Destiny (Civil War series):
Beloved Enemy (Battle of First Bull Run)
A Heart Divided (Battle of Mobile Bay)
A Promise Unbroken (Battle of Rich Mountain)
Shadowed Memories (Battle of Shiloh)
Joy from Ashes (Battle of Fredericksburg)
Season of Valor (Battle of Gettysburg)
Wings of the Wind (Battle of Antietam)
Turn of Glory (Battle of Chancellorsville)

Hannah of Fort Bridger series (coauthored with JoAnna Lacy):
Under the Distant Sky (Book One)
Consider the Lilies (Book Two)
No Place for Fear (Book Three)
Pillow of Stone (Book Four)
The Perfect Gift (Book Five)
Touch of Compassion (Book Six)
Beyond the Valley (Book Seven)

Mail Order Bride series (coauthored with JoAnna Lacy):
Secrets of the Heart (Book One)
A Time to Love (Book Two)
Tender Flame (Book Three)
Blessed Are the Merciful (Book Four)
Ransom of Love (Book Five)
Until the Daybreak (Book Six)
Sincerely Yours (Book Seven)

DAMASCUS JOURNEY

BOOK EIGHT

AL AND JOANNA LACY

Multnomah•Publishers *Sisters, Oregon*

This book is a work of fiction. With the exception of recognized historical figures, the characters in this novel are fictional. Any resemblance to actual persons, living or dead, is purely coincidental.

DAMASCUS JOURNEY
© 2001 by ALJO PRODUCTIONS, INC.

published by Multnomah Publishers, Inc.

International Standard Book Number: 1-57673-630-X

Cover illustration by Frank Ordaz
Cover design by Left Coast Design

The Holy Bible, King James Version (KJV)

Multnomah is a trademark of Multnomah Publishers, Inc.,
and is registered in the U.S. Patent and Trademark Office.
The colophon is a trademark of Multnomah Publishers, Inc.

Printed in the United States of America

ALL RIGHTS RESERVED
No part of this publication may be reproduced, stored in a retrieval system, or transmitted, in any form or by any means—electronic, mechanical, photocopying, recording, or otherwise—without prior written permission.

For information:
Multnomah Publishers, Inc.•Post Office Box 1720•Sisters, Oregon 97759

Library of Congress Cataloging–in–Publication Data
Lacy, Al.
   Damascus journey /c by Al and JoAnna Lacy.
      p.cm.—(Hannah of Fort Bridger series ; bk. 8)
   ISBN 1-57673-630-X (pbk.)
   1. Women pioneers—Fiction. 2. Jewish pioneers—Fiction.
3. Fort Bridger (Wyo.)—Fiction. I. Lacy, JoAnna. II. Title.
   PS3562.A256 D36 2001   813'.54—dc21   00-011790

01 02 03 04 05 06—10 9 8 7 6 5 4 3 2 1 0

And as he journeyed, he came near Damascus: and suddenly
there shined round about him a light from heaven:
And he fell to the earth, and heard a voice saying to him,
Saul, Saul, why persecutest thou me?

And he said, Who art thou, Lord? And the Lord said,
I am Jesus whom thou persecutest: it is hard for thee
to kick against the pricks.
And he trembling and astonished said,
Lord, what wilt thou have me to do?
And the Lord said unto him, Arise, and go into the city, and
it shall be told thee what thou must do.

ACTS 9:3–6

This book is affectionately dedicated to
Connie Bennett,
our dear Christian neighbor, devoted fan, and faithful friend.
We love you!

EPHESIANS 1:2

CHAPTER ONE

The cavalry unit of sixteen men and one civilian rode out of Helena, Montana, at ten o'clock in the morning on Tuesday, August 8, 1871, and headed northeast toward Fort Logan.

The fort was on the Smith River, some thirty miles from Helena, which would take them through a narrow canyon in the rugged Big Belt Mountains into a twenty-mile-wide valley that stretched all the way to the Little Belt Mountains. Both ranges were segments of the northern Rocky Mountains and were encircled with belts of limestone.

It was almost noon as the column of riders rode the blistering, sunbaked prairie and neared the lower slopes of the Big Belts, which were covered with thick oak brush. Just above the oak brush, the shimmering aspen trees skirted the mountains, and higher still—all the way to the rocky peaks—the towering blue spruce cast their deep shadows. Periodically, each man shoved his hat back and mopped his forehead with his bandanna, while keeping a sharp eye out for Indians.

When they reached the gurgling stream that flowed out of the canyon they were about to enter, they stopped to water the horses and fill their canteens. They took a few minutes to eat some beef jerky and hardtack, then mounted up and rode cautiously between the lofty rock walls of the canyon, appreciating the cool contrast of the shade to riding in the sweltering heat of the sun.

It was just after four o'clock that afternoon when Colonel Cole Hammer sat at his desk, writing a letter, and his attention was drawn to a knock at his door. "Yes, Corporal?"

The latch clicked and the hinges complained as the door came open. Corporal Bob Whalen said, "Colonel, the unit you sent to Helena has returned, and I have Pastor Lee out here."

"Good!" exclaimed Hammer. "Bring him in."

When Pastor Wayne Lee was ushered into the office, Colonel Hammer rounded the desk, saying, "Thank you for coming, Preacher! It's good to see you again."

The two men shook hands, then with a puzzled look on his face, Lee said, "Lieutenant Carson didn't even give me a hint as to what you wanted to see me about, Colonel. I pressed him hard all the way from Helena, but all he would say was that he was not at liberty to discuss it with me. He said you had specifically commanded him to keep mum."

"That I did, Pastor," said Hammer. "I wanted to tell you about it myself. Here, sit down in this chair in front of the desk. May I offer you some refreshments?"

"Something cool to drink would be great," said Lee, removing his hat. "It's been a long, hard ride from town."

"I could use something myself," said Hammer as he hurried toward the door. Opening it, he ordered Corporal Whalen to bring some lemonade and oatmeal cookies from the fort's kitchen.

When Hammer returned to his desk and sat down, Lee said, "So I assume whatever it is you want to discuss with me has to be quite important."

"Yes. Very important. Are you aware of the attack the Blackfeet launched on the fort on Sunday?"

"I heard about it yesterday, but there were no details in the information going around town."

"Well, the attack came when I was leading my men into a battle with the Shoshonis some ten miles to the north, up the Smith River. As usual, I had left a detail of men to guard the fort. The Blackfeet used the depth of the river to swim underneath the surface from around the bend and spring a sudden attack. There were about a hundred warriors, I am told. I had left some sixty men here."

Lee was moving his head back and forth, his brow puckered.

Hammer sighed. "It was bad, Preacher. The Blackfeet caught everybody in the fort off guard. They came out of the river quickly, storming the walls and the gates. It all happened so suddenly that they caught many of the women and children in vulnerable places all over the compound. Our gallant men were able to send them scurrying for the gates and walls within minutes, but not before three soldiers were killed and six wounded. Two officers' wives were killed, and three children."

"Oh no," Lee said.

Hammer drew a deep breath, let it out slowly, and said in a tight voice, "One of the wives killed was Mary Kirkland."

Lee's jaw slacked and his eyes widened.

Before he could speak, Hammer went on. "One of the children killed was the Kirklands' five-month-old son, Donnie. Mary had Donnie in her arms when the attack came and was running across the compound toward shelter when Blackfeet guns cut her down from behind. One of the bullets went through her body and killed the baby."

Lee's face was white. Shaking his head, he said, "This...this is terrible. And what about Dane, Colonel? How's he taking this?"

"Very hard. We were battle weary when we returned at sundown and found that the Blackfeet had attacked the fort. Having several wounded men and four dead ones with us was bad enough, but we were stunned beyond belief when we found the carnage here. When Captain Kirkland viewed the bodies of his wife and little son, he broke down and had to be escorted to his house on officers' row by two of the men.

"The other officer whose wife was killed, Pastor, was Lieutenant Darrel Whitmore. I believe you've met him."

"Yes."

"Well, Lieutenant Whitmore was killed that day in the battle with the Shoshonis."

Lee bit his lower lip. "I'm so sorry to hear this."

Hammer sighed. "The parents of the other two children who were killed are being counseled by the chaplain, but I felt that since the Kirklands are members of your church, it should be you who counsels Captain Kirkland; and it should be you who conducts the funeral service for Mary and the baby."

"Of course. I'd better go to Dane. Is he at his house?"

"Yes, but he's probably still asleep. The fort doctor gave him a strong sedative about three and a half hours ago. Said he'd sleep about four hours. You've got time for those refreshments, which should be showing up any minute."

There was a light tap on the door.

"Ah, here they are now," said Hammer. "Come in, Corporal!"

The adjutant entered, bearing a tray with a pitcher of lemonade, two cups, and a plate of oatmeal cookies.

When Corporal Whalen was gone, the preacher eyed the cookies and said, "My appetite has deserted me, Colonel. I can't eat any of the cookies, but I will take some lemonade."

While Hammer was pouring lemonade into the cups, Lee said, "It's hard to believe that Mary and little Donnie are gone. It is almost inconceivable how rapidly one's seemingly well-ordered life can be snatched away, even at an army fort."

"That it is, Pastor," said Hammer as he set Lee's cup before him.

Lee took a couple of swallows. "The Bible talks a lot about our frail life here on earth and how unsure tomorrow is. There's that passage in James that says, 'Whereas ye know not what shall be on the morrow. For what is your life? It is even a vapour, that appeareth for a little time, and then vanisheth away.' We never know when we wake up on any given morning, but what it could be our last day on earth. As I so often say in my sermons, the most important thing in life is to be ready to face death."

Hammer nodded. "And nobody's ready to do that unless they know our Lord Jesus Christ, Pastor."

"Amen, Colonel," said the preacher. He downed his lemonade, stood up, ran a shaky hand over his face, and said, "I'd better get on over to the Kirkland house. Dane's probably awake by now."

The colonel rose to his feet. While rounding the desk, he said, "The burials are slated for tomorrow morning, Pastor. Chaplain Downing is set to conduct the other funeral services, but if you can stay over and take care of the services for Mary and Donnie, we can send a wire to your wife and let her know what has happened. After the services, I'll have a cavalry unit escort you home."

"Of course I can stay, Colonel," said Lee.

"Good. I know it will mean a lot to Captain Kirkland to have you here."

The preacher picked up his hat, clamped it on his balding head, and took a deep breath. "My heart is so heavy for Dane."

Colonel Hammer placed his hand on Lee's back and gave him a reassuring pat.

The pastor weakly smiled his thanks, and headed for the door. Hammer followed him into the outer office and watched him step outside and head across the compound toward officers' row.

Turning to Corporal Bob Whalen, who sat at his desk, he sighed and said, "I wouldn't want that preacher's job."

CHAPTER TWO

I t was a banner day in Fort Bridger, Wyoming, on Saturday, September 23, 1871, for a double wedding was taking place at the church.

A cool afternoon breeze wafted over the mountains, hills, and plains of southern Wyoming as the people in the crowded church building looked on while Pastor Andy Kelly had the couples repeat their vows. When the grooms had kissed their brides, Kelly asked the couples to turn and face the audience.

Many in the crowd were wiping tears from their cheeks as the pastor smiled broadly and said, "It is with great pleasure that I introduce to you Dr. and Mrs. Patrick O'Brien and Marshal and Mrs. Lance Mangum."

Organist Lila Sparrow pumped hard and played fast lilting music, and the couples—faces beaming—hurried up the aisle and out the front door of the church. Those who comprised the separate wedding parties followed on their heels.

Moments later in the church's fellowship hall, the people crowded in to see the happy couples standing behind tables that bore two identical wedding cakes. Dr. and Mrs. Frank O'Brien were standing close by their son and new daughter-in-law's table, their own faces beaming. Patrick had done them proud by marrying Sundi Lindgren, the town's schoolmarm.

Town marshal Lance Mangum had married Heidi Lindgren, Sundi's sister, who was two years older. Being owner and operator of Heidi's Dress Shop, Heidi had made both wedding dresses with the assistance of Julianna Bower, wife of Fort Bridger's deputy marshal, Jack Bower. Julianna had proven herself a competent seamstress and often helped Heidi in the shop when the workload became heavy.

Glenda Williams had made the cakes in the kitchen of her café, Glenda's Place.

While people were still filing into the fellowship hall, many of the women who stood close by were complimenting Sundi and Heidi on their identical dresses. The sisters smiled at each other as the compliments came one after another. They had agreed that they wanted their wedding dresses stylish but simple. They had chosen white on white stiff dotted Swiss material over the palest of pink taffeta slips and wide crinoline petticoats.

Heidi's veil was attached to a circlet of pink and white flowers, while Sundi's veil was attached to an old comb of silver engraved with flowers. Their golden hair and fair skin were beautifully accentuated by the pastel colors and their faces were aglow with happiness.

The Lindgren sisters had experienced a great deal of sorrow in their young lives, but at that moment, they allowed only happy thoughts to enter their minds.

At one spot in front of the tables, Adam Cooper—Hannah's brother-in-law—and Doug McClain of the *Fort Bridger Bugle* set up a camera. Pictures of the newly married couples would go on the front page of Monday's edition of the town's new and only newspaper.

As Sundi stood beside her physician husband waiting for everyone to arrive, she looked at her joyful sister at the next table and thought of just over an hour ago when they were in a Sunday school room, dressing for this most special occasion...

Sundi giggled at something Heidi had said as she was adjusting her sister's veil, then said, "Honey, this is a day we will never live again. Let's make happy memories that will last forever."

"Yes, let's do that," said Heidi, turning to embrace her sister.

They hugged each other tightly, with tears threatening to well up in their eyes and spill down rosy cheeks.

Heidi and Sundi missed their parents dreadfully, and both were trusting that they were looking down from heaven's portals, ready to observe the double wedding.

The sisters successfully held back the tears, and as they pulled apart, they heard the organ begin playing in the auditorium. Bright smiles lit their faces.

"Oh, Sundi," said Heidi. "God has been so good to us."

"So very good," agreed Sundi. "Now, if you'll make sure my veil is just right, we'll go join our bridesmaids."

"Yes," said Heidi, making a slight adjustment of the veil, "and in just a few minutes, we'll go meet our nervous, waiting grooms and begin the first day of our lives as Mrs. Patrick O'Brien and Mrs. Lance Mangum!"

Careful of their finery, they joined arms and left the room...

Sundi saw Pastor Andy Kelly weaving his way through the crowd, leading his wife, Rebecca, by the hand. Both Kellys smiled at the couples, then they turned around, faced the bright-eyed onlookers, and said, "Well, folks, it's time to cut the cakes."

Kelly offered a brief prayer, then the cakes were cut and the reception was under way. Soon people were passing by the newly married couples congratulating them and wishing them well.

Sundi was being hugged by Sweet Blossom, squaw of Two Moons, chief of the Crow village nearby. While Sweet Blossom was speaking softly into Sundi's ear, the new bride looked up and saw that Hannah Cooper and her family were just moving away from the Mangums, and were next in line to greet Patrick and herself. With them was Jacob Kates, manager of Cooper's General Store.

As the Indians moved on, Hannah motioned for her children to move ahead of her. Six-year-old Patty Ruth was first. This was the precocious redheaded child's first year in school, and Sundi was thrilled to have her in her class.

When Patty Ruth looked up into her teacher's eyes, she smiled warmly and said, "Congratulations, Miss Lindgr—" Patty Ruth's hand went to her mouth. "I mean, Mrs. O'Brien," she said, giggling.

Sundi bent down and said, "I see your front teeth have grown in enough so you don't lisp anymore, Patty Ruth."

"Yeah, now my brothers can't tease me anymore."

Sundi and Patty Ruth shared a special hug, then came Mary Beth, who would turn fourteen next month. Next was the oldest Cooper son, Chris, followed by nine-year-old B. J., who was carrying his baby brother, Eddie, now six months old. Patrick took Eddie from his big brother, hefted him, and said, "Eddie, you're a husky boy. Your papa would be real proud of you."

"Oh, Papa is proud of him, Dr. O'Brien," said B. J. "He looks down from heaven every day and watches him grow."

"Can't argue with that, B. J.," said Patrick.

Hannah embraced Sundi, and both were shedding tears.

"Sundi, I'm so glad for you," said Hannah. "I know you and Patrick are going to be very happy...even as Heidi and Lance will be."

"Of course," said Sundi. "First of all because we have the Lord. Second, because we have each other, but also because we have wonderful friends like you to make our lives happy."

Hannah kissed her cheek and said, "This is for you, and I have one more left for the doctor, here."

There was a chuckle from the doctor, who said, "You'd better save me a kiss, Hannah. After all, I'm never going to have another one, so I have to make the best of it today!"

Since there was no time for either of the couples to take a honeymoon trip, they were in church the next day. Heidi and Sundi sang a duet in the morning service, their faces still glowing as they had at the wedding the day before.

On Monday it was back to the normal routine for the doctor and the schoolmarm, and for the marshal and the dressmaker. As they parted in their separate homes, each going to their own jobs, their minds were filled with rejoicing, each looking forward to the end of the day when they could return home again and be with the one they loved.

As Sundi walked toward the schoolhouse, she prayed, "Lord, please help my husband in his work today. Give him wisdom as he takes care of the sick, and bless him with just Yourself."

As she met people on the street, Sundi greeted them with a smile that mirrored the joy that bubbled in her heart. Everyone who met her along the way felt better for it.

Heidi's countenance was the same as her sister's as she walked the opposite direction toward the dress shop. Her radiant smile and the warmth of her personality brightened the day for people who met her along the street.

As Heidi neared the shop, she said, "Dear Lord, as I have prayed for Lance ever since I fell in love with him...please keep Your hand on him this day. That badge on his chest makes him vulnerable to every outlaw and troublemaker who rides into this town."

Heidi smiled when she saw Julianna Bower cross the street and head toward the shop door. They would be working together today on dress orders that came in last week. Thinking of Julianna's husband, she said, "And, Lord, please keep your hand on Jack, too, as he sides Lance this day."

After waiting on a couple of customers who were at the door of the general store when they opened up for the day, Hannah and Jacob took advantage of the lull that followed to stock shelves. Little Eddie played nearby while his mother and Jacob worked side by side.

As Jacob handed Hannah five-pound bags of flour to place on a shelf, he said, "I'm so glad your parents have been able to come and stay for these two months. Have they said anything about when they plan to go home to Missouri?"

"No," replied Hannah. "They are enjoying their stay, and nobody in my household has said one word to them about when they might go home. The children and I are so happy to have them in Fort Bridger. We'd like for them just to move here. In our prayer time each night, we're praying that they will."

Jacob nodded. "It sure is nice of Gary and Glenda to put them up at the hotel for free."

"As small as our apartment is, there's just no way we could keep Mama and Papa. Gary and Glenda are so kind and generous to do this for us."

"I understand that both your parents help around the hotel to sort of earn their room."

"Papa does small repairs, and Mama not only cleans their room, but helps the maids at times when they need it."

"Have you any idea if they're thinking they might move here?"

"Well, both of them have said things that sort of tell me it has crossed their minds. They seem to have aged considerably just since Solomon and I left Independence to move here a little more than a year ago. I'd love to have them near so I could keep an eye on them and take care of their needs as they grow older."

"That would be good," said Jacob, placing the last flour sack in her hand. "Well, that takes care of this section."

"All right. Want to do another one?"

"Not right now. I need to go to the hardware store. Since things are quiet at the moment, I think I'll do that right now, if that's all right with you."

"Certainly," Hannah said with a smile. "You go on. Eddie and I will keep an eye on the store."

Jacob hurried out the door and walked briskly down the boardwalk toward the Fort Bridger Hardware Store and Gun Shop, greeting people along the way. Just as he reached the store, the door opened, and the owner, Justin Powell, came out.

Powell smiled and said, "Good morning, Jacob."

"And the same to you, Justin. You leaving?"

"Yes, but my new man, Bill Wolfram, will take care of you. Have you met him, yet?"

"I did. He came into the store a couple of days after arriving in Fort Bridger, but we only had a few seconds to talk."

"You'll like Bill. He's a nice guy. See you later, Jacob."

"Sure enough," said Jacob, and moved inside.

Bill Wolfram, who was in his early thirties, was behind the counter and smiled as Jacob approached. "Good morning, Mr. Kates. What can I do for you?"

"I need a new wood file, Bill. I'm making Hannah's little Eddie a crib and a little toy horse, and my file broke."

Moving out from behind the counter, Wolfram said, "Let's go back here where the files are. I'm sure you'll find one that'll work."

It only took a few seconds to pick out the file Jacob wanted. They returned to the counter, Jacob paid Wolfram, then said, "You've been in Fort Bridger for better than two weeks, now, Bill. You liking your job and the town all right?"

"I sure am. Lots of friendly people here, and I really like the Powells. They're nice folks to work for."

"So, if you don't mind my asking, where did you come from and what brought you to Fort Bridger?"

"Well, I was living in Cheyenne City, working in a hardware store there, and was engaged to a young woman."

"I can see it in your eyes," said Jacob. "Something bad happened."

"Yeah. Nelda left me for another man just a month before we were to be married."

"I'm sorry."

Wolfram sighed. "I was so grieved over it that I couldn't stay in Cheyenne City. Nelda would still be living there. I couldn't have stood it to see her with this other guy. So a couple of days after she left me, I quit my job, got on my horse, and rode west out of town. I went to Laramie first and tried to get a job in the hardware store there, but they didn't need me. So I kept moving west, trying to find a job. Since hardware is what I know best, I wanted to stay with it. I tried in Rock Springs and Green River, but neither of those hardware stores had jobs open. When I came to Fort Bridger and talked to Justin Powell, it just so happened that Justin's business was doing so good that he had decided only days previously to look for a man to hire. So with my experience in the hardware business, Justin hired me. Of course, as you probably know, Justin pretty well takes care of the gun shop. I can sell guns, all right, but when it comes to repair, I know nothing about it."

"He'll probably teach you if you want to learn gun repair," said Jacob. "I'm sure sorry for the way that woman treated you, Bill. But maybe you'll find another one who'll treat you right."

"I sure hope so."

"Well, I'd better get going. Business will be picking up right soon, and Hannah will need me at the store."

It was almost six o'clock on Tuesday evening as Hannah, her mother, and Mary Beth were about ready to dish up supper and put it on the table. A savory aroma filled the entire apartment.

Chris, Patty Ruth, and Grandpa Singleton were in the parlor area with Eddie. Looking toward them, Hannah said, "Patty Ruth, will you go to the boys' room and tell B.J. it's almost time to eat, please?"

"Yes, ma'am," said Patty Ruth, and hurried toward the rear of the apartment.

Hannah glanced toward the door and said to her mother and Mary Beth, "I wonder what's keeping Jacob. He's never late for supper."

Overhearing her words from the parlor area, Ben Singleton said, "You want me to go down and tell Jacob supper's ready, Hannah?"

Before Hannah could reply, Patty Ruth came running into the kitchen, saying, "Mama, B. J.'s not in his room." Biggie, the family's pet rat terrier, was on her heels.

"He's not? Where could he possibly—Oh, then he's got to be downstairs with Jacob. Usually B. J. can smell pork chops a mile away. I'm surprised he isn't in here at the table with fork in hand." Turning toward the parlor, she said, "Chris, will you save Grandpa the steps and go down and tell those two that supper is ready?"

Just as Chris opened the door to do is mother's bidding, everyone heard a clattering on the stairs. Chris stepped out onto the deck, smiled when he saw what his brother and Uncle Jacob were carrying up the stairs, and stepped back into the apartment. "Mama, you're going to love this."

Hannah headed toward the door, and the others followed, including Biggie. Ben had Eddie in his arms.

Jacob and B. J. were just reaching the top of the stairs with the crib when Hannah stepped through the door. Her eyes widened, and her hands went to her mouth. "Oh, Jacob, it's beautiful! Little Eddie's going to love it! And the way he's growing, he really needs it."

"That's what I figured," Jacob said as he and B. J. set the cradle down for her inspection. The grandparents and the rest of the Coopers gathered around the crib.

"Look, Eddie!" said Ben. "That's your new crib! Uncle Jacob made it for you."

Tears rushed to Hannah's eyes as she hugged the little man. "Jacob, you precious dear! You've been keeping a secret from me." Even as she spoke, tears of delight rained down her cheeks. "Thank you! You are such a good friend. What would this family ever do without you?"

Easing back, Jacob looked into her watery eyes through tears of his own. "And what would I have done without you, Hannah? When I came here, I was destitute. You gave me a job and a home. I'll always be grateful. You and these wonderful children have given me love like I have never known since my precious wife died so many years ago."

Chris announced that he and B. J. would carry the crib inside, and Mary Beth held the door wide for them.

Patty Ruth stepped up to her baby brother who was still in his grandfather's arms, took hold of a fat foot, and jiggling it, said, "Wasn't it nice of Uncle Jacob to make that crib for you, Eddie?"

The baby smiled at her and gurgled a wordless reply.

As the boys entered the apartment and headed for the hall that led to their mother's bedroom, B. J. sniffed the mouth-watering aroma and said, "Hey, we're having pork chops! Yippee, let's eat!"

"Not till we get this crib to Mama's room," said Chris.

Following them, Hannah said, "Mama, Mary Beth, I'm going to show the boys where I want the crib. If you'll go ahead and dish up the food, we'll all be ready to sit down in a few minutes."

"Consider it done, dear," said Esther Singleton.

When her sons carried the crib into her bedroom, Hannah moved a chair that stood against an inside wall and had them stand the crib in its place.

"Is it where you want it, Mama?" Chris asked.

Hannah ran a hand along the dark, smooth wood of the crib, nodded, and said, "Yes, honey. Exactly. Let's go eat before we have to mop up your brother's drool!"

When supper was over, and B. J. had made four pork chops disappear along with a substantial amount from all the side dishes, Hannah set adoring eyes on him and said, "There's still another pork chop on the platter, B. J."

The boy raised a palm toward her, and shaking his head, said, "Mama, I can't possibly eat another bite."

Letting her eyes roam the other faces, Hannah said, "Anybody want that last pork chop?"

When everyone else had refused, Patty Ruth said, "Biggie will eat it, Mama."

"Oh, really?" said Hannah, raising her eyebrows. "After the generous portions you have been smuggling him under the table, do you really think Biggie could eat that whole pork chop?"

Patty Ruth's freckled face crimsoned.

Jacob scooted his chair back, ran his gaze around the table, and said, "Please excuse me. I have to go down to my quarters for a moment. I'll be right back."

Hannah picked Eddie up off the blanket where he was

lying on the floor, laid him on her lap, and looked at B. J. "Does Uncle Jacob have some other big secret?"

Shrugging his shoulders, the boy said, "Not that I know of."

"It was awfully sweet of him to make that crib," said Esther.

"Uncle Jacob is such a nice man, Grandma," spoke up Mary Beth. "I want to see him saved so very much."

Ben was about to comment when the sound of the little man coming up the stairs met their ears.

When Jacob appeared, he had one hand behind his back and a sly grin on his face. As he drew near the table, he said, "I have something else for the newest member of the Cooper family."

Stepping up to Hannah, he bent down, grinned at the baby on her lap, and brought his hand around. In his grasp was the toy horse. "There you are, Eddie! I carved it with my own hands."

Eddie reached for it with his chubby hands, smiling broadly. Instantly, the horse's muzzle went in his mouth. There was laughter all around the table.

"Don't worry, Hannah," said Jacob, "it's clean."

Hannah chuckled, then said, "Oh, Jacob, you are just full of happy surprises tonight! I thank you again with all of my heart."

A lopsided grin graced Jacob's wrinkled features. "It's my pleasure, Hannah."

Patty Ruth spoke up. "Mama, before we do the dishes and clean up the kitchen, could we all go and see where you put Eddie's crib in your room?"

"Yes!" said Mary Beth, "I want to see."

Rising with the baby in her arms, Hanna supported the horse—whose muzzle was still in Eddie's mouth—and led the troops down the hall. When everybody was in the room, they all agreed that the crib fit best where it stood.

Hannah asked Mary Beth and Patty Ruth to place a couple of pillows from her bed in the crib so she could let Eddie try it out. When it was done and she placed Eddie in the crib with the horse still in his hands, he giggled and kicked his fat legs.

"He likes it!" said B. J.

"I knew he would," said Patty Ruth.

Hannah turned to Jacob, who stood beside her, laid a hand on his arm, and said, "Jacob, the cradle you made for Eddie before he was born is such a treasure to me. I will always keep it."

Jacob gave her a warm smile.

"That cradle was the very first bed for my little Eddie," she said, running her gaze over the faces that formed a half-circle around her. "But the first bed for the little Lord Jesus was a manger in a stable in Bethlehem."

Jacob said, "It's too bad Jesus' father hadn't made better arrangements and made sure he had a nice clean room somewhere for his wife to give birth to their child."

Hannah gave him a slight smile and said softly, "Joseph was not the father of Jesus Christ, Jacob. Jesus is the virgin-born Son of God. You know the thirty-nine books of the Old Testament, and you know that Isaiah 7:14 foretold that Messiah would be born of a virgin."

"Well, yes, but—"

"Jesus came into this world to die for sinners on the cross as the Lamb of God, Jacob, which Isaiah chapter 53 states that Messiah would do. He wouldn't be born in a nice clean room somewhere but in a stable, where lambs are born. The fact that He was born in a stable and laid in a manger was arranged by God. It was all in His perfect plan."

"But Hannah," said Jacob in a kind and gentle tone, "what Isaiah wrote would be true of the Jews' Messiah, but He hasn't come into the world yet."

Tears misted Hannah's eyes. She knew her family was praying in their hearts for this man they loved so dearly. "Jacob, Jesus Christ *is* the true Messiah, and if you will just give Him a chance to speak to you through His Word, He will make it so clear that you will see it and understand it."

Jacob said weakly, "I don't mean to be rude, Hannah, but I really need to get back down to my quarters."

Hannah hugged him once more, and said, "Of course. We'll talk more about this later."

The Cooper children hugged Uncle Jacob, telling him good night, and thanking him once more for what he had done for Eddie. Jacob told each one he loved them, repeated it to Hannah, and said the same thing to the Singletons as he headed for the door.

Hannah turned to her parents and said, "I've witnessed to Jacob little by little ever since he came to Fort Bridger and went to work for me in the store, but he will only listen for short periods then gets very nervous and has something he needs to do. My heart goes out to him."

"Chris and B. J. and I have said little things to him now and then," said Mary Beth. "He is always polite but tries not to hear what we're saying. We all want Uncle Jacob to see that Jesus is the true Messiah and Saviour."

Deep lines penciled themselves across Ben's brow. "Hannah, kids, I'm sure you will win Jacob to Jesus if you keep loving him and keep showing him with Scripture that Jesus is the promised Messiah. The Holy Spirit can use the Word to convince him, even as He has many other Jewish people."

Tears were streaming down Mary Beth's cheeks. "Uncle Jacob just has to get saved, Grandpa. He just *has* to. I want him in heaven with us."

CHAPTER THREE

T he Montana sun was halfway up the morning sky
when Lieutenant Lloyd Carson's cavalry unit trotted
through the gate at Fort Logan with Pastor Wayne Lee
amongst them. There was a creak of dusty saddle leather and
the clank of canteens and metal gear that blended with the
muffled thumping of hooves on the soft earth of the compound.

Lee thanked the lieutenant and his men for the escort,
then veered his horse toward the colonel's office.

As Carson and his men trotted toward the stable, other
uniformed men glanced at them from the smithy shed, the bar-
racks doors, and the quartermaster's porch.

Hauling up in front of Colonel Cole Hammer's office, Lee
dismounted, spoke to two soldiers who were passing by, and
stepped up on the porch. Suddenly the door came open, and
Corporal Bob Whalen moved out and said, "Nice to see you,
Pastor Lee. I just told Colonel Hammer you're here. His office
door's open. Just go on in. I'll go get Captain Kirkland."

Whalen dashed across the compound to officers' row and
knocked on Captain Dane Kirkland's door. The tired face and
sad eyes of Kirkland appeared. "Hello, Corporal," said Kirkland,
offering him a thin smile.

"Colonel Hammer sent me to get you, sir. Pastor Lee is
here, and they want to talk to you."

"Oh? I didn't know Pastor Lee was coming today."

"I didn't either, sir," said Whalen. "Must be something special."

Kirkland lifted his campaign hat off a peg by the door, placed it on his head, and said, "Well, let's go."

Moments later, the captain entered Colonel Hammer's office, was welcomed by the colonel and the preacher, and the three of them sat down at a small table.

Hammer said, "Captain, I have kept in touch with Pastor Lee about the counseling sessions he has had with you each week since Mary and Donnie were killed. At the beginning, I asked him to just give me a brief report after each time he had counseled you."

"Pastor Lee told me you had requested this, sir," said Kirkland, "and I appreciate your concern about me."

Hammer smiled. "After your counseling session yesterday, the two of us discussed the situation at length. We agreed that you are still weighted down so heavily over the deaths of your wife and baby son that you can't function properly as a leader of men."

"I'm sorry, sir, that I have not been the soldier I ought to be, but the loss of Mary and Donnie is ever with me. I have asked the Lord to take the pain away, but so far, it just keeps hurting. And...and I know it's because there is so much all around here to remind me of them."

"That's the key to it, Dane," said Lee. "I told Colonel Hammer that I have seen you gaining at least a measure of strength from the Lord through these counseling sessions, and I believe to a degree, you've learned better how to lean on His everlasting arms. Wouldn't you say so?"

"Yes, Pastor. The Lord has used you to be a tremendous help to me, and indeed, He has given me strength. But every day I wake up in the house where Mary and Donnie used to be, and they're gone. And it isn't just the house. Every day I picture

Mary walking across the compound carrying Donnie. I see them at the sutter's store. I see them at the laundry shack, and at other places where the women gather. It's the whole place. So many memories."

Lee nodded. "It's been my experience in the ministry, Dane, that people are different. With some, it helps when someone dear has been taken from them in death to stay near the constant reminders. But with others, it is the opposite. The constant reminders are a source of pain and further heartache."

"This is your case, Captain," said the colonel, "and that's why I talked to your pastor, here, about getting you transferred to another fort."

"Oh?"

"We feel it would be best for you to get away from Fort Logan," said Lee. "We know you're a career man and wouldn't want to leave the army, but it is obvious that things cannot go on as they are. Being here just keeps the memories too fresh."

Tears welled up in the captain's eyes. "I…I thought about asking for a transfer, Colonel, but I didn't feel I should approach you about it. You worked hard with Washington to get me here in the first place."

"That I did," said Hammer, "and you've been even more than I expected in your service here. You're a born soldier and leader of men. But this tragedy has taken its toll on you."

Lowering his head, Dane wiped the tears from his eyes. Swallowing hard, he raised his head and his sad eyes went from one man to the other. "I know the Lord never fails, and I feel His peace and strength, but the constant reminders continue to tear me apart. It's especially hard when I walk past the very spot on the compound where they fell."

Having his well-worn Bible in hand, Lee began flipping pages.

Colonel Hammer laid a firm hand on Kirkland's shoulder. "Don't feel guilty, Captain. We each handle grief in a different way. Your pastor and I want to do what is best for you and will make it possible for you to continue your life in the army. I'm going to wire army headquarters in Washington, explain the situation, and request that you be transferred to another fort. I think it would be best if it was in another territory...get you completely out of Montana."

"Though I will miss having you in the church, Dane," said Lee, "it is best for you and that's what matters."

"I appreciate your attitude, Pastor," said Dane. Then he said to Hammer, "And, Colonel, I thank you for being so understanding. I will await my orders and trust God to see that I am sent where He wants me."

The preacher had the Bible lying open on his lap. "Dane, I've taken you to many Scripture passages in our counseling sessions. Let me read you a couple more."

"I can always use more of that wonderful Book, Pastor."

Lee smiled. "The first one is Isaiah 49:13. 'Sing, O heavens; and be joyful, O earth; and break forth into singing, O mountains: for the LORD hath comforted his people, and will have mercy upon his afflicted.' Dane, the heavens, the earth, and the mountains have good reason to sing joyfully. The Lord does comfort His people, and He does have mercy on His people who are afflicted. You certainly are in need of comfort and mercy from your heavenly Father. This has been a horrible ordeal for you, but better days are ahead of you, my brother. God's comfort and mercy will be more and more evident as time passes."

Lee flipped more pages. "Dane, here's the other one I want to read to you. Isaiah 58:9, the first half of the verse. 'Then shalt thou call, and the LORD shall answer; thou shalt cry, and he shall say, Here I am.' I know you've been calling and crying to the Lord with all of this agony in your heart."

"That I have, Pastor."

"Then listen for that still, small voice to say, 'Here I am.'

He is with you every step of the way, Dane, and you will hear His comforting voice in the depths of your soul if you will listen for it."

Tears were in Dane Kirkland's eyes again as he set them on his pastor and friend and said in a low, heartfelt tone, "Thank you. I'm going to commit these passages to memory and let them comfort and encourage me in the days to come."

"Good," said the preacher. "You will always find God's Word sufficient."

Colonel Hammer rose from his chair. "I'm going to work on my wording for the wire, Captain, and I'll let you know as soon as I get a reply."

Dane and the preacher stood up.

"Thank you, Colonel," said Dane, extending his hand. Hammer met it, and they gripped each other firmly.

Dane then turned and gripped the preacher's hand in the same manner. "Pastor, we'll advise you when my orders come from Washington. And thank you, again, for what you've done for me."

"I'm glad God gave me the privilege," said Lee.

The colonel and the preacher accompanied the captain to the outside door and watched him as he headed across the parade ground toward officers' row. They noted that he walked a little straighter, and his head was not hanging so low as before.

On the second Monday in October, Jacob Kates was eating supper with Hannah Cooper and her children. Chris brought up something Pastor Andy Kelly had said in the morning service the day before about how the gospel had been given to the Jews first, then to the Gentiles.

"Yes," said Hannah, noticing Jacob's ears perk up when the Jews were mentioned. "I thought the Pastor did a marvelous job of showing how God had planned it that way from the very beginning because Israel was His chosen earthly nation, and through Israel the Messiah would come."

"And it was so good when Pastor went to Matthew 15," said Mary Beth, "and pointed out that Gentile woman from Canaan who came to Jesus, wanting Him to deliver her daughter who was vexed with a devil. And Jesus told her He was not sent but unto the lost sheep of the house of Israel. But even though she and her daughter were Gentiles, she wouldn't give up."

"Yeah," said Chris, "and when Jesus saw her faith, He said how great it was and delivered her daughter."

"And it was so good the way Pastor brought his sermon to a close by going to Romans and pointing out that Paul could say there was no difference between the Jews and the Gentiles, that the same Lord is rich unto all that call upon Him for salvation."

Everybody at the table could see that the conversation had Jacob's rapt attention.

"Mr. Carver's lesson in my Sunday school class was sort of tied with Pastor's sermon," spoke up B. J.

"How was that, honey?" asked Hannah.

"Well, you said a minute ago that God had it planned that the Messiah would come through Israel. I don't think most of the boys in our class had ever realized that Jesus was a Jew. I sure hadn't. It really surprised me. Mr. Carver said that even though God was Jesus' Father, since His mother, Mary, was a Jew, Jesus was a Jew."

Chris chuckled. "I remember how surprised I was to find that out when I was about your age, B. J."

There was a brief silence, then Patty Ruth said, "Uncle Jacob, you're a Jew too, aren't you? Just like Jesus."

Jacob's face tinted slightly. "Yes, honey."

Patty Ruth grinned from ear to ear. "I think that's neat."

"Uncle Jacob, it *is* true that your Messiah had to be a Jew, right?" Mary Beth said.

When a nervous Jacob told Mary Beth that was correct, Hannah said, "Jacob, this brings up what we were talking about that evening when you gave Eddie his crib and toy horse. We were going to discuss it further. Could you stay after supper so I can show you some more things in the Bible about Jesus?"

Jacob felt a cold ball form in his stomach. Forcing a smile, he said, "Yes. I guess I could stay for a little while."

After supper, Hannah and Jacob sat in the parlor area of the apartment with the children gathered around. Mary Beth was holding little Eddie. Jacob was a bit fidgety as Hannah opened her Bible. She went first to the Old Testament and read several prophecies about Israel's promised Messiah. With each one, Hannah asked Jacob if the prophecy was definitely about the Messiah, and he agreed that it was.

Hannah then carefully showed him in the New Testament how every one of the prophecies they had looked at were fulfilled by Jesus Christ.

Trying not to show it, Jacob was stunned at what he saw.

"What do you think about what I just showed you, Jacob?" Hannah asked.

Jacob cleared his throat. "Well, I…ah…I will have to think about it, Hannah."

"Good enough," she said. "When you've had sufficient time to ponder it, we'll talk about it again. All right?"

"All right," he said, pressing a smile on his lips.

That night as Hannah prayed with her children before they went to sleep, each child prayed for Uncle Jacob's salvation.

On the second Tuesday in October, a lone rider drew up at the gate of the Bar-W ranch a few miles west of Medicine Bow,

Wyoming. Two cowboys were riding toward the gate with the ranch house, barn, and outbuildings in the distance behind them.

Touching spurs to his mount, the lone rider trotted toward them and smiled as they drew rein.

"Howdy," said the lone rider. "You fellas work here at the ranch?"

"Well, we put in our time," said the long, slender one.

"Yeah," the short, chubby one said, "we even work once in a while. You lookin' for a job?"

"Ah, no. Actually, I'm lookin' for a man I was told is one of the cowhands here on the Bar-W. Spike Denny. He and I are old friends. I just happened to be passin' through town, and havin' heard that he was workin' at the Bar-W, I thought I'd come by and see him."

"Oh, sure," said the lanky one. "Spike's at the bunkhouse right now. Can't miss it. It's the log buildin' just north of the barn and corral."

"Much obliged," said the lone rider, smiling.

Putting the horse to a gallop, he raced across the level land, waving at a cowhand who showed himself friendly near the ranch house and slowed as he passed it and drew near the bunkhouse.

Two more men were just coming out of the bunkhouse as he reined in and slid from the saddle. "Howdy," he said to them, "I was told by a couple of your hands that Spike Denny is in there."

"Shore is," said one. "He's playin' checkers with a couple guys."

Stepping through the door, the lone rider spotted three men at a small table in a corner, and one of them was Denny. None of them had looked up, but all three did as he stepped to the table.

Suddenly Denny shoved is chair back, stood up, and said

with a wide smile, "Well, shoot me now and bury me later! If it ain't my ol' pal, Rafe!"

The two old friends shook hands, then Spike said, "What are you doin' in these parts, and how'd you find me, Rafe?"

"Well, if you could break away from this checker game and we could have a few minutes together, I'd answer your questions."

"Well, of course! Judd Walters and Barry Smythe, meet Rafe Ketcham."

Both men nodded at Ketcham, then Spike said, "I was about to beat you two dudes, anyhow. Start yourselves a new game. I'll see you later."

When the two old friends stepped out on the bunkhouse porch, Spike said, "Let's take a walk out toward the creek."

Rafe followed Spike's line of sight and his gaze focused on a winding creek lined with cottonwood trees. As they moved that direction, Rafe said, "Been a long time since our days in the old Jake Mallory gang."

"Sure has. What, about seven years now?"

"More like eight."

"Time gets by, doesn't it? So what are you doin' now?"

"Still on the outlaw trail…hittin' banks and stagecoaches. Train robbery now and then. But mostly banks. Looks like you've settled down to an honest life of ranchin'."

"Yeah. After Jake was killed and the gang split up, I got into another gang down in New Mexico. Didn't do too good, so I ended up takin' a steady job on a ranch in Colorado. Coupla years later, I came up here and hired on with Jim Wright."

"So's it goin' okay for you?"

"Oh, so-so. Not much pay in this business."

There was a brief silence, then Rafe said, "Ever think about goin' back on the outlaw trail?"

"Every time my pockets get empty before payday rolls around. You keepin' your pockets stuffed?"

"Pretty well. Some of the banks we've hit lately didn't have as much around as we thought they would, but I'm still doin' a lot better than you, I can tell you that for sure."

They were drawing up to the creek. Cattle were drinking from it about fifty yards upstream.

"So tell me, Rafe," said Spike, "how did you find me?"

"Well, the gang I'm runnin' with is holed up in an abandoned farmhouse over by Rock Springs. Couple of us were in Medicine Bow yesterday afternoon, lookin' the bank over, and I happened to spot you when you came out of the Gun Barrel Saloon. You said somethin' to an old codger there on the boardwalk, then jumped on your horse and took off before I could get to you."

"Oh, so that's it. You asked Abner Perkins if he knew where I lived."

"That's it."

They stopped on the bank of the creek. Letting his eyes drift up to the spot where the cattle were drinking, Spike said, "Well, I'm sure glad you took the time to ride over here and pay me a visit. It's good to see you."

Rafe bent down, picked up a fist-sized rock, tossed it into the creek and said, "Actually, Spike, this is more than just a social call. I'm here on business, too."

"What kind of business?"

"When I got back to the hideout yesterday afternoon, I talked to the boss and told him about you and me bein' in the old gang together, and that I'd seen you over at Medicine Bow. His name's Dutch Hendrix."

Spike's eyebrows arched. "Dutch Hendrix! I've heard about his gang. Got lawmen pullin' their hair out all over Wyomin'. Didn't know you were runnin' with Hendrix."

"Well, now you do…and I'm here to ask if you'd like to join the gang."

Spike's eyes widened. "Really?"

"Dutch likes to have four other men in the gang besides himself. Well, we've been runnin' one man short since early August. You'd be fillin' Mo Froggate's place if you'd join the gang. When I told Dutch about you yesterday, he got excited and said for me to ride over here today and recruit you if I could. How about it? I guarantee you'll line your pockets real good."

A grin spread over Spike's face. "Well, since my ol' pal Rafe Ketcham is in the gang, and I'm bein' offered a spot, I'd be a fool to pass it by. Spike Denny knows a good deal when he sees one."

When Ketcham and Denny arrived at the hideout, Dutch Hendrix was alone in the old farmhouse, and welcomed Denny into the gang. At that time, gang member Durbin Mitchell came in from the barn, and Hendrix introduced him to Denny.

Rafe looked around and said, "Where's Rex?"

"He's in Rock Springs buyin' ammunition and supplies," said Dutch. "Should be back pretty soon. Did you explain to Spike that we've been runnin' a bit short in what we're gettin' from the banks lately?"

"No details. Just mentioned it to him."

"Well, let's sit down here and let me explain it so you'll get the picture, Spike," said Dutch. "This shortage of cash-on-hand started last week, Spike, when we hit the bank over in Rawlins. I never saw a bank in a town the size of Rawlins that had less than a thousand dollars in their vault, but that one did. Then a couple days later, we hit the bank in Lamont, and they only had six hundred dollars in their vault."

"Strange."

"And then just day before yesterday, we hit the bank in Saratoga, and they only had a little over eight hundred in their vault. In each one of those, we cleaned out the tellers' cages, of course, but still…it ain't natural to be carryin' so little cash in them banks."

Spike rubbed his jaw. "Sounds to me like they were expectin' you."

"That's my assessment of it," put in Rafe. "I think because we've been pullin' so many bank robberies in southern Wyomin', they're stashin' their money elsewhere and only keepin' a limited supply 'cause they're expectin' the Dutch Hendrix gang to show up."

Spike looked at the gang leader. "Dutch, maybe it's time to put Wyomin' behind you and head for fresh territory. Colorado or Nebraska. Or maybe even Dakota Territory."

Dutch began moving his head back and forth.

"I know why you're shakin' your head, Dutch," said Durbin, "but not only are the banks catchin' on, but one of these days some posse is gonna catch up to us."

Dutch eyed Mitchell stonily. "Since you know why I'm shakin' my head, Durbin, why waste your breath? You know we ain't leavin' these parts till I get my hands on that low-down Mo Froggate."

"But Mo's probably hightailed it to some distant place by now," Durbin said.

"You know how much he loves Wyomin'. Especially the southern half. I tell you, I've got this gut feelin' that dirty rat is still around these parts, and is probably clerkin' in a hardware store under an assumed name, actin' like he's poor."

Spike said, "Dutch, since I'm takin' this Mo Froggate's place, how about fillin' me in on him? Rafe didn't tell me much. I think he was wantin' to let you fill me in."

"Okay," Dutch said. "Right off, I'm tellin' you…Mo Froggate is a dead man. I'm gonna catch up to that snake in the grass, and when I do—he's a dead man!"

Spike licked his lips. "I'm listenin'."

"Well, Mo and I had a fallin' out one night in early August

at a hideout we had near Cheyenne City. He was actin' like he might be wantin' to be boss of this outfit, so I called his hand on it. He denied that was his intention, sayin' he just wanted more say about what went on in our holdups and robberies. We had us a hot argument. It still wasn't settled by the time the gang hit the sack that night, and I was too tired to go on with it, so I told him we'd finish our talk the next mornin', and if he wasn't ready to pull in his horns, he could ride.

"Well, that next mornin', when me and the rest of the boys got up, that low-down Froggate was gone. That would've been all right, except fifty thousand dollars of the gang's money that I had stashed in a closet upstairs was gone, too." Dutch's face was crimson. He hissed through clenched teeth, "That's why I told you, Spike—Mo Froggate is a dead man."

Spike said, "I don't blame you. How long had Mo been with you?"

"Four years. I met him up in Billings when I went into the hardware store there to buy somethin'. He was complainin' about the low pay he was gettin'. I was needin' another man, so I met with him privately later that day and talked him into joinin' the gang. Wish now I'd never done it." Dutch took a deep breath. "The need to catch that dirty, ungrateful thief is festerin' inside me, Spike. My life is gonna be miserable till he pays for what he did. I've *got* to find him."

"Hey, boss," spoke up Durbin Mitchell, who happened to be looking out the parlor window. "Rex is back."

CHAPTER FOUR

E very eye was on Rex Holt as he entered the front door of the old farmhouse, carrying a heavily loaded canvas bag in each hand. His line of sight flashed to the face of the stranger, then he said, "Got everything we needed, Dutch. Who's this?"

"An old friend of mine," spoke up Rafe Ketcham. "Set those bags down and shake hands with Spike Denny."

Spike stepped up to Holt, and as they shook hands, Rafe said, "Spike and I used to be in a gang together years ago. He's takin' Mo's place. Believe me, he's top notch."

As the two men released each other's hand, Holt smiled and said, "Welcome to the Hendrix bunch, Spike. Any friend of Rafe's is a friend of mine."

Holt then ran his gaze over the faces of the other gang members and said, "I've got some interesting news. While I was in the hardware store and gun shop buyin' ammunition, the Rock Springs Wells Fargo agent came in. While he was waitin' for the proprietor to finish up with me, he got to talkin' to him and told him about an important shipment one of his stagecoaches would be haulin' in a few days.

"After the proprietor finished up with me, the two of them went into a back room to talk. Instead of leavin' the store, I tiptoed to the door of the back room and eavesdropped. I learned that the stagecoach is gonna be haulin' a large amount of cash exactly a week from today from the bank in Green River to its new affiliate bank in Evanston."

Dutch's eyes were bright. "Did you hear the Fargo agent say how much cash there'll be?"

"If he told the proprietor, it had to have been when they first stepped into the back room. But I figure it has to be a pretty good chunk of change to open up a bank."

"Be enough to go after, that's for sure," said Rafe.

Rex grinned. "The Fargo agent said the regular cash box, normally kept under the driver's seat, will have a little money in it as a decoy for potential robbers, but the large amount of cash will be in a normal-looking suitcase in the overhead rack with the rest of the luggage."

Dutch leaped to his feet, rubbing his hands together briskly. "Rex, you've done yourself proud! This'll make up for the last three banks that cheated us!" He paced a moment, still rubbing his hands together. When he stopped, he looked around at his men and said, "We'll waylay the stage between Green River and Fort Bridger. In the meantime, we'll stay holed up right here, except that yours truly is gonna check the hardware stores in every town in this part of Wyomin'. I've got to find that slitherin' snake, Mo Froggate."

On a Friday afternoon in Fort Bridger, Chris Cooper and his best friend Travis Carlin walked home from school together and went to the Carlin home inside the fort. It was warm for a fall day in southern Wyoming, and Donna Carlin had placed lemonade and cookies on a small table on the front porch for the boys.

While the boys were enjoying their cookies and lemonade, Chris said, "Travis, when will your dad be back from Montana?"

"He and his men are supposed to be back either today or tomorrow."

"So where'd they go in Montana?"

"Fort Logan. I'm not exactly sure where Fort Logan is, but Dad said it's in the central part of the territory north and south, and on the western side."

"How come Colonel Bateman sent them there?"

"From what Dad told mom and me, it was to escort a Captain Dane Kirkland from Fort Logan to Fort Bridger. Indian threat, you know."

"Yeah."

"Dad said Captain Kirkland has been assigned to Fort Bridger because back in August, a war party of Blackfeet attacked the fort, and Captain Kirkland's wife and baby were killed."

Chris shook his head. "Aw…that had to have been tough."

"Yeah. Dad said that Captain Kirkland has had a hard time with them being killed, and is being assigned to Fort Bridger in order to get him away from the scene where it happened."

"I sure hope when I become an army officer, something like that doesn't happen to my wife and children if I have them."

"It's things like that that keep me from committing myself to being a soldier when I grow up."

"Your dad isn't pushing you toward a military career, is he?"

"I think he would like it if I did, but he's told me several times that he wants me to do what I feel is best for my life."

"If my father was alive today, he'd tell me the same thing. But I can't picture myself being anything other than an army officer." The boys talked about other careers for some time, then there was a stirring at the front gate of the fort.

Travis pointed toward the gate and said, "Look, Chris! There's Dad and his unit now."

Rising to their feet, the two fifteen-year-olds watched with interest as the dusty riders filed into the fort. All but two guided their horses toward the stable. Lieutenant Dobie Carlin and the man with captain's bars on his shoulders rode to the commandant's office and dismounted.

Travis hurried to the front door of the house, opened it, and called, "Mom, Dad's home!"

As Travis moved back to stand beside his friend, he saw Colonel Ross Bateman come out of his office and greet Captain Kirkland.

While the commandant chatted with the captain and Lieutenant Dobie Carlin, Mrs. Carlin came out and stood on the porch beside the boys.

"Thank the Lord they're home safely," said Donna.

Chris noted the position of the sun in the western sky and said, "I'd better be getting home. Mama will have my hide if I'm late for supper. Thank you, Mrs. Carlin, for the cookies and lemonade. See you at church Sunday, Travis. I'll be busy all day tomorrow doing things for my mother at the store."

As Chris hurried toward the gate, he kept his eyes on the three officers talking in front of the colonel's office. The man with the captain's bars on his shoulders had a sad look in his eyes. Lieutenant Dobie Carlin happened to notice Chris. He smiled and waved to him. Chris waved back.

While Carlin was waving to Chris, Colonel Ross Bateman said to the man with the sad face, "Captain, I'm very glad that the powers that be in Washington decided to send you here."

"I am too, sir," said Dane Kirkland. "If the rest of the men in Fort Bridger are like Lieutenant Carlin and the other men who escorted me here, I know I'm going to like it."

"They are, I assure you," said Bateman. "Well, Captain, I'll have Lieutenant Carlin take you to the officers' quarters and let you get settled in your room. You will be eating with Mrs. Bateman and me this evening. Lieutenant Carlin will show you my house. If you'll be there by six o'clock, Mrs. Bateman will be ready to feed you."

"Thank you, Colonel," said Kirkland. "I won't be late."

"You'll enjoy Mrs. Bateman's cooking, Captain," said Dobie. "I promise."

When the two men were in Kirkland's room, Dobie said, "I told Pastor Kelly about you, and I know he's eager to meet you as soon as possible. I'd be glad to take you to the parsonage and introduce you to him and his wife after you've eaten with the Batemans."

"That would be good. I'm looking forward to meeting him. It has already helped just to get away from Fort Logan."

"Okay, I'll show you my house while I'm pointing the Bateman house out to you. When you're done with supper, just come and knock on my door, and I'll take you to the parsonage in town. Then, so I won't interfere with your time with the pastor, I'll head on back home. That all right?"

"You wouldn't be interfering as far as I'm concerned, my friend, but I'm sure you need to be home with your family."

"All right. But let me say something right here. Anything I can do for you—I mean anything—you let me know."

"Thank you, Dobie," said Dane. "You've been a tremendous encouragement to me already."

"I'm glad. I sure want to be. Since there are a few minutes left before I escort you to the colonel's house, let's pray together."

"I'd like that," said Kirkland.

Laying a hand on the captain's shoulder, Dobie Carlin led in prayer, asking the Lord to give Dane peace and strength, and to give Pastor Kelly the wisdom to help him.

It was after ten o'clock that night when Captain Dane Kirkland left the parsonage and walked down Main Street toward the fort, which was on the town's northwest side.

A cool breeze swept through the town and moaned

through the trees that lined the street, rustling the leaves that were turning yellow and gold.

The wild yelps of coyotes could be heard just outside of town in the darkness, mingled with the howl of a lonely wolf somewhere in the distance. The wolf's doleful cry made Dane think of his own loneliness with Mary and Donnie gone. He shook his head and immediately did as Pastor Andy Kelly had told him to do.

"Lord," he said, swallowing the lump in his throat, "I need Your special grace right now. I'm hurting. Please ease my pain as only You can do. Right now, Lord. Please." He stopped, took a deep breath, and after a few seconds said, "Thank You, Lord. You did exactly what the pastor said You would. Your amazing grace is on me, and I sense Your glorious presence right now. Thank You."

His pain of heart and soul lightened measurably, as if the Lord had come physically and wrapped His arms around him.

Dane took another deep breath and looked at the heavens above him. The sky was a wonderful pitch-black dome, spangled with white stars. He breathed another prayer of thanks, and moved on down the street.

The town's street lamps were burning on the corners on each side of the street, creating great rings of light at the intersections, but leaving the middle of each block in the business district in deep shadows.

As Captain Kirkland crossed one intersection and headed into the shadows in the next block, he saw a dark form emerge from a door. Just above the door, he could make out the large letters on a sign overhead that informed him it was the marshal's office. As he drew closer, the figure became clearer, and he saw that the man was tall and broad-shouldered. A soft glint of reflected lamplight from the man's chest told him it was coming from a badge.

The lawman saw Kirkland, and as they drew up, facing

each other, he said, "Good evening, soldier. I'm Marshal Lance Mangum. I can see enough of your face to know that we haven't met. You must be new at the fort."

"Yes, Marshal," said the captain, extending his hand. "I'm Captain Dane Kirkland. I was transferred here from Fort Logan, Montana. Just got in today. Lieutenant Dobie Carlin headed up the unit that escorted me here through hostile Indian country."

After they had shaken hands, Mangum said, "Just taking a late-night walk, Captain?"

"No, sir. I won't go into it now, since you're probably on your way home, but I've just been to see Pastor Andy Kelly at the parsonage."

"Are you a Christian then?"

"Yes, sir, I am."

A smile broke over the marshal's face that was clearly visible, even in the shadows. "Well, Captain, I'm one of those born-again fellows, myself. Just young in the Lord, but I'm growing and walking closer to Him all the time."

"Well, wonderful, Marshal! It's always good to meet a brother in Christ. I hope we get to know each other real well."

"I'm sure we will. You'll be coming to church whenever possible, won't you?"

"I'm planning on being there Sunday."

"Great! I'll see you there. Well, I'll be moving on. Got to get home to my new bride."

Though it felt like an icicle had been plunged into his heart, Dane covered it well, and said, "Newlyweds, eh?"

"Three weeks. I guess that still qualifies us as newlyweds, doesn't it?"

"I'd say so."

"You married, Captain?"

"I...ah...was, Marshal. My wife is dead."

"Oh, me and my big mouth. I'm so sorry."

"Please don't be. You had no way of knowing. Good night,

Marshal. If I don't see you around town tomorrow, I'll see you Sunday in church."

As the two men parted and Dane Kirkland moved on down the street toward the fort, he said, "Once more, Lord. I need Your grace right now. "

The next morning, Hannah Cooper came into the general store from the back door, carrying little Eddie, as Jacob Kates was unlocking the front door to open for business. He heard her come in.

As he turned the Closed sign around to read Open, Jacob said over his shoulder, "Good morning, boss-lady. And how are you, today?"

"We are just fine," said Hannah, a smile spreading over her features.

Jacob pivoted, and it was his turn to smile big when he laid eyes on the baby. "Oh!" he said, hurrying toward mother and child. "Hello, Eddie! Let's have a big hug for Uncle Jacob!"

Hannah smiled as her baby squealed with delight when he saw Jacob.

Taking the baby boy in his arms, Jacob hugged him good, then began tickling him under his double chin. Eddie was laughing, squirming, kicking, and wiggling, enjoying Uncle Jacob's attention when the bell over the front door jingled, and the day's first customers came in.

Hannah smiled when she saw Dobie and Donna Carlin coming in. Both of the Carlins' attention was drawn to Jacob and Eddie as the tickling continued.

Drawing up, Dobie said, "You know, Jacob, you're more like a grandpa to Eddie than an uncle."

Jacob laughed. "Be all right with me if he called me Grandpa when he gets bigger. That is, as long as his Grandpa Singleton didn't care."

Hannah laughed. "Well, I don't think my father would care if Eddie called you Grandpa."

"Good!" said Jacob, hugging the baby to his chest. "As soon as he starts talking, I'll teach him to call me Grandpa!"

Hannah said, "Dobie, I'm glad you and your men got home safely from your trip to Fort Logan. Chris told me some things about Captain Dane Kirkland. What a horrible thing…to lose his wife and baby like that. I can understand why he needed to go elsewhere."

"Especially since they were gunned down right there on the compound where Captain Kirkland had to walk past the very spot every day."

"Oh my. How awful!"

"One thing Chris couldn't have known, since Travis didn't know either, Hannah, is that Captain Kirkland is a born-again man. We had plenty of time to talk, riding side by side on the trip. His testimony is clear as a bell."

"I'm glad to know that. Then his wife was probably a Christian, too."

"Without a doubt. He told me a lot about her. Sometimes he broke down and cried, but from what he said, she was a faithful Christian woman. I tried to encourage him all I could by reminding him that both Mary and Donnie are in the presence of the Lord, the angels, the blood-washed throng of saints who have gone on before us, and all the heavenly host."

From the corner of her eye, Hannah saw Jacob's face lose color. "This has got to give him at least a measure of peace," she said, "but my heart goes out to him in his loss."

"Mine too. I took the captain to see Pastor Kelly last night, then left and went home, so I don't know how it went. But I sure hope Pastor will be able to help him through this very difficult time in his life. I detected a trace of bitterness in him."

"It's quite possible. He's only human," Hannah said. "I…well, I came close to getting bitter toward God when

Solomon was taken from me. I'm glad I can say that with His help, I was able to avoid it, but it was the most difficult thing I have ever faced in my life."

"Dobie and I were talking about the captain's bitterness, Hannah," said Donna. "If that's what it is. We were going to suggest that you get to know him. You just might be able to help him, since you lost Solomon in such a tragic way."

"And especially since you came so close to becoming bitter toward the Lord, yourself, as you just said," Dobie added.

"I will do my best," said Hannah. "I assume Captain Kirkland will be coming to church."

"He said he would be in church Sunday. It's already set that Donna, Travis, and I will be walking him to church in the morning. He doesn't know that yet, but we'll be his escorts."

"Well, I'm glad to know that the captain isn't so bitter that he would stay out of church."

"I've seen Christians get bitter at God over unpleasant things that have happened in their lives," Donna said, "even much less severe than a death of someone they loved dearly. They fail to see that harboring bitterness toward the Lord will accomplish nothing but to pull them away from Him, and that can never bring about anything but more heartache."

"It's one thing to have questions in your heart about tragedies and unpleasant things the Lord has caused or allowed to come into your life," Hannah said, "but it's something else to get bitter toward Him, and in essence, to charge Him with cruelty and wrongdoing."

"I so often think of Job," said Dobie. "With all the tragedies upon tragedies that came into his life, the Bible says he never charged God foolishly."

"Lord, help us to be like Job," said Hannah.

The bell jingled at the front door, and Chris came in from the storeroom in the back of the building. Jacob headed for the counter as Chris said, "Hello, Mrs. Carlin, Lieutenant."

The Carlins responded with a warm greeting.

Jacob greeted the three customers who had just come in as Chris said, "Mama, I got all the boxes stacked in the storeroom."

"Thank you, son," she said, putting an arm around him. "You're a good boy. I'll have you start filling the pickle barrels next."

"I'll get right on it."

"Before you do, there's something I'd like you to know. You prayed so sweetly last night for Captain Dane Kirkland and asked the Lord to use this tragedy in his life to bring him to Jesus. Remember?"

"Yes."

"Well, Lieutenant Carlin just told me that the captain is definitely a saved man, Chris. And so was his wife. She's in heaven with their baby."

"Oh, praise the Lord!" said Chris, his eyes misting with tears. "I'm so glad to hear this. The Lord has a plan for his life, and I'm sure things will get better for him."

"I'm sure you're right, son," said Hannah.

CHAPTER FIVE

T he church bell was ringing on Sunday morning under a clear azure sky as people were arriving for the morning service. Word had spread rapidly through town, fort, and surrounding area about Captain Dane Kirkland and the tragedy that had taken his wife and baby son.

The pump organ was playing a heart-touching gospel song as Dobie and Donna Carlin led Dane inside. As usual, the only seats available by that time were near the front. All eyes turned Kirkland's direction as he moved down the aisle, following the Carlins.

On the platform, Pastor Andy Kelly was talking to his song leader, but his line of sight found the captain. He smiled and nodded. Kirkland nodded in return.

As the captain was moving past the pew where Hannah Cooper sat with her children, her parents, and Curly and Judy Charley Wesson, Kirkland saw the bright smile of the dark-haired teenage boy on the pew. The boy was looking at him as if he knew him. Dane nodded back, and for an instant, his sad eyes met those of the woman who sat next to the boy.

Hannah was aware of the same deep grief reflected in his eyes that she had seen in her own after Solomon's death. She smiled at him tentatively and he nodded at her, his lips making a thin smile.

Hannah's soft heart felt Kirkland's pain, and she sent a

silent prayer heavenward, asking the Lord to bestow His grace and comfort on the man.

The song leader stepped to the pulpit, announced the hymn number, and asked the congregation to stand. When two songs had been sung, the crowd was seated, and the pastor came to the pulpit for announcement and offering time. Before beginning the announcements, he welcomed the visitors and asked them to stand. After two ranch families from west of town introduced themselves, he asked Captain Kirkland to stand and do the same. In brief, the pastor shared the captain's sad story with the people, and asked them to hold him up in prayer.

After the service, the church members converged on Dane Kirkland to give him a special welcome, to speak their heartfelt condolences, and to assure him they would be praying for him. Kirkland was deeply touched, and fought tears as the kind words came from Christian brothers and sisters.

A couple in their early sixties stepped up, and the man said, "Captain Kirkland, my name is Ben Singleton and this is my wife, Esther. We're from Independence, Missouri. Our daughter, Hannah Cooper, owns Cooper's General Store here in town. She was widowed last year. We're visiting her and our grandchildren."

"I'm very happy to meet you folks," said Kirkland. "Will you be staying long?"

Ben looked at Esther, who shrugged her shoulders, and looked back at Kirkland. "I think if she had her way, we'd just move here. Anyway, we haven't set a time to head for home, yet."

"Captain," said Esther, "please know that my husband and I will be praying for you."

"I appreciate that more than I can tell you," said Kirkland.

Several other families spoke to Kirkland, and when Hannah and her brood approached him, Hannah could tell that God had already lifted some of his burden.

Stepping up and offering her hand, Hannah said, "Captain Kirkland, I'm Hannah Cooper."

"Oh yes, ma'am," he said, his countenance brightening somewhat. "I met your parents a few minutes ago, Mr. and Mrs. Singleton."

"Yes. They're visiting us from Missouri."

"That's what they told me. They also told me that you were widowed last year."

"Solomon lost his life while protecting the children and me from a rattlesnake while we were in a wagon train on our way here to Fort Bridger to start a new life. It was the hardest thing I've ever been through. I can certainly sympathize with you."

"I'm sorry for your loss, Mrs. Cooper," Kirkland said softly. "Most certainly you know how I feel."

"Yes, sir. And please be assured, Captain, that my children and I will be holding you before the throne every day. You won't live a day that we don't bring you before the Lord. We will ask Him to bless you, encourage you, and give you a happy new life."

Tears misted Kirkland's eyes, and a smile that was having trouble breaking through finally materialized. "Thank you, ma'am."

"Captain," said Hannah, "I want you to meet my children."

Starting with the oldest, Hannah introduced Kirkland to Chris, who impressed him with his warmth and the news that he had been praying for him since Friday. Chris explained that his friend, Travis Carlin, had filled him in on the captain's reason for coming to Fort Bridger, so he told his family what Travis had passed on to him, and they prayed together for him both Friday and Saturday nights.

"Chris," said the captain, "I appreciate this more than I could ever say. Thank you."

Hannah brought forth her two girls quickly. Both Mary Beth and Patty Ruth impressed Kirkland with their warmth and courtesy.

Kirkland then let his eyes trail to B. J., who had Eddie in his arms when he stepped up.

Hannah said, "Captain Kirkland, this is B. J., and the little one is Eddie."

The captain's brow furrowed, and his face pinched as he set eyes on the baby. Swallowing hard, he looked at B. J. and said, "I'm glad to meet you, B. J. How…how old is your little brother?"

"He's almost seven months old, sir," said the nine-year-old.

"My little Donnie would be almost seven months old now, too. He was born March 16."

"Eddie is just two days older, Captain," said Hannah. "He was born on March 14." She bit her lip. "I'm sorry if seeing Eddie has upset you."

"I wouldn't call it upset, ma'am," the captain said in a tender tone. "Just…it makes me miss Donnie. You understand."

"Yes," said Hannah. "Captain, it has been nice meeting you. I see Pastor and Mrs. Kelly are waiting for you, so we'll be on our way."

Kirkland thanked the whole Cooper family for their concern and their prayers as they turned to leave, and the Kellys moved up beside him. The captain's eyes followed Hannah and her brood as they walked away.

"What a nice family," he said to the Kellys.

"That they are," said the pastor.

"My heart goes out to that young widow. It must have been horrible for her. I mean to lose her husband and have the responsibility of the four children to provide for, plus carrying another one in her womb."

"It was very difficult," said Rebecca.

Still watching the Coopers as they moved down the street toward home, Kirkland asked, "Did she have a tough time accepting her husband's death?"

"In some ways she did," said the pastor, "but she weathered it because she is a very strong Christian. She really knows how to draw strength from the Lord, and how to let Him fill her life with His grace."

In his heart, Dane said, *Lord, help me to have the same kind of strength Mrs. Cooper has, and teach me how to let You fill my life with Your grace.* Then he said to Kelly, "Pastor, I want to be strong like that dear lady. Please pray for me."

"I will, Captain. The counseling sessions we have planned will help you a great deal, I'm sure."

Rebecca touched her husband's arm. "Andy, did you tell the captain that you sent the Carlins home?"

"Ah…no."

"I noticed they aren't anywhere around," said Kirkland.

"I told them Rebecca had prepared enough Sunday dinner for a third party, and that we'd feed you," said Kelly.

"That's very nice of you folks," he said. "I'll just take you up on it."

On Monday evening, Jacob Kates sat down to supper with Hannah and her children, and after Chris had prayed over the food, Jacob said, "That new army captain Lieutenant Carlin told Chris about, was he at church yesterday?"

"He sure was," said Chris.

"And did you get to meet him?"

"Sure did. All of us."

"And my heart is so heavy for him, Jacob," said Hannah. "Losing his wife and only child at the very same time has taken its toll on him."

"That would be tough," said Jacob, "especially having them die so violently, as Chris told me."

"The captain is really a nice man, Uncle Jacob," said B. J.

"And handsome too," put in Mary Beth. "I mean, he really is a good-looking man."

Chris chuckled, grinned slyly, and said, "Mary Beth, Captain Kirkland is too old for you."

Mary Beth picked up her cloth napkin, wadded it into a tight ball, and threw it at him, striking him in the face. "I know that, smart aleck! I wasn't saying that I wanted to marry him. I was only commenting that he is handsome!"

Chris folded the napkin and sailed it over the table so it landed on Mary Beth's head. She jerked it off, gave him a mock scowl, and said, "Mama, don't you think Captain Kirkland is handsome?"

"Yes, honey, " said Hannah. "He is quite handsome."

Patty Ruth covertly slipped a morsel to Biggie under the table and said, "I think Captain Kirkland is very, very handsome, Mary Beth."

"I sure hope the young man will have relief from his broken heart soon," said Jacob.

"He will," said Hannah. "When a person has the Lord Jesus in his heart, he has something the lost person doesn't have. Jesus can give peace and joy in the midst of the greatest storms life can bring. Those who are not saved have no access to this peace and joy, for it's found only in Jesus."

Patty Ruth said, "Uncle Jacob, you can have Jesus in your heart, too, if you will let Him come in. He would help you a lot, like he does us. I've sure been happier since I took Jesus into my heart."

Mary Beth, Chris, and B. J. looked at each other, then to their mother, who was as surprised as they were to hear these words from Patty Ruth.

Jacob swallowed hard, forced a thin smile, and said, "I'm

very glad for you, Patty Ruth."

"When are you gonna ask Jesus to come into your heart and save you, Uncle Jacob?"

Jacob scrubbed a shaky hand over his mouth, cleared his throat, and said, "Sweetie, as a Jew, I'm waiting for my Messiah to come to earth. Your Jesus Christ isn't my Messiah."

Hannah fixed the little man with eyes of compassion and said softly, "Jacob, why is your Messiah coming to earth?"

"Well, according to the Scriptures, He is coming to give forgiveness and cleansing of sin to the people of Israel, and to do battle with the nations who are our enemies, and to conquer them."

"And where is this spoken of in the Bible?" Hannah asked.

"In several places. But the one I like best is in the book of Zechariah."

Looking at B. J., Hannah said, "Honey, will you go get the Bible in the parlor so Jacob can show it to us?"

"Sure," said the nine-year-old, shoving his chair back. As he got up, he noticed Biggie licking Patty Ruth's fingers underneath the table, and their eyes met. Patty Ruth's face flushed. B. J. grinned at her but said nothing.

B. J. returned quickly and handed the Bible to Jacob, who turned to Zechariah chapter 13.

"Here in Zechariah 13:1," said Jacob, "listen to what it says. 'In that day there shall be a fountain opened to the house of David and to the inhabitants of Jerusalem for sin and for uncleanness.' Then over here in chapter 14, it says in verses 3 and 4: 'Then shall the LORD go forth, and fight against those nations, as when he fought in the day of battle. And his feet shall stand in that day upon the mount of Olives, which is before Jerusalem on the east, and the mount of Olives shall cleave in the midst thereof toward the east and toward the west, and there shall be a very great valley; and half of the mountain shall remove toward the north, and half of it toward the south.'

And over here in verse 9, it tells that the Lord shall be king over all the earth. That king is my Messiah. And…and in verse 11 it says Jerusalem shall be safely inhabited because in the next verse it says, 'The LORD will smite all the people that have fought against Jerusalem.' Hannah, this is why Messiah is coming…to set His people free."

"There in Zechariah 13:1, who will open the fountain for cleansing?" Hannah said, giving him one of her kind looks.

"Why, Messiah, of course."

"I agree. Now, over here in chapter 13 and verse 5, it speaks of a husbandman. Who is that?"

"That's Messiah, seen in His humility."

"Mmm-hmm. Then, Jacob, look at verse 6," she said, placing her finger next to it on the page. "'And one shall say unto him, What are these wounds in thine hands?' And He answers, 'Those with which I was wounded in the house of my friends.' Jacob, Messiah is a Jew, isn't He?"

"Yes."

"So his 'friends' would be Jews, wouldn't they?"

"Yes."

"What about those wounds in His hands? How and where did He get those wounds?"

Jacob's wrinkled features turned gray. "I…well, I don't know."

The children were looking on and listening intently.

"Jacob, you know when the nation of Israel was under Roman rule, that the Romans used crucifixion as a means of execution for Jews who broke Roman laws."

"Yes."

"When the Romans crucified the Jews, how did they fasten them to the crosses?"

"They drove nails through their hands and feet."

Hannah then took him to Psalm 22 and asked, "Jacob, who is speaking here when it says, 'My God, my God, why hast thou forsaken me?'"

"David."

"You mean God forsook David?"

"He must have."

"Then how could David say in Psalm 37:25, 'I have been young, and now am old; yet I have not seen the righteous forsaken'?"

The little man got a blank look on his face.

"I believe that the Person speaking in Psalm 22:1 is the Messiah, Jesus Christ, who was forsaken by God when He bore the sins of the world on the cross of Calvary. When was David ever crucified?"

"Well, never."

"But the man who cries that God has forsaken Him says in verse 16 of this same psalm, 'they pierced my hands and my feet.' This is your Messiah, Jacob. He was crucified for your sins and mine."

Jacob Kates blinked, but had nothing to say.

Hannah said softly, "Jacob, wouldn't you say that Jesus Christ bears a very strong resemblance to your Messiah?"

Jacob licked his lips, cleared his throat, and said, "Well... yes."

Reaching across the table, Hannah took hold of his hand, and with tears in her eyes, said, "Jacob, if Jesus isn't the Jews' Messiah, what could your Messiah do or be differently than Him?"

Jacob closed his eyes and rubbed his forehead. "I...I have to think about all of this."

"All right," Hannah said quietly. "And while you're thinking on it, I want you to think about something else."

She took him to a few passages on hell and the wrath of God, then showed him some verses on salvation. She then closed the Bible and said, "Please, Jacob, give God a chance to show you who Jesus really is. Where you will spend eternity depends on it. These children and I love you very much, and we want you in heaven with us."

Jacob's eyes filled with tears. "Hannah, dear, I know that you and these precious children of yours love me and care about me. And I appreciate that very much. But please understand what I have been taught all of my life, and that I must think about all of this."

Hannah squeezed his hand. "We do understand. And we are so glad that you know we love you."

On Tuesday morning, Hannah was changing the window display at the store while Jacob was at the counter waiting on customers. Little Eddie was on a pallet on the floor near the table at the rear of the store where some of Hannah's male customers often came in and played checkers. Eddie was holding his toy horse and "talking" to it.

From the corner of her eye at the window, Hannah saw a man on the boardwalk as he stepped up to the door. Hannah smiled at him, and was relieved to see that there was less anguish in Dane Kirkland's eyes than there had been on Sunday. When his hand touched the latch, she backed away from the window and headed for the door. Still smiling as it came open, she said, "Captain Kirkland, how nice to see you!"

"It's nice to see you too, Mrs. Cooper. I need some shaving supplies."

"Well, you came to the right place. I'll show you where we keep them."

As she led him along the long rows of shelves, the captain commented on how well the store was stocked.

"Thank you, Captain, but I couldn't do it alone. I'll introduce you to the man who actually carries the load in a moment. Well, here's what you're looking for: razors, various shaving soaps, brushes, and cups."

It took Kirkland only seconds to gather what he wanted,

and then Hannah led him toward the counter. Jacob's customers had gone, and the little man was looking at the captain as they drew up to the counter.

Hannah introduced Kirkland to Jacob, and said, "Now, here is the one who really runs the store."

Jacob grinned from ear to ear as he shook hands with Kirkland and said, "Don't let her fool you, Captain. This store wouldn't be here if it weren't for Hannah and her hard work. It was her grit that put the store here in the first place, and her bulldog determination that has kept it going in spite of many hardships."

The bell over the front door jingled.

"Well, enough of that kind of flowery talk," Hannah said, swinging a playful fist at Jacob's chin. "You two have a nice chat and get acquainted. I'll take care of the customers."

Hannah went to greet the customers and guide them to what they needed, and Kirkland laid his items on the counter. "I'll take these, Mr. Kates."

As Jacob totaled the bill, he said, "Captain Kirkland, Hannah and her son, Chris, told me about what happened at Fort Logan. Let me say, sir, that you have my heartfelt sympathy in your loss."

"Thank you."

"My wife died a few years ago, so I know the pain that goes with it...but with your wife and little baby both being taken from you in such a terrible manner, I know you are suffering much more than I did."

"Well, sir, I'm sure there are degrees of pain in this kind of thing, but I'm sure your suffering was bad enough."

"Worst thing I've ever experienced."

"I detect some eastern accent in your speech, Mr. Kates. Where are you from?"

"New York City."

"I spent a week there a few years ago and got to visit all five boroughs."

Jacob went on to tell the captain where he lived in Manhattan, and in what part of the business district the mercantile store was located where he used to be in business with his brother before coming to Wyoming. The little man's eyes lit up when Kirkland told him he had been on the very street where the mercantile store was.

Hannah waited on her customers, took Eddie to a back room to change his diaper, then placed him back on the pallet. As she approached the two men, Jacob looked at her and said, "Hannah, the captain and I have a lot in common. He's even been to New York, right where I used to live."

"We both like the West better than the East, though," said Kirkland. "He's never been fishing. One of these days, if his hard taskmaster boss will let him off, I'm going to teach him how to fish."

"I don't know," said Hannah, a mock scowl forming on her brow, "if he learns to fish, I might never get any work out of him!"

Jacob laughed. "You're right, Captain. She is a hard taskmaster!"

"Since you two have become friends already, how about coming to supper this evening?" Hannah said to Kirkland. "Jacob will be there, as well as my parents—and my children, of course. Will you come?"

The captain licked his lips uneasily.

Hannah smiled and said, "Please say you will come, Captain. It'll be good for you to be with people. I know by experience, that if it hadn't been for my new friends here in Fort Bridger who kept me so occupied that I could hardly think of my broken heart, losing Solomon would have put me under. Won't you please let us be your friends and help support you through this difficult time?"

A softening look crossed Dane's features. "Thank you, Mrs. Cooper. I would be glad to come." The smile that had gone into hiding found its way back, and he turned it on Hannah as he asked, "What time should I come?"

"Six o'clock would be fine. Our apartment is upstairs above the store. You'll find the stairs on the alley in back."

"I'll be there. Mr. Kates, nice to meet you. We'll get better acquainted in the days to come."

"Sure will," said Jacob. "I'm glad you're coming to supper this evening. You'll like it, I guarantee you."

"I have no doubt of that."

Hannah chuckled. "It'll be good because my little Mary Beth does most of the cooking. Along with Patty Ruth's help, of course."

"Sweet girls," said Kirkland, his head whipping around as little Eddie let out a squeal. He smiled at the baby. "Would it be all right if I pick him up, ma'am?"

"Of course. The child doesn't know a stranger. He's such a friendly little guy."

The bell above the front door jingled, and Jacob turned his attention toward the new customers as Hannah followed the captain to the pallet.

Dane dropped to his knees, saying, "Hello, Eddie. Okay if I pick you up?"

The baby let go of the horse whose head was wet with slobber, and lifted his hands up toward the man. Dane gathered him into his arms and stood up. Tears stung his eyes as he looked into the friendly little face and said, "I used to have a little boy like you, Eddie. Only Jesus took him to heaven so he and his mommy could be together up there."

Lowering the smiling baby from his chest, Dane said, "You're right, Mrs. Cooper, he sure is a friendly little guy."

Hannah reached out to take Eddie, but Dane shook his head. The familiar scent of soap and talcum powder had reached his senses, and a flood of memories assailed him.

His mind flashed back to the times when he held little

Donnie just like this—a tiny chubby hand patted his cheek, and a stubby little finger tried to poke into his mouth…

Dane gave Eddie a light chuck on the chin, then handed him to his mother. Hannah took him, but Eddie made a squeal and held his arms out for the man who had been holding him.

Taking hold of a tiny fat hand, Dane said, "Well, little guy, I guess you and I are going to be friends."

Hannah smiled warmly, laid Eddie back on the pallet, and placed the toy horse in his hands.

"Well, I guess I'd better get back to the fort or Colonel Bateman will have the militia looking for me!"

Hannah chuckled. "See you around six, Captain. I'm so glad you're going to have supper with us."

"Thank you, ma'am," he said sincerely, his eyes misting.

Hannah patted his muscular arm. "Captain, I'm not telling you anything you don't know, but keep in mind that you will see your little boy one day in heaven…as well as your dear wife."

In a choked voice that could barely be heard, Dane said, "Yes. Thank you for reminding me. And thank you for inviting me to supper. Maybe being with you and your family is just what I need."

Hannah walked him to the door, and as he stepped out and closed it behind him, she moved to the window and watched him walk away. Pain gripped her heart for this man, and again a prayer for God's strength and mercy in his life wended its way heavenward.

CHAPTER SIX

T he Wyoming sun sloped westward as Dutch Hendrix dismounted at the hitching rail in front of Webber's Hardware Store in Granger. A man and woman, walking arm in arm along the boardwalk, greeted him as he headed for the door. Hendrix's mind was on his mission, and he didn't bother to return the greeting.

As he reached for the knob, he saw a silver-haired man hanging a Closed sign on the window. "Hey, wait a minute!" bawled Hendrix.

"Sorry, sir," the man said loud enough to be heard through the door. "I'm already late closing. Come back tomorrow."

"All I want to do is ask you a question!" snapped the outlaw leader, a deep scowl etching itself on his brow.

The man opened the door. "What's the question?"

"Do you have a man employed here named Mo Froggate?"

"No, I don't."

"Well, you see, he's a friend of mine, and he's supposed to be workin' in a hardware store somewhere here in southern Wyomin'. Maybe he came in, lookin' for a job. Early thirties. Sandy hair. Blue eyes. Hundred and seventy pounds. Five-feet-ten. Part of his left earlobe is missin'."

"Haven't seen him," said the proprietor.

Hendrix bit his lower lip and nodded. "Okay." With that,

he wheeled, crossed the boardwalk, mounted, and rode away.

"You're welcome," said Dirk Webber.

Twilight was rapidly succeeding the sunset as Dutch Hendrix rode up to the barn behind the old abandoned farmhouse and left the saddle. He glanced toward the Uinta Mountains in the distance to the southwest and saw the night shadows trooping down from the black and looming peaks.

He removed saddle, blanket, and bridle from the horse inside the barn, and turned it out into the corral with the other horses.

When Dutch opened the back door of the house, the aroma of fried elk met his nostrils. Spike Denny was at the stove in the kitchen, stirring gravy in a skillet. The other men were already seated at the table, sipping coffee.

They all spoke to their boss, then Dutch said, "Spike, every time you do the cookin', it smells so good."

Spike grinned. "Maybe I shouldn't let that happen, boss. I sure don't want this job full time."

There was a round of light laughter, then Rex Holt asked, "So how'd it go today, Dutch?"

"Same ol' thing," said Hendrix with disgust as he tossed his dirty hat on a peg by the door. "Nothin'. I've been to four towns today: McKinnon, Burntfork, Lonetree, and Granger. Nobody in those hardware stores knows any Mo Froggate or a man of his description."

"Boss," said Rafe Ketcham, "I still think that skunk has hightailed it outta Wyomin'."

"You might as well forget findin' him, Dutch," said Rex Holt. "He's headed for new territory a long way from here, sure as you're breathin'."

Hendrix shook his head. "Don't you guys remember how much Mo talked about lovin' Wyomin'? He used to say he'd never leave here."

"Well, if he's stayin' in Wyomin', boss," said Mitchell, "he's probably gone north."

"Nope. I tell you, I got a gut feelin'. The dirty rat is still in southern Wyomin'. And I'm gonna find him, and when I do, he's a dead man. I won't be able to rest until Froggate gets what's comin' to him."

That evening at the Cooper apartment, Captain Dane Kirkland, Jacob Kates, and the Singletons were enjoying the meal that Hannah and Mary Beth had prepared, with some help from Patty Ruth.

While the meal was in progress, Ben Singleton told stories of sweet things Hannah did as a child. Soon Ben was weeping, and had Esther and Hannah doing the same.

Everyone was just about finished eating as Ben wiped tears and said, "Now, let me tell you a very special story. Esther is the only person I've ever told about this. Of course Hannah knows because this story is about her."

"Oh, boy!" spoke up B. J. "I just love these stories about Mama when she was a little girl!"

"Well, this one isn't about when she was a little girl, B. J.," said Ben. "This one is about the day she married your papa."

"You mean something Mama did at the wedding?"

"Exactly. It—" Ben choked up, swallowed hard, and cleared his throat. He ran his gaze over the faces around the table. "It was when Hannah and I were in the vestibule of the church just before I walked her down the aisle. She—" He choked up again.

Esther laid a steady hand on his arm and smiled at him.

Everyone saw tears in Hannah's eyes.

Ben cleared his throat once more, looked at his daughter, then the others and said, "She kissed my cheek and said, 'Papa, you'll always be my special boyfriend.'"

Hannah's hand went to her mouth, and Ben left his chair, bent over her, and hugged her, saying, "Sweet baby, I love you with all of my heart."

"I love you with all of my heart too, Papa," Hannah said.

Everyone else at the table was fighting back tears, including Jacob Kates and Dane Kirkland.

Suddenly Mary Beth shoved her chair back, sniffling, and ran down the hall.

"Excuse me," Hannah said, rising to her feet and following her.

All eyes watched Hannah until she passed from view, then Chris said, "It's probably about Papa. Your story about the wedding must have touched her tender nerve concerning Papa, Grandpa."

"Oh, I shouldn't have told it."

"Don't feel bad, Grandpa," spoke up B. J. "You didn't mean to upset Mary Beth. All of us still cry now and then over Papa's death, but the one who does it the most is Mary Beth."

"That girl is so sweet and tenderhearted," said Jacob.

"Mary Beth is the sweetest sister in the whole world," put in Patty Ruth.

Chris and B. J. looked at each other and grinned impishly, trying to think of what to say to that. Esther saw it and said, "Boys, it would be best to leave it alone."

Patty Ruth smiled at her brothers and said, "Isn't it wonderful, boys? You have the two sweetest sisters in all the world!"

In the girls' room, Hannah found Mary Beth lying face down on her bed, sobbing. Sitting down beside her, she laid both hands on her shoulders, squeezed gently, and said, "Sweetheart, what is it?"

Mary Beth kept on sobbing, and it took Hannah several minutes to quiet her down. When the sobbing finally subsided,

Hannah said, "Now tell me what it is."

Drawing a shuddering breath, Mary Beth said in a quavering voice, "When…when I was watching you and Grandpa together at the table, I was glad for you, that you still have your father. But…but it made me miss Papa so terribly. Then when Grandpa talked about how he walked you down the aisle to marry my papa, it hit me, Mama."

Again, Mary Beth choked up, and couldn't speak for a few seconds. Finally, she said, "It hit me that when the day comes for me to marry, Papa—Papa won't be here to walk me down the aisle."

Mary Beth broke into sobs again.

Hannah's own tears began to fall as she drew her cherished daughter into her arms, and they wept together. After several minutes, the weeping eased, and when the healing tears were dried, Hannah gave Mary Beth an extra hug and said, "Sweetie, do you remember the old saying Pastor Kelly refers to now and then, 'When God closes a door, He always opens a window'?"

"Uh-huh."

"Well, when the time comes for you to marry that special young man the Lord has all picked out for you, and a man is needed to walk you down the aisle, He will open that window, and it will be the man God has chosen to do it."

Mary Beth lowered her eyes and thought on it for a moment, then looked up and gave her mother a watery smile. "I love you, Mama. You always know exactly what to say."

Taking hold of both her daughter's hands, Hannah squeezed them and said, "I've got to get back to our guests. Wash your pretty face, and when you're ready, come out and join us."

Mary Beth nodded.

When Hannah returned to the kitchen, she explained to everyone what had upset Mary Beth.

"Is she all right now, Mama?" Chris asked.

"She'll be fine, son," said Hannah. "We had a little talk about it all, and it helped her. She'll be out in a moment."

"Should I go be with her till then, Mama?" asked B. J.

"There's no need, honey. She's just washing her face."

"You look like you've been cryin', too, Mama," said Patty Ruth.

Hannah smiled. "Yes, honey. Talking about Papa brought the tears."

Ben wiped a palm over his face and said, "I shouldn't have told that story. My timing wasn't so good. But…well, I just didn't think about how it might affect that sweet girl."

"You had no way of knowing what would go through her mind, Papa," said Hannah, bending over and kissing his cheek. "Don't chastise yourself."

Ben reached up, patted her cheek, and said, "Thank you for your understanding."

"Hannah's right, dear," said Esther. "You certainly didn't mean to upset her."

"Of course you didn't, Grandpa," came Mary Beth's words as she entered the kitchen and headed straight for her grandfather.

Ben rose from his chair, opened his arms, and enfolded her, saying, "I'm sorry, honey. Please forgive me."

Hugging him tight, Mary Beth said, "Grandpa, you needn't apologize. The story you told is very sweet. I could just hear my mother saying that to you. It's just that, hearing you tell it, I couldn't help thinking of Papa, and—well, it struck me that Papa won't be here to walk me down the aisle when I get married."

"Aw, honey," said Ben, "I should be horsewhipped for not using my brain."

Mary Beth shook her head. "No horsewhip, Grandpa, but I have an idea."

"What's that?"

"Well, if you and Grandma would move to Fort Bridger, you'd be here to walk me down the aisle and give me away when I get married."

"Yeah!" exclaimed Patty Ruth, clapping her hands.

Ben and Esther exchanged glances, smiled thinly at each other, and Hannah's heart skipped a beat just at the thought that her parents might decide to move to Fort Bridger.

Mary Beth kissed her grandfather's cheek as he let go of her, and said, "Please don't feel bad about telling the story, Grandpa. It's just that sometimes I miss Papa so terribly."

Esther left her chair, wrapped her arms around the girl and said softly, "Mary Beth, someday you'll be with your Papa again…in heaven."

Esther's words touched Chris, B. J., and Patty Ruth, and sniffling was heard among them. Hannah was fighting tears again as Mary Beth said, "That will be a wonderful day, Grandma. I am so very much looking forward to being in Papa's arms once more."

B. J. left the table and picked up little Eddie from the pallet on the floor nearby. Looking down at the baby's smiling face, B. J. said, "Eddie, even though you've never seen Papa, you'll get to see him and be with him forever in heaven."

More tears were shed by Hannah and her other children. Jacob was also wiping tears.

Hannah noticed a look of discomfort on Dane Kirkland's face and said, "Captain, I'm sorry this family has been so open and emotional in front of you."

"Oh, there's no need to apologize, ma'am. I count it an honor that you felt you could be so open. It helps to realize that others have endured the same kind of sorrow I'm going through and have weathered the storm, though they still miss their loved one. Thank you for letting me share these special moments with you."

A gentle smile touched Hannah's lips. "You are always welcome here, Captain."

"I appreciate that, Mrs. Cooper. You sure have a wonderful family. It's such a blessing to see how much you all love each other."

Patty Ruth said, "Captain Kirkland, even though Uncle Jacob isn't our real uncle, we love him the same as if he was."

"He *is* our uncle as far as we're concerned," said Chris.

Jacob's lower lip quivered. "That works both ways, Chris. All of you are family to me."

Mary Beth slipped up to Jacob, hugged his neck, kissed his cheek, and said, "I really do love you a lot, Uncle Jacob."

Patty Ruth crawled up on Jacob's lap, kissed his cheek, and said, "I love you so-o-o-o much, Uncle Jacob."

Once again, Jacob was blinking at tears. His voice broke as he said, "I love *you* so-o-o-o much too, sweetheart. In fact I love everyone in this precious family."

Patty Ruth kissed his cheek again, and he squeezed her tight.

Late in the afternoon on Wednesday, Dutch Hendrix entered the Rocky Mountain Hardware Store and Gun Shop in Lyman, Wyoming, some twelve miles east of Fort Bridger.

The man behind the counter smiled and said, "Howdy, stranger. How can I help you? I'm Les Munson."

"I'm John Barton, Mr. Munson," Hendrix said. "Just need some information."

"I'll try."

"I'm lookin' for an old friend of mine I've been told is livin' somewhere in southern Wyomin'. His name's Mo Froggate, and he's probably workin' in a hardware store. Does he happen to work here?"

"Nope. I run the store by myself."

"I see. Well, my friend would've only been in the area a short time, and—"

"Wait a minute!" said Munson, snapping his fingers. "I do remember a man coming in something like a month or so ago, asking for a job. But as I recall, his name was Bill something."

Hendrix frowned. "Was he blond? Early thirties?"

"Yeah. Pale blue eyes."

"Just under six feet?"

"I'd say so. Thing I remember the most was his left ear. Part of the lobe was gone. Looked like it had been chewed off."

Dutch's heart was pounding. "Yes, that's him! Come to think of it, ol' Mo talked about bein' called Bill somethin' sometimes." He laughed hollowly. "Wonder what that scalawag has to hide!"

Munson chuckled. "Don't know, but I do know where your friend is."

"You do?"

"Yep. Just last week I went to Fort Bridger to see if my friend Justin Powell—who owns the Fort Bridger Hardware Store and Gun Shop—had some paint in stock that I needed for a customer, and I found your friend Bill working there."

"Well, whattya know?" said Dutch, laughing. "This is great! Thanks for the information, Mr. Munson."

The other gang members were just sitting down to supper when Dutch Hendrix came through the kitchen door, smiling broadly.

"Hey, guys!" said Rafe Ketcham. "Look at the grin on the boss's face. Did you find him, Dutch?"

Dutch tossed his hat on the peg. "I found out where he is. Owner of the hardware store over in Lyman told me Mo's workin' at the hardware store in Fort Bridger. He's goin' by the name of Bill somebody. See, didn't I tell you guys? Don't ever disregard ol' Dutch's gut feelin's!"

"So when do we go after him?" asked Rex Holt.

"Yeah," said Spike Denny. "I wanna see the look on the face of this guy I replaced when he realizes he's about to get what's comin' to him."

"Well, since we're doin' the stage holdup tomorrow," said Dutch, "Mo will get what's comin' to him on Friday." He took a quick breath. *"But..."*

"But what, boss?" said Spike.

"None of you boys will get to see the look on Mo's ugly face when he's about to get what's comin' to him. I'm doin' this alone."

"Dutch, the rest of us should go with you," Rafe said. "You never know what you might run into."

"I appreciate your concern, Rafe, but the privilege of exactin' justice on that low-down snake is gonna be mine and mine alone." Adjusting the gun belt on his hip, Dutch said, "When I get back here after takin' Froggate out, we'll pack up the money we've taken off that stage and ride into Colorado. We'll rob some banks and stagecoaches there, then when the law gets hot on our trail, we'll ride for New Mexico. Sound all right?"

"Sure, boss," said Rex. "We're gonna stuff our pockets full!"

"See what I told you, Spike?" said Rafe. "You're gonna be plenty glad you joined up with us."

Spike laughed. "I can see that. Sure am glad we got together again, ol' pal!"

When it was time to go to the midweek service that evening, Hannah and her children stepped out of their apartment, and as they started down the stairs, they saw the Carlins and Captain Dane Kirkland coming around the back corner of the store.

"Right on time!" said Hannah.

"Of course, Hannah," said Donna. "We're military!"

Everybody laughed.

Hannah looked up into Kirkland's eyes as the group headed alongside the store toward the street. "So how was your day, Captain?"

"Fine. Even in the few days that I've been here, I'm getting a grip on things. Thanks to the Lord and some very good friends He has given me."

"Your counseling sessions with Pastor Kelly are helping?"

"Oh yes, he *and* Mrs. Kelly are included in those very good friends I just mentioned."

There was lighthearted conversation among the group as they made their way down Main Street toward the church. When they drew near, people were mounting the church steps and made it a point to speak to Captain Kirkland.

One couple appeared on the boardwalk, coming from the opposite direction. Mary Beth said, "Uh oh, Patty Ruth. There's Uncle Curly and Aunt Judy."

"Yeah," said Chris, "and Uncle Curly's got that look in his eye, Patty Ruth."

Dobie Carlin chuckled and said, "Captain, get ready for a real cute scene. This happens quite often."

"Okay," said Kirkland. "And who are these people?"

"Curly is the Wells Fargo agent here, and also the Western Union agent. Judy is his wife, and helps him with both jobs."

"They talk kind of funny, Captain," said Mary Beth, "but they are wonderful Christian people."

As they drew up, the skinny little couple greeted them and made a special effort to make Captain Kirkland feel welcome. Then Curly stepped in front of Patty Ruth, bent over, and through toothless gums, said, "Wal, lookee here! What's your name, li'l girl?"

Patty Ruth bent her head down, looked up at him and said, "Patty Ruth."

Curly gasped, eyes wide. "What? Your name is Patty Ruth?"

Her feet were planted solid, and the little redhead was moving her shoulders back and forth. "Yes, sir."

"Wal, Patty Ruth, how old are you?"

"Six."

Curly gasped again, bobbing his bald head. "You're six years old?"

"Yes, sir."

Putting his face close to hers, he said, "Wal, Patty Ruth, do you know what I do when I meet a li'l girl who is six years old an' her name is Patty Ruth?"

"Huh-uh."

A wide grin captured Curly's face as he opened his arms and said, "I hug her!"

With that, Curly folded Patty Ruth in his arms, and she hugged him back.

The group that had gathered—most who had seen the act more times than they could count—applauded.

Judy Charley Wesson moved close to Patty Ruth when the embrace was finished, smiled, exposing her one snaggle tooth, and hugged the child, saying, "Wal, P. R., Aunt Judy will hug you without all that thar hoopla!"

The group applauded again as the skinny woman and the little girl embraced.

Hannah picked out some faces in the group that had gathered and motioned to them. When they stepped up, she introduced Captain Dane Kirkland to her brother-in-law, Adam, and his wife, Theresa, and their children, Seth who was seven, and Anna, who was nine months old. She also introduced him to Doug McClain and his little daughter, Jenny, who would soon be two years old. She then introduced the captain to Carrie Wright, who was holding Jenny.

Dane smiled and said, "I recall you passing by to welcome

me on Sunday, and now that I see you again, I remember, Mr. Cooper, that you told me you were brother-in-law to the woman who owns Cooper's General Store. It's nice to see all of you again."

Hannah then made a brief explanation about Kathy McClain being killed on the train when the Adam Coopers and the Doug McClains were coming to Fort Bridger from Cincinnati to establish the *Fort Bridger Bugle*.

"Mr. McClain, I'm so sorry for your loss," Dane said. "As you know, I can sympathize because of losing my wife."

"Yes," said Doug.

Dane then smiled down at little Jenny and said, "Aren't you a doll? If your daddy looks the other way, I'm liable to steal you!"

Jenny giggled.

"Well, we'd better get inside," said Dobie Carlin, "or we're going to be late to the service!"

CHAPTER SEVEN

After the service, Captain Dane Kirkland was walking toward the general store with Hannah Cooper and her children. B. J. was carrying little Eddie.

Hannah said, "Captain, I should explain to you about Doug McClain and Carrie Wright, since you saw them together with little Jenny in Carrie's arms. Carrie is a widow. Her husband was killed by a cougar last winter. As you can imagine, it was very difficult for her."

"Can I ever."

"Well, recently Doug and Carrie fell in love, and they plan to marry next spring."

"Wonderful! I'm glad for them, and for little Jenny. She's such a cutie."

"That she is," Hannah said. "It was so good that the Lord worked things out for both Doug and Carrie."

"That's great," said Dane. "I—"

"Yes?"

"I was just going to say that although I'm still grieving over the loss of Mary, I know life must go on, and I'm only thirty-five, so I'm hoping that in the future, God will have someone for me."

"Oh, I'm sure He will, Captain. I have no doubt He has some fine Christian lady all picked out for you. And when the time is right, He'll bring her into your life."

They were passing under the street lamp that was on the corner near the general store. Hannah saw a smile curve the captain's mouth.

When they reached the store, Dane walked the Cooper family to the alley, and when they drew up to the stairs, he said, "Well, I'll say good night, now. Thanks for letting me walk all of you home."

"We enjoyed your company," said Hannah.

"We want you to walk to and from church with us whenever you can, Captain," said Mary Beth.

"Captain Kirkland…" said Patty Ruth.

Smiling down at her, Dane said, "Yes, Patty Ruth?"

"I'll give you a good night hug if you want one."

The captain's smile widened as he bent low and said, "I sure do want one!"

After he and Patty Ruth had embraced for a long moment, Dane thanked her, then tenderly patted Eddie's chubby cheek and said, "Good night, little pal."

"God bless you, Captain," said Hannah. "I'm so glad to see that your grief is easing."

"You and your children have a great deal to do with that, Mrs. Cooper. Thank you for being so kind to me. Good night."

The Coopers watched Dane fade into the night, then Chris took his mother's arm to walk her up the stairs, and the others followed.

Biggie was there to meet them at the door, tail wagging. Patty Ruth picked him up, kissed the top of his head, and hugged him.

Later, when Eddie was asleep in his crib, and everyone else was ready for bed, they gathered in the parlor for prayer and Bible reading. When that was done, and Hannah was about to take them to their rooms so she could tuck them in and kiss them good night, Chris said, "Mama, could I ask you something?"

"Sure, honey."

"You know what you said to Captain Kirkland about the Lord bringing someone into his life when the time is right?"

"Yes."

"Do you think the Lord has planned someone for you to marry, or is He going to make you live the rest of your life alone?"

Hannah took a few seconds to prepare her answer, then said, "Honey, I'm not alone. I have you, Mary Beth, B. J., Patty Ruth, and Eddie."

"But, Mama," said Chris, "we're all going to grow up, get married, and have our own families someday. Then what?"

Hannah brushed a stray lock of hair from her forehead. "Well, Chris, I'll just have to leave this in the Lord's hands. He has His plan for my life. If…if He should want me to marry again, He will bring the man of His choice into my life."

Patty Ruth said, "Mama, would that man be someone like Captain Kirkland, who doesn't have a family anymore?"

"Well, sweetie, to be honest about it, I really don't think such a thing is going to happen. My life is quite full. Now it's time to get to bed."

"Mama," said Mary Beth, "Chris is right. Your children are getting older, and one day we will all marry and be out of your home. Take me, for instance. I'll turn fourteen on October 25. Most young women marry by the time they're nineteen, which means if I do, I'll be gone in five years. Chris turns sixteen come February, and most young men get married by the time they're twenty-one. So he could be gone in five years, too. The years pass so quickly, Mama, and before you know it, all your children will be grown up. I know we all miss Papa, and think of him many times a day, but why wouldn't the Lord do for you what you said He'd do for Captain Kirkland? Why wouldn't He have some fine Christian gentleman all picked out for you, and when the time is right, bring him into your life?"

"Mama, I think we should be praying that the Lord will bring a man into your life real soon," Chris said. "Sure, we all miss Papa, but it would be wonderful if we could have a stepfather in the years that are left for all of us to grow up—especially Eddie. Shouldn't we start praying that way?"

Hannah chuckled. "Chris, it would take an exceptional man if it was anytime soon, because how many men would want to marry a widow with five children? And besides, at this point I can't imagine anyone filling your papa's shoes, or filling his place in my heart and life."

"Never, Mama?" asked B. J.

"Well, maybe in time, son. Come on now, everybody. It's bedtime."

Dawn came with a clear, steely sky sweeping over the land in southern Wyoming. The air was cool, and on the eastern horizon, a faint redness was shining and growing brighter.

In Rock Springs, three people were about to board the westbound Wells Fargo stage. Driver Chuck Stroud and shotgunner Malcolm Evans were getting acquainted with their passengers. The young couple in their early twenties were Bob and Ellie Smith, and the woman in her midfifties was Alma Rader.

Alma was a widow who was going to Fort Bridger to visit her niece and family who had a farm a few miles outside of town. The Smiths had just been married in June and were going to change stagecoaches at Evanston, then go on to Boise, Idaho, to visit Ellie's parents.

By the time the introductions were over, the luggage had been loaded, and the passengers were climbing aboard the stage, the steely sweep of sky had been transformed by the rising sun. It was now a world of red earth, golden rocks, and purple sagebrush. On the prairie all around the town were endless green cedars and blue spruce casting their long shadows.

The passengers chatted together as the stage rolled westward, and soon pulled into Green River. When Chuck Stroud guided the stage to a halt in front of the Wells Fargo office, the agent was standing outside the door, talking to a middle-aged couple who had their arms around a young girl.

The passengers listened as the Fargo agent explained to driver and shotgunner that Susie Joslyn was ten years old. She was being put on the stage by her grandparents, whom she had been visiting for three weeks, and was returning home to Evanston.

The grandparents asked the stage crew to take good care of Susie. Stroud and Evans assured them that they would.

As the grandfather was helping Susie board, Bob Smith leaned toward him and said, "Sir, my name is Bob Smith, and this is my wife, Ellie, here beside me. Ellie and I will be going all the way to Evanston. We'll see that Susie is taken care of."

"Thank you, Mr. Smith," said the grandfather, helping blond, blue-eyed Susie onto the seat beside Alma Rader.

Soon the stage rolled out of Green River and headed for Fort Bridger. Alma introduced herself to the child and helped her to get more comfortable on the seat. The Smiths spoke kindly to her, and Susie warmed up to all three adults.

As the coach rocked and swayed, Alma said, "Susie, how could you visit your grandparents during schooltime? Don't you have to be in school?"

"My mother and father had to go to California to visit my Aunt Bess, ma'am," Susie explained. "She's my mother's sister, and she was very, very sick. So my parents explained to my teacher that I had to stay with my grandparents in Green River while they were in California. My teacher gave me schoolwork to do while I was in Green River."

"Sounds like you have a real nice teacher, honey," said Ellie.

"Oh yes, ma'am. She is very nice."

When the stage was some twenty-five miles from Green River, Chuck Stroud was guiding the six-up team slowly through a narrow passage between two huge rock formations when suddenly three riders in hooded masks with double-barreled shotguns leveled on the crew rode out in front of the stage.

Evans stiffened, and from the side of his mouth said, "Chuck, I can get at least two of them, should I—"

"No!" said Stroud, pulling rein. "It isn't worth it! They'll take what little we've got in the cash box, and be gone."

At the same time, Evans looked back over his shoulder and saw two more masked riders behind the stage, also bearing shotguns. "Oh, boy. There are two more behind us."

"See what I mean?" said Stroud. "If you'd opened up with that shotgun of yours, they'd have blasted you. Maybe both of us. Like I said, it isn't worth it."

Calling down to his passengers as the stage rolled to a halt between the towering rocks, Stroud said, "We've got a holdup on our hands, folks! Everybody stay calm, and we'll get through this all right."

Inside the coach, Susie Joslyn's body went slack and her face lost color.

"Don't be afraid, honey," said Bob Smith, reaching over to take hold of her hand. "Like the driver said, if we stay calm, we'll get through this all right."

The child was trembling. Alma Rader picked her up and placed her on her lap, holding her tight.

Outside, all but one of the gang dismounted and held their guns on the crew, one of them watching the man inside the stage. Rex Holt peered menacingly through the eyeholes of his hood and snapped, "Throw your weapons down! One false move—you die!"

Evans was quick to toss his shotgun to the ground, and then he and Stroud threw down their revolvers.

Dutch Hendrix stayed in the saddle directly in front of the stage, watching the scene closely.

Stroud reached under the seat and lowered the cash box to Rex Holt. Holt took it, handed it to Durbin Mitchell, then looked back up at Stroud and said curtly, "All right, now we want the suitcase with the money in it!"

Stroud frowned. "What suitcase?"

"The one in the rack that's full of money for the Evanston bank! And don't tell me it ain't up there! I want it now, or else!"

Stroud said in a low tone, "Get it for him, Malcolm. There ain't no amount of money worth dying for."

When Evans was handing the small suitcase to Holt, Dutch left his saddle, stepped up to him and said, "Let me check it out."

Dropping to his knees, Dutch laid the suitcase on the ground and opened it. His eyes widened at the sight of the compact bundles of currency neatly packed together, filling the suitcase. Closing it, he stood up, took it by the handle, and said, "Okay, boys, take the valuables from the passengers."

Rafe Ketcham jerked the stagecoach door open, pointed his shotgun at the passengers, and snapped, "Everybody out!"

Susie Joslyn drew in a shuddering breath and let out a strangled cry, breaking into sobs.

"Hey, you!" Ketcham said. "Stop that bellerin'!"

This frightened Susie more, and her crying grew louder.

Spike Denny shouldered his way past Ketcham, grasped Susie's arm, and yanked her out of the coach, snapping at the others to get out. Susie fell to the ground, wailing in blind terror.

As Bob Smith helped his wife and Alma Rader out of the coach, Ketcham stood over the wailing child, roaring at her to shut up. Anger flared in Bob's eyes as he shouted at Ketcham, "Leave her alone!"

Ketcham swore at Bob and cracked him on the head with

his revolver. Ellie screamed as Bob went down, and dropped to her knees beside him. He was unconscious, and blood was beginning to seep from a cut in his scalp.

Susie was still wailing in terror.

Ketcham picked her up, gripped her shoulders, and shook her. "Stop that bawlin', kid!"

"That's enough, Rafe!" Dutch said. "Mount up, boys. We don't need their valuables, anyhow. There's plenty of money in the suitcase."

Ellie bent over Bob, dabbing at the cut on his head with her handkerchief, and Alma wrapped her arms around Susie, holding her tight as the gang mounted up and galloped away. Stroud and Evans climbed down, and while Evans picked up the guns he and the driver had tossed aside, Stroud knelt beside Bob, facing Ellie.

"We'll put him in the stage, ma'am," Stroud said. "I'll drive the horses hard and get us to Fort Bridger as soon as possible. The town has two doctors, and they're both excellent."

"Thank you," said Ellie, tears evident in her eyes.

Susie had stopped crying when Alma helped her back into the stage. Stroud and Evans carried Bob Smith, and Ellie climbed inside the stage. Bob was placed next to Ellie, and she held his upper body on her lap.

At Fort Bridger, Drs. Frank and Patrick O'Brien were standing at the desk in the reception and waiting room talking to Edie when they heard a pounding of hooves and a squeal of brakes. All three looked out the window and saw the Wells Fargo stage skidding to a stop in a cloud of dust.

"Somebody's hurt, Dad," said Patrick, hurrying to the door.

Seconds later Patrick returned, helping Malcolm Evans support Bob Smith as they brought him into the office. Blood was trickling down the side of Bob's pallid face. Patrick explained quickly to his father and mother that the stage had been robbed halfway between Green River and Fort Bridger, and that one of the robbers had cracked Bob on the head. Doc led the way as his son and the shotgunner assisted Bob into the examining and operating room.

Evans appeared again quickly, saying he and Stroud needed to hurry to the Wells Fargo agent and report the robbery. They would be back in a little while.

Ellie was just ahead of Alma and Susie, anguish showing on her face. Edie asked, "Are you his wife, dear?"

"Yes," said Ellie in a tremulous voice.

"Here, honey. Sit down."

Suddenly Doc appeared at the back room door and said, "Edie, will you see if you can find someone on the street to run and bring the marshal, please? These ladies need to tell him about the robbery."

"Will do, dear."

Edie stepped out on the boardwalk and saw two soldiers from the fort and called to them. She made a quick explanation and asked if they would run to the marshal's office and bring him to the clinic.

As the soldiers took off running, Edie stepped back into the office and told Ellie and Alma that she would go and see if her husband and son needed her help.

Ellie rose to her feet and began pacing the floor, wringing her hands. "Oh, Alma," she said in a strained voice, "what if that blow fractured his skull? He will die."

With an arm around Susie, Alma said, "Now, honey, don't cross your bridges before you get to them. It probably isn't that bad at all."

"I wish I could believe that," said Ellie, still pacing and wringing her hands. "That outlaw hit him awfully hard."

The two soldiers returned, looking around for Edie as

they stepped into the office. "Where's Mrs. O'Brien?" asked one of them.

"She's in the back room with my husband," said Ellie. "I guess it would be all right if you knocked on the door."

"I don't want to bother her, ma'am. We have to get back to the fort. Would you tell her that Marshal Mangum and his deputy are both out of town? The deputy's wife is at the office and said they should be back soon. She'll send them over here immediately."

"I'll tell her," said Ellie. "Thank you."

Hardly had the soldiers departed when Edie came in. Ellie rushed to her, took both of her hands with her own, and almost afraid to utter the words, asked, "How is he?"

Edie squeezed her hands. "I don't know for sure yet, but from what my husband and son told me, their preliminary diagnosis is that it isn't serious."

Ellie let out a big gust of air.

Edie smiled. Releasing her hands and patting them lightly, she glanced at Alma and Susie and said, "I think you ladies could both use a cup of hot mint tea."

Alma looked at Ellie, then at Edie, and said, "That would be wonderful."

Edie smiled at Susie. "And how about some hot chocolate for you, little miss?"

"I would love some, ma'am," replied the ten-year-old, giving her a fragile smile.

"Please sit down, Ellie," said Edie. "Pacing the floor isn't going to change a thing." With that, she bustled from the room.

When Edie returned several minutes later, bearing a tray laden with fragrant mint tea and hot chocolate and a plate of soft molasses cookies, she found Ellie standing at the window, staring at the street and the people passing by.

Turning about, Ellie sniffed the aroma of the hot mint tea and said, "That really does smell good." She went to the settee and sat down beside Alma and Susie.

As the ladies sipped their hot drinks, the tension eased, and their nerves settled down. Standing over them, Edie said, "There, now. Isn't that better?"

Susie swallowed a mouthful of cookie and smiled.

Ellie said, "It helps, Mrs. O'Brien. Thank you."

"Yes," said Alma. "There's very little that a strong cup of hot tea won't help."

Ellie had just drained her cup when the door of the back room opened, and the three men emerged with Bob walking between the doctors, a bandage around his head. She put her cup down and rushed to her husband.

"Bob's going to be fine, ma'am," said Patrick. "He has a slight concussion, but I'm sure it will clear up by the time you get to Evanston."

"It took four stitches to close up the wound in his head, Mrs. Smith," said Doc, "and as I told Bob, he should see a doctor when you get to Boise. He'll decide when the stitches can come out."

Ellie blinked against the tears that rushed to her eyes. "Thank you both for taking care of him." The door opened, and four men entered the office as she quipped, "I was afraid of becoming a widow before I even got used to being a bride."

Edie, Alma, and the two doctors chuckled.

Bob put an arm around Ellie's waist, partly for support, since he was still feeling a bit shaky, but mostly to reassure her that he was indeed all right. Ellie kept her eyes on her husband and slipped a supporting arm around him.

Marshal Lance Mangum and Deputy Jack Bower were flanked by Chuck Stroud and Malcolm Evans.

"So Bob's all right, Doc?" Stroud asked.

"He's going to have a whopper of a headache, but yes, he's going to be fine."

"Well, that's good news," said the driver.

Doc introduced the lawmen to the stagecoach passengers, and Mangum said, "We'll need to talk to you and the crew about the holdup."

"Could I do something first, Marshal?" asked Susie.

"What's that, honey?"

Susie moved to Bob, put her arms around his waist, and looked up at him. "Thank you, Mr. Smith, for trying to keep those bad men from frightening me and hurting me."

Bob put an arm around her neck, hugged her close to his side and said, "You're very welcome, honey."

Bob then reached into his hip pocket and took out his wallet. Looking at the doctors, he said, "Before we talk to Marshal Mangum and Deputy Bower, I want to pay you for your services."

"That won't be necessary, Mr. Smith," spoke up Chuck Stroud. "Wells Fargo will send a check to pay for it as soon as we get a bill from the clinic."

"I'll take care of that," said Edie.

Mangum and Bower then quizzed the crew and passengers about the men who robbed the stage. When they were told that the robbers were masked, Mangum asked if the horses had any markings that could identify them.

Nobody recalled any special markings on any of the horses. Chuck Stroud told the lawmen that the robbers rode away eastward, but he could give no descriptions that would be useful to identify the robbers.

Mangum sighed. "Well, without significant descriptions of men or horses, there's really nothing I can do. The robbers are no doubt a long way from that spot by now. The Green River Bank has been notified of the robbery, and they will advise the U.S. marshal's office in Denver. There will probably be some federal men show up to ask questions."

The door opened and Adam Cooper came in with Doug McClain at his side. Doug was carrying a camera, tripod, and flasher. They wanted to get a picture of the crew and passengers, and an interview for an article in the *Fort Bridger Bugle* about the robbery.

Just as Adam and Doug were finishing, Alma Rader's niece, Leah Morley, and her husband, David, drew up in their farm wagon, and whisked Alma away.

Moments later, the crew put their passengers aboard the stage, and with a light-headed Bob Smith sitting between Ellie and Susie, the stage pulled out of Fort Bridger.

Dutch Hendrix and his gang arrived at the hideout and sat down excitedly at the kitchen table to count the money in the suitcase. When they found that they had $70,000 of the bank's money, they lifted up a rousing cheer.

Spike Denny slapped his boss on the back and said, "Well, Dutch, your cut of this loot oughtta make you one happy man!"

Dutch set his mouth in a grim line and looked at Denny with cold eyes. "I won't be happy, Spike, until Mo Froggate has paid his dues. And I'll take care of that tomorrow."

CHAPTER EIGHT

Hannah Cooper awakened deep in the night, and at first was not sure what had pulled her from her slumber. Was it Eddie crying? Raising up on an elbow, she turned her sleepy eyes on the crib. In the chalky wash of moonlight that came through the windows, she saw the baby lying still and sleeping soundly.

But it was somebody crying, she thought. *I'm just sure it was the sound of weeping that—*

There it was again.

Hannah sat up, tossed the covers back, left the bed, and put on her robe and slippers. "It's Mary Beth," she whispered to herself.

Hurrying down the hall, using the wall to guide her, Hannah drew up to the girls' room. But the low sound of weeping was not coming from there. It was coming from the front of the apartment.

The weeping grew louder as Hannah passed the kitchen and headed into the moonlit parlor area. There she found Mary Beth curled up on the couch in her robe, sobbing. She was not aware of her mother's presence until Hannah sat down beside her and put a hand on her shoulder.

Mary Beth swallowed a sob and threw her arms around her mother. "Oh, Mama...I'm sorry. I didn't mean to wake you up. That's why I came out here, so I—"

"Honey, what is it? What are you crying about?"

"I...well, I had a bad dream, and, oh, Mama, it was so real and so awful!"

"What, honey?"

Mary Beth sniffed, wiping tears from her cheeks. "It was about Uncle Jacob. I dreamed he died, Mama! Died lost and went to hell! Oh, it was so awful!"

"Well, sweetheart, we've prayed daily for his salvation and witnessed to him over and over again. The seed of the Word has been planted in his heart and been well-watered. We have to trust the Lord to take the darkness from him and open his understanding to the truth."

"I know, Mama. It's just that...well, so few Jews ever see the truth about Jesus and come to Him for salvation."

Hannah stroked her daughter's tear-stained face. "We'll keep loving Jacob, Mary Beth. And we'll keep praying for him and witnessing to him. I know how you feel. Sometimes it almost seems like he will never be saved. But we can't give up. We have to keep praying and witnessing to him."

"I know it's the devil causing me to doubt, but I'm having an awful time with it."

"Let's read a little, shall we?" said Hannah, letting go of her and rising from the couch. Lighting the lantern on the table at the end of the couch, she picked up the Bible that lay next to the lamp and sat down once again beside Mary Beth. "I've often quoted James 5:16: 'The effectual fervent prayer of a righteous man availeth much.'"

"Yes, and you've taught us what effectual and fervent mean."

"Now, look here with me in 1 John 5:14 and 15. 'And this is the confidence we have in him, that, if we ask anything according to his will, he heareth us: And if we know that he hear us, whatsoever we ask, we know that we have the petitions that we desired of him.' Do you understand?"

"I have some problem with the part about according to His will. We don't always know God's will when we pray about things we desire."

"True, but we do know God's will when we pray for Jacob's salvation. Second Peter 3:9 says God is not willing that any should perish, but that all should come to repentance. Since He is not willing that anybody should go to hell, then He is willing that all should be saved. So when we pray for Jacob to be saved, we most definitely know that we are praying in God's will. And what does it say here? 'If we ask anything according to his will, he heareth us: And if we know that he hear us, whatsoever we ask, we know that we have the petitions that we desired of him.'"

Mary Beth wiped a palm over her face. "Please don't misunderstand me, Mama, but since God is not willing that anyone should go to hell, why doesn't He just save people without our praying?"

"Honey, the Lord never saves anyone against his will. He does not force salvation on anybody. When we pray for a person's salvation, the Lord hears our prayers, and because of them, He sends things into that person's life to put him in a position where the Word of God can convict him of his lost state. He brings about circumstances that will make that person so miserable or so wretched that he will turn to Him. But remember...it takes effectual, fervent praying to bring this about.

"This is why you've seen Christians who were burdened over the lost condition of some friend or loved one, and they have even prayed, but that person has died lost. The key to seeing our friends and loved ones saved, once we've made sure to witness to them in love, is the effectual, fervent praying we do. So many Christians are not willing to pay the price. And what is 'effectual'?"

"It means to work at or labor in."

"And what is 'fervent'?"

"Eager. Impassioned. Zealous."

"The kind of prayer that brings about the salvation of devil-blinded souls is the kind where we labor zealously in prayer without ceasing till we see them saved."

"Then we should pray harder for Uncle Jacob, shouldn't we?"

"Yes, we should."

"Then we will. I will. But where my faith is weak, Mama, is knowing Uncle Jacob clings hard to his Jewish faith."

Hannah smiled. "Let me remind you of a Jew in the Bible who was more stubborn by far than Jacob. He was not only stubborn, but he hated Christians and persecuted them, even unto death. You know who I mean, don't you?"

Mary Beth nodded. "Saul of Tarsus."

"But he was stopped on the Damascus road by the Lord Jesus Himself, and was put under such conviction that he got saved right then and there. If the Lord could save Saul of Tarsus, honey, he can save Jacob of Fort Bridger."

Mary Beth smiled. "I can imagine that there were a lot of Christians effectually and fervently praying for Saul to get saved."

Hannah laughed. "I never thought about that, but I'm sure you're right."

Mary Beth took a deep breath and sighed. "Mama, you've strengthened my faith. We are going to see Uncle Jacob saved. There's no way to know what circumstances the Lord might send into his life to bring this about, but whatever it is, I know Uncle Jacob is going to get saved."

Hannah hugged her. "That's what I wanted to hear. Let's pray for Jacob right now. Then we both need to get back to bed."

Mother and daughter prayed together effectually and fervently for Jacob Kates to come to faith in Jesus Christ.

When they rose to their feet, Hannah folded the girl in her

arms and said, "Thank you, Mary Beth, for being so tender and sweet."

Mary Beth kissed Hannah's cheek and said, "I learned it from my mother."

Early on Friday morning, Dutch Hendrix rode into Fort Bridger, vengeance on his mind. There were a few people on the street, but the day's business had not yet begun.

Angling to the east side of Main Street, Hendrix fixed his attention on the sign above a door a half block away: *Fort Bridger Hardware Store and Gun Shop—Justin Powell, Prop.*

Passing slowly by the place, he noted a small sign on the door that told him the store would open at eight o'clock. Noting the clock on the sign of the Fort Bridger Bank a little further down the street, he saw that it was 7:48.

Dutch swung to the hitching rail in front of the shoe and boot store next door and dismounted. He tied the reins loosely to the hitching rail, then adjusted the sheath on his gun belt and touched the handle of the large hunting knife in the sheath.

Moving in a casual manner so as not to draw attention from the few people moving about on the street, he eased up to the edge of the hardware store's large window and peered inside. Mo Froggate was behind the counter talking to a tall, lanky man Hendrix assumed was Justin Powell.

Hendrix eased back from the window and leaned against the wall of the shoe and boot store next door as if he were waiting for it to open.

Moments later, he heard the lock turn on the door of the hardware store and saw Justin Powell come out. When Powell was several doors down the street, Dutch gripped the handle of the hunting knife, looked both ways to make sure no one close by was heading for the hardware store, and slipped inside.

A few minutes later, banker Lloyd Dawson was crossing

the street on his way to the bank when his attention was drawn to a man running out of the hardware store with a large knife in his hand. The man sheathed the knife, vaulted into the saddle of his horse, and galloped away in a cloud of dust.

Dawson headed for the hardware store, and just before he reached the door, the man he recognized as the new clerk came staggering out and fell, holding his midsection. Kneeling beside him, Dawson saw the blood running between the man's fingers and looked around until he saw a farmer passing by in a wagon and shouted, "Hey, Mack, Bill Wolfram's been stabbed! Go get one of the doctors!"

As the farmer nodded and put his horses to a gallop, Dawson saw the town's pharmacist across the street about to open the drugstore and shouted, "Eugene! Bill Wolfram's been stabbed! Mack Harley is going for a doctor. Go get the marshal, will you?"

As the pharmacist hurried toward the marshal's office, Dawson leaned over the bleeding man and said, "Bill, we'll have one of the doctors here shortly."

Through clenched teeth, the wounded man said, "Lloyd, I'm...not...gonna make it. The guy...who stabbed me was Dutch Hendrix."

Dawson's eyebrows arched. "The outlaw?"

"Yes. I'm...I'm not Bill Wolfram. My real name is...Mo Froggate. I used to be...in Dutch's gang. Stole money from... the gang. Dutch stabbed me as...payback. I—"

Froggate threw his head back, then went limp, eyes closed.

Seconds later, Marshal Lance Mangum, Deputy Jack Bower, and Dr. Patrick O'Brien arrived at the same time.

Lloyd Dawson looked up at them and said, "He's dead." Then he informed them of what Froggate had told him about himself, naming the gang leader as his killer.

Mangum said, "Hendrix is wanted all over Wyoming for

robbery and murder. Jack and I will go after him."

"He rode east out of town, Marshal," said Dawson.

Holding his horse to a full gallop, Dutch Hendrix felt safer every minute as he rode toward Rock Springs, looking back over his shoulder. He was about six miles out of Fort Bridger when he spotted two riders coming behind him at full speed, kicking up dust clouds.

He swore and snapped the reins against his horse's neck. Another few minutes showed him that the two riders were gaining on him. There was less than a hundred yards between them. Lashing the animal beneath him even harder, he screamed at him to go faster.

Suddenly the horse threw a shoe from his right front hoof. He stumbled, then went down headfirst, throwing his rider from the saddle. The horse ejected a shrill whinny as he rolled over and over, and Dutch slammed the ground hard. By the time he stopped rolling, he found himself in a cloud of dust, a bit dazed.

The two riders drew up, skidded to a halt, and slid from their saddles. A dizzy Dutch Hendrix clawed for his gun, but it had fallen from his holster.

"Yep, it's Hendrix, all right, Jack," the marshal said. "Looks just like the picture on the wanted poster we've got on him at the office. Put the cuffs on him."

While Jack Bower was cuffing Hendrix, the marshal said, "I'm Lance Mangum, marshal of Fort Bridger. You're under arrest, Dutch. Murder is the charge, and the latest is the murder of Mo Froggate, alias Bill Wolfram."

As Hendrix was being lifted into the saddle of his limping horse, Mangum said, "We have a nice uncomfortable jail cell for you, Dutch. The circuit judge will be in Fort Bridger in about a week, so you can stand trial for murder. With all the murders on your record, my deputy and I might as well get our portable gallows ready. As you no doubt know, when outlaws are hung in a Wyoming town, it is done on Main Street so the public can witness it. We do it this way so some young would-be outlaws can see what happens to men like you…hoping it will cause them to take a different path in life."

Dutch only glared at the marshal with hate-filled eyes.

When Mangum and Bower rode into Fort Bridger with their prisoner riding between them, they saw a crowd gathered in front of the hardware store. Adam Cooper and Doug McClain were there with a camera, and Lloyd Dawson was telling his story with Justin Powell standing beside him.

Suddenly a man in the crowd pointed to the three riders and shouted, "Hey, they're back, and they've got him!"

When the lawmen drew up with Dutch Hendrix in tow, Adam Cooper rushed up and said, "Marshal, will you give us a statement for the *Bugle*?"

"Sure," replied Mangum, dismounting.

"And could we take Hendrix's picture, Marshal?" asked Doug. "We want to put it on the front page of our next edition."

"Anything you want, gentlemen. Go ahead and take the picture. Then we'll lock him up."

At the hideout near Rock Springs, Rex Holt, Spike Denny, Rafe Ketcham, and Durbin Mitchell stood in the cool autumn air on the front porch, gazing toward the west as the sun was setting in long-fingered, blood red clouds.

"Somethin's gone wrong," Durbin said.

"We don't know that for sure," Spike said. "It just might be that Dutch is havin' a hard time gettin' to Mo. Him workin' in that hardware store keeps him where there's probably people all day long. Dutch may have to wait till after dark to get him."

"That could be exactly it, Spike," said Rafe. "Let's give it some time before we panic. How about we go ahead and eat supper?"

"Sounds good to me," said Durbin. "I'm glad it's your turn to do the cookin', Spike."

While Spike was preparing the meal in the kitchen, the other three sat on the porch, talking about when they would go south to Colorado. By the time Spike called them in to eat, twilight was stealing across the rugged land and slowly turning into gloom.

After supper the four gang members stood at the parlor window, observing the black vault of sky overhead as it brightened with blinking stars. Then came the serene, silent Wyoming night.

They sat down and Rex and Durbin listened while Rafe and Spike talked about the "old days" when they were in the Jake Mallory gang. Though there were some moments of humor, at the back of their minds was Dutch Hendrix and the fear that something had gone wrong.

Finally when it was almost eleven o'clock, Rex said, "Boys, I think we'd better go find him."

"You mean ride into Fort Bridger and start askin' if anybody's seen the famous outlaw with the price on his head?" said Durbin.

"Well, I didn't mean that, exactly. But we can't just sit here. We gotta do something."

"I think Spike hit the nail on the head when he said Dutch might be havin' a hard time gettin' to Mo," said Rafe. "Mo likes the saloons, you know. And if that's where he is, Dutch will have to wait till he heads for home to get him."

"And for all we know, there might be some other complications," said Rafe. "Dutch is so set on killin' Mo that he no doubt will hang around town till he gets his chance. It might even take a couple of days. I think we'd better just sit tight."

Rex sighed. "You're right, Rafe. We'd better just stay here. Ol' Dutch knows what he's doin'."

Sunday came with heavy clouds that looked like they could begin dropping snow at any time.

Gary and Glenda Williams had invited Captain Dane Kirkland to Sunday dinner that afternoon, along with Hannah and her children, and the Singletons. The Williamses' foster daughter, fifteen-year-old Abby Turner, had helped Glenda prepare the meal early on Sunday morning so it would be almost ready when everyone arrived from church. The Williamses had hurried home after the morning service so Glenda and Abby could take care of last-minute details before their guests arrived.

When the knock came at the door, a smiling Gary opened it and welcomed them.

Various delicious aromas greeted the guests as they stepped into the house and began shedding their coats, scarves, and hats. Glenda and Abby made a brief appearance to greet them, then hurried back to the kitchen.

Ben Singleton sniffed the air, and speaking loud enough for his voice to carry back to the kitchen, called out, "Smells like turkey and dressing to me!"

Glenda appeared in the hallway and said, "You're right on target, Mr. Singleton. And if everybody will gather in the dining room, it will be ready in about three minutes."

Glenda's dining room table sparkled with a snowy white damask cloth. Her best china was gleaming in golden candlelight.

Just as everyone was sitting down, they looked out the big dining room window and saw that the heavily laden clouds had let go of the burden they had been carrying all morning. Fat, fluffy snowflakes swirled around the house as the wind picked up and buffeted them as they fell.

As Glenda sat down and ran her gaze around the table, she said, "I apologize for the table seating being a little crowded, but—"

"Glenda, dear," cut in Esther, "don't fret about that. Everything is perfect. On such a snowy day, sitting close together only adds to the comfort of being in here away from the elements!"

"You've got that right, Mama," said Ben. "Let's pray and dig in!"

Gary asked Ben to pray over the food, which he did quickly.

During the meal, Hannah talked about her experience in losing Solomon in an attempt to encourage Dane Kirkland. When the meal was almost over, and he had finished his apple pie, Dane said, "Mrs. Cooper, you have been such a help to me. You know the bitterness I was carrying..."

"You mean the bitterness you felt toward the Lord for allowing the deaths of Mary and Donnie?"

"Yes. Well, I want to say right here in front of everybody that your words concerning your husband's having been taken from you, and how you've handled it by letting the Lord work in your heart and life, have helped me to get over the bitterness. I was dead wrong to feel that way toward the Lord, and I have asked Him to forgive me."

"Which, of course, He has," said Hannah. "Captain, one of the lessons I had to learn through my own heartache is that bitterness is like a disease, and it will destroy all of the joy in a Christian's life if you let it consume you. You can never get peace in your grief if you continually feed on bitterness. And worst of all, it robs you of God's blessings."

"You are so right," said Dane. "You and the Kellys have helped me so much to see this and to rid my heart of bitterness and of blaming the Lord for letting it happen."

"I'm so glad," said Hannah. "During those first few

months after Solomon's death, I spent a lot of time in the book of Job. Think of all the tragedies that befell him, yet in the midst of it all, Job said of the Lord, 'Though he slay me, yet will I trust in him.'"

Abby spoke up. "Mrs. Cooper, when my family was killed by the Indians and I came here to live with Mom and Dad Williams, they had me in the book of Job a lot. And it has stayed with me that in the midst of it all, Job had confidence in God that He would lead him through the storms that assailed him, and that there are precious blessings to be found in trials. All we have to do is find them."

"Yes," said Hannah. "One of the verses I memorized in Job was 5:18. I've had over a year now, since Solomon was taken from me, to let the Lord heal my wounded heart. And though it hasn't been an easy road, Job 5:18 rings so true. It says of the Lord: 'For he maketh sore, and bindeth up; he woundeth, and his hands make whole.' God's Word has been my constant companion in all of this, and my greatest source of comfort."

Reaching across the corner of the table Hannah smiled and placed a tentative hand on Dane's arm. "It will be that way for any child of God, Captain Kirkland, and it can be *your* greatest comfort too, if you will immerse yourself in it and hide it in your heart."

Dane nodded. "Pastor Kelly told me the same thing, and I've been reading my Bible more than ever and memorizing verses he has shown me. I'm going to work on Job 5:18, too." He patted her hand and released a smile that reached his eyes, erasing some of the sorrow there. "I wish I could tell you how much you've helped me, ma'am."

Hannah smiled again. "Captain, right after my children and I arrived here in Fort Bridger almost fifteen months ago, Pastor Kelly told me that the Lord would use me to help others because of my losing Solomon. I'm glad to know He has used me to help you."

That evening after church, Dane was walking the Cooper family home as snowflakes pelted them, driven by the wind. Escorting Hannah and her children to and from church was becoming routine for Dane, and he loved it. Chris carried Eddie, and there was very little talk as the small group walked rapidly through the night.

When they arrived at the foot of the stairs behind the apartment, Dane said, "Mrs. Cooper, could I have a private word with you before you go upstairs?"

Hannah wiped snowflakes from her eyelashes and said, "Of course. Children, you go on up. I'll be there shortly."

The Cooper children entered the apartment and Hannah waited for Dane to speak.

"Mrs. Cooper," he said, "I'll only keep you a moment. I want to say again what a marvelous blessing you have been to me, and—well, I just wanted to ask if you will call me by my first name from now on. I feel like we have become friends."

"All right, Dane," she said, warming him with a smile. "But of course this works two ways. I certainly feel that we have become friends, so you will no longer address me as *Mrs. Cooper.* You will call me Hannah."

A smile spread over his face from ear to ear. "I'll just do that, Hannah. Thank you. Now, I will tell you good night and let you get in out of this weather."

Hannah told him good night and hurried up the stairs. Dane waited till he saw her enter the apartment, then turned and headed for the fort. "Lord," he said, bending his head against the wind, "that is one wonderful woman. And those children of hers are wonderful, too."

Chapter Nine

Hannah stepped into the apartment, closed the door, and removed her coat and hat. She shook the snow from them, then hung them on a peg by the door, along with those of her children.

A warm feeling was flooding her heart, but she couldn't quite put her finger on the source of it. She stood there for a moment, shrugged her shoulders, gave her head a small shake, then turned around to see Mary Beth standing in the kitchen area. She had a paper bag in her hands and was rolling the top down.

Moving to her, Hannah said, "What's in the bag, honey?"

"The oatmeal cookies I made especially for Uncle Jacob yesterday. Since it was the Sabbath, I couldn't go down and give them to him. May I take them down now?"

Hannah hugged her. "It's snowing, honey. Couldn't it wait till morning? Besides, I was about to fix a snack for all of us."

"I'm not hungry, Mama. Please. May I take them down to him?"

Hannah smiled. "You want to talk to him some more about Jesus, don't you?"

"I've got my small Bible tucked in my coat pocket. There's some Scripture I want to show Uncle Jacob, if he will let me."

Hannah's face was beaming as she kissed Mary Beth's cheek and said, "Mary Beth Cooper, you are such a blessing. Don't stay too long."

"Just a little while," she said, and with paper bag in hand, hurried to the door. Setting the bag down, she put on her coat and scarf, picked up the bag, and stepped out onto the snow-laden deck. She took a few steps toward the stairs, then stopped in her tracks. Something was scratching at the back of her mind, but she couldn't identify it.

Suddenly she knew what it was.

A tiny smile started, then burgeoned into a wide grin. "It's Mama!" she said aloud as the snow pelted her face. "That's it! There is definitely something different about her. She...she seems in better spirits than I've seen her since Papa—well, since Papa was taken from us. Thank you, Lord!"

And with that happy thought she made her way down the stairs, holding onto the handrail, with a prayer in her young heart for Uncle Jacob's salvation.

When Jacob Kates answered the knock on his door, a smile broke across his face. "Well, hello, Mary Beth! Come in!"

Mary Beth stepped inside Jacob's quarters, which were part of the back side of the store building. "I brought you something!" she said cheerfully.

Jacob closed the door, looked at the paper bag in her hand, and said, "Is it what I'm thinking?"

She giggled. "That depends on what you're thinking."

The little man bent over and sniffed the bag. "Yes! I was thinking my favorite kind of cookies, and that sack sure smells like oatmeal cookies to me!"

Mary Beth giggled again as she handed the bag to him.

Jacob took it from her and said, "Honey, this means so much to me. Thank you."

She hugged him. "I made them for you because I love you, Uncle Jacob."

"And I'll eat them because I love *you!*" he said.

Mary Beth's eyes took on a more serious look. "Uncle Jacob, I actually had two reasons for coming down here tonight. One was to bring you the cookies, and the other was that this morning in Sunday school, Mrs. O'Brien was teaching us some history related to the Bible, and it was really interesting. I'd like to show it to you."

"I'd like to see it."

Mary Beth slipped the small Bible from her coat pocket, laid it on a nearby table, and Jacob helped her out of her coat. Leaving coat and scarf draped over a chair, she picked up the Bible and followed Jacob to a small couch, where they sat down side by side.

Turning to face him, she said, "Uncle Jacob, when Mama showed you some Scriptures about Jesus Christ and asked you what your Messiah could *be* or *do* different than Him, you couldn't come up with anything. You said you'd have to think about it. Have you thought about it?"

"Well...some."

"And?"

Jacob cleared his throat lightly. "Mary Beth, I haven't been able to put much time to it."

Mary Beth nodded. "Well, let me show you this, and see what you think."

With a prayer in her heart and butterflies in her stomach, Mary Beth opened her Bible to Luke 19. Scooting a little closer to him, she held the Bible so both of them could see it and said, "You follow along as I read it out loud, okay? I want you to see a prophecy the Lord Jesus gave about Jerusalem. This is Him speaking."

"All right. Go ahead."

Mary Beth read slowly and carefully. "'And when he was come near, he beheld the city, and wept over it, saying, If thou hadst known, even thou, at least in this thy day, the things which belong unto thy peace! but now they are hid from thine eyes. For the days will come upon thee, that thine enemies shall cast a trench about thee, and compass thee round, and keep thee in on every side, and shall lay thee even with the ground, and thy children within thee; and they shall not leave in thee one stone upon another; because thou knewest not the time of thy visitation.'"

When Mary Beth looked at Jacob, he frowned and blinked as if he had heard something that disturbed him.

"Uncle Jacob, this prophecy was fulfilled exactly as the Lord Jesus said it would be. Do you know when it happened?"

Dry of mouth, Jacob licked his lips. "I most certainly do. I studied about it in school, and since then, I've heard the rabbis talk about it. But..."

"But what?"

"I...I was never told that Jesus Christ had foretold it."

"Well, you see now that He did."

Jacob swallowed hard, licked his lips again. "Yes. It...it happened in the year 70. That would have been nearly forty years after Jesus Christ made the prophecy, wouldn't it?"

"That's right."

The little man wiped a hand across his brow. "The Roman emperor Titus Vespasianus led his army to destroy Jerusalem, and it happened exactly as we just read."

Mary Beth smiled at him. "So, Uncle Jacob, Jesus' prophecy was fulfilled to the letter, wasn't it?"

Slowly his head began to nod. "Yes, honey. It was." He licked his lips again. "Mary Beth...what did Jesus mean when He said: 'thou knewest not the time of thy visitation'?"

"Mrs. O'Brien explained that this morning. The Lord Jesus Christ came to earth as Israel's true King and Messiah and visited Jerusalem, but the people of Israel rejected Him. Therefore they would be punished by God. He would let their enemies destroy their city and the temple."

Jacob's head bent down, and he rubbed his forehead with a shaky hand.

"Mrs. O'Brien explained that the Old Testament clearly prophesied the coming of the Messiah and gave a perfect picture of Him. The Jews refused to believe that Jesus was the Messiah in spite of all the evidence He had shown to prove it."

Jacob continued to rub his forehead. "But if Jesus was the true Messiah, my people didn't know it. Somehow, they didn't know it. Why would God punish them?"

"Mrs. O'Brien talked about that, Uncle Jacob. She said that when a man drunk on whiskey commits some crime without knowing what he's doing, it doesn't remove his guilt. Because he is responsible for getting himself into this drunken condition, he must pay for breaking the law. So God holds us all accountable for an ignorance which He knows is due to our neglect."

Jacob's head came up. Deep lines penciled themselves across his time-weathered brow. "Neglect?"

"This was the case with the Jews in that day. If they had earnestly and sincerely studied the Scriptures written by their own prophets, they would have seen in Jesus of Nazareth the divine Visitor whose coming Israel had been expecting for long ages. But they neglected the Scriptures, and because of this self-inflicted ignorance, they knew not the time of their visitation by their Messiah, King, and Saviour. God, therefore, would punish them for it."

Jacob Kates was like a man who had been struck by lightning. His eyes were wide, and his face void of color.

Seeing the state that the little Jewish man was in, Mary Beth flipped to the first chapter of the Gospel of John. Pointing her finger to verse 11, she said, "Look here, Uncle Jacob. It says of Jesus, 'He came unto his own, and his own received him not.' His own were the people of Israel. Now look at the next verse. 'But as many as received him, to them gave he power to become the sons of God, even to them that believe on his name.' Do you see that? We human beings born in the image of

Adam are not the children of God when we are born into God's world. We are His *creation,* but not His children. We must *become* the sons of God. In order to enter God's family, we must believe that Jesus Christ is the true and only Saviour and in repentance of our sin, receive Him into our hearts. Ephesians 3:17 says, 'That Christ may dwell in your *hearts* by faith.'"

Jacob was bending forward, staring at the floor.

Tears filled Mary Beth's eyes as she bent lower so she could look into his face. "Uncle Jacob, you can receive Jesus into your heart and become a child of God. You can be saved if you will believe on His name and open your heart to Him."

Jacob swallowed with difficulty and scrubbed a palm over his eyes, but continued to stare at the floor.

Laying a tender hand on his shoulder, she said, "Will you, Uncle Jacob? Will you receive my Saviour into your heart and make Him your Saviour, too? The Bible says, 'Whosoever shall call upon the name of the Lord shall be saved.' I'll help you."

Jacob turned and looked into her tear-filled eyes. The muscles in his jaw were rippling under the skin.

Leaning to him and placing her soft cheek against his, she said, "I love you. And more than anything in the whole world, I want you to be saved."

Jacob placed a hand on the other side of her head and held it there.

Putting an arm around his shoulder, Mary Beth sniffed as tears spilled down her cheeks and said, "Uncle Jacob, Jesus loves you. He died for you on the cross so you could be saved if you will believe on Him. And I love you so much that if giving up my life would cause you to call on Jesus and be saved, I would do it."

This brought tears to Jacob's eyes. Releasing her head from his hand, he straightened up, looked into her eyes, and said, "You are such a sweet girl. This is all so foreign to the way I have been taught since I was a little child. You have shown me things here that I didn't know. But I must have time to think on them."

"I'll be praying for you, Uncle Jacob, that the Lord will help you to understand it all."

"Thank you," he said softly.

Rising from the couch, she said, "I'd better get upstairs. It'll soon be bedtime."

Jacob helped her into her coat. She slipped the Bible into a pocket, put on her scarf, and hugged the little man one more time. They bid each other good night, and Mary Beth stepped out into the storm. Jacob watched her till she turned the corner of the building toward the stairs, then closed the door.

Turning slowly, he moved like a man in a trance as he readied himself for bed, put out the lantern, and slipped between the covers.

Slumber, however, eluded Jacob Kates.

He could not sleep for thinking about the things that both Hannah and Mary Beth had shown him in the New Testament, which he had always been taught to disregard and disbelieve.

As he tossed and turned with the sound of the wind moaning outside in the eaves, Mary Beth's words came back to haunt him: *I love you so much that if giving up my life would cause you to call on Jesus and be saved, I would do it.*

Finally, after over two hours of hearing those words echo through his head, Jacob Kates fell asleep.

At midmorning on Monday, Rafe Ketcham, Rex Holt, Durbin Mitchell, and Spike Denny rode into Rock Springs just to get out of the hideout for a while. The snow in the street was almost gone.

"This cold air is gettin' to my bones," said Rex. "How about us goin' into the Wagon Wheel Saloon and drinkin' a little firewater?"

"Sounds good to me," said Rafe.

When the four outlaws had dismounted, they crossed the boardwalk toward the saloon door. Next to the saloon was a general store. From the corner of his eye, Rafe noted a newspaper rack in the big window of the store, and what he saw on the front page of the *Fort Bridger Bugle* froze him in place.

Spike was on his heels and bumped into him. The other two were almost to the saloon door. Halting, they looked at Rafe, who pointed at the newspaper rack and said, "There's Dutch!"

Suddenly the other three saw the large photograph on the front page of Saturday's edition of the *Bugle* with bold headlines that read:

OUTLAW DUTCH HENDRIX JAILED FOR MURDER!

"Dutch is in jail, it says!" reported Durbin.

Rafe moved toward the door, saying, "Be right back." Less than two minutes later, he returned with a copy of the paper and said, "Let's go sit down at a table in the saloon and read this."

Entering the saloon, they sat down at an isolated table, ordered drinks, and Rafe read the front-page article to them, keeping his voice low. They learned that Dutch had been arrested for stabbing Mo Froggate alias Bill Wolfram to death on Friday, and would face the circuit judge for his string of murders.

Rafe banged a fist on the table. "They'll hang him, guys!"

Looking around, Spike said, "Hey, not so loud, Rafe!"

Rafe shook his head. "Sorry," he said, once again keeping his voice low. "We've got to get Dutch outta that jail quick! It says here that the circuit judge will be in town later this week."

"Okay," said Spike, "how are we gonna get him out of that jail?"

Durbin said, "Somehow we'll have to go into the marshal's office, get the drop on him and any deputies he might have, and force 'em to let Dutch outta the cell. We'll lock the marshal and his deputies in the cell and ride outta town with Dutch a free man."

Rafe shook his head. "No! As you guys know, I've been around these parts some, and believe me, you don't want to mess with Marshal Lance Mangum. He's tough as nails, and he's nobody's fool. He's too smart to let that happen. We could all end up in jail. I've got a better idea."

"Okay," said Rex, "let's hear it."

"Fort Bridger's got a school."

Spike's face twisted. "So what's that got to do with gettin' Dutch outta jail?"

Raising a finger, Rafe said, "Just hear me out. The four of us could enter the schoolhouse suddenly tomorrow mornin' when school is in session and hold the teacher and the students as hostages."

A grin spread over Rex Holt's face. "Ah...now I'm gettin' the picture. Go ahead."

"Well, the last I knew, there's only one teacher. While we're holdin' guns on her and the students, we'd send an older student to tell the marshal we have the teacher and the children at our mercy, and we'll start shootin' 'em within fifteen minutes if Dutch ain't delivered to us."

Spike laughed. "This is good, ol' pal! Even though this Mangum may be tough and smart, your plan will put him in a corner. He'll have to give in to our demands."

"Okay," said Rafe, "once Dutch is free, we'll take two children with us. We'll warn Mangum that if we're followed, the kids will be killed. And then, if we're not followed—which we won't be—we'll leave the kids at some ranch or farm when we're a safe distance away, then ride on."

Durbin Mitchell was frowning. "I'll go along with it, Rafe, as long as we all agree that no child will be hurt or killed, no matter what."

Rafe guffawed, slapped him on the shoulder, and said, "Don't worry, Durb! We ain't gonna hurt no kids."

"Looks like a foolproof plan to me," said Rex.

"Good," Rafe said, looking at the other two. "You guys in agreement?"

"Sure," said Spike.

"Me too," Durbin said, "as long as no kids get hurt."

Rafe fixed him with steady eyes. "Like I said, Durb, we ain't gonna hurt no kids."

Late on Monday afternoon—after the Cooper children had come home from school and Mary Beth had taken Eddie upstairs to the apartment—Hannah and Jacob took care of their last customers for the day and closed the store.

While they were behind the counter counting the money and working on the day's receipts, Jacob eyed Hannah when she wasn't looking at him, a question stirring in his mind. Hannah was always a very pleasant person to be around, and most of the time was a happy soul, but all day, Jacob had been aware of a subtle softness about her demeanor. He hadn't given it a lot of thought since it had been an unusually busy day, but now, as they worked together at the cash drawer, he noticed her inability to stay focused on her work.

Even as she was supposed to be counting money and adding up checks, Jacob caught her staring off into space, a soft sigh escaping her lips.

"Hannah…" he said in a low tone. "Hannah…"

Jacob laid a hand on her shoulder, and she jumped and said, "Oh, Jacob, I'm sorry. Did you say something?"

A wee secret smile beamed from Jacob's lips. "It's nothing. We just need to get our work done."

"Oh yes. Yes," she said, a guilty look in her eyes. "Just woolgathering, I guess. Now, where were we?"

Jacob hid another smile. "I was making records on the financial sheet, and you were counting the money."

"Of course," she said, returning to her work.

Jacob went back to his task. However, his heart felt a little lighter, though he wasn't sure just why.

A few minutes later, as Hannah was endorsing the checks, she said, "Jacob, did you and Mary Beth have a nice talk last night?"

The little man chuckled. "Any time spent with that girl is nice, Hannah, but I'll say this. If Mary Beth were a boy, I'm sure she would end up being a preacher. She has a marvelous way with words, and she really knows her Bible."

"I hope she wasn't overbearing."

"Not at all. She just has it in her heart to see that I become a Christian."

"I know."

"Of course you do. Your whole family—except little Eddie for obvious reasons—has the same thing in your hearts."

"We love you, that's why."

"I know," he said, scratching his head, "but Hannah, in order for me to become a Christian, I would have to give up what the rabbis have taught me about Jesus Christ. I'd have to change my thinking completely to put my faith in Him as the Messiah and Saviour."

Placing the checks in an envelope, Hannah looked at him and said, "Jacob, many Jews have done that very thing. There were two Jewish families in Independence who became Christians when I was in my teens, and became faithful members of our church. Later they were able to bring a few of their relatives to Jesus."

"Really?"

"Yes. And, Jacob, are you aware that the book of Hebrews in the New Testament was written to Jews who had become Christians?"

"Well, I've heard of that book in the New Testament, but I didn't know why it was called Hebrews."

"Well, that's why. Didn't you tell me once that you are of the tribe of Benjamin?"

"That's what my parents told me."

"Have you ever heard of Saul of Tarsus in the New Testament?"

"He was the one who became Paul the apostle, wasn't he?"

"Yes. Well, Paul—Saul was also of the tribe of Benjamin."

"Are you sure?"

Hannah always kept a Bible under the counter. Pulling it out, she opened it to the book of Philippians, and said, "Right here. Philippians 3:5. Paul speaks of himself and says, 'Circumcised the eighth day, of the stock of Israel, of the tribe of Benjamin, an Hebrew of the Hebrews.' There it is. Plain as day."

Jacob nodded. "Sure enough. He was of Benjamin's tribe, just like me."

"And he became a Christian, Jacob. Have you ever read the account of when and where that Jew of the tribe of Benjamin became a Christian?"

"No, I haven't."

Flipping pages, Hannah said, "It's in Acts chapter 9. Saul of Tarsus took a journey from Jerusalem to Damascus with the intention of persecuting Christians there, Jacob, and it was on that Damascus journey that he became a Christian. Here. Follow along as I read aloud. Verses 1 through 8…

"'And Saul, yet breathing out threatenings and slaughter against the disciples of the Lord, went unto the high priest, and desired of him letters to Damascus to the synagogues, that if he found any of this way, whether they were men or women, he might bring them bound unto Jerusalem. And as he journeyed, he came near Damascus: and suddenly there shined round about him a light from heaven: And he fell to the earth, and heard a voice saying unto him, Saul, Saul, why persecutest thou me?

"'And he said, Who art thou, Lord? And the Lord said, I am Jesus whom thou persecutest: it is hard for thee to kick against the pricks. And he trembling and astonished said, Lord, what wilt thou have me to do? And the Lord said unto him, Arise, and go into the city, and it shall be told thee what thou must do.

"'And the men which journeyed with him stood speechless, hearing a voice, but seeing no man. And Saul arose from the earth; and when his eyes were opened, he saw no man: but they led him by the hand, and brought him into Damascus.'"

Jacob's eyes were fastened on the page, unblinking.

"Jacob, when Jesus stopped Saul on the Damascus road, it shook him so hard that he was trembling. The man of Benjamin's tribe had come face to face with the true Messiah, and it astonished him to learn that it was Jesus Christ."

Jacob was still staring at the page.

Touching his arm, Hannah said, "I'll ask you again, Jacob dear…what could your Messiah *do* or *be* that would make him different than Jesus Christ?"

Jacob scrubbed a palm over his eyes.

Hannah squeezed his arm. "Will you put your faith in Jesus to save you like Saul of Tarsus did? I'll be glad to help you."

The little man took a deep breath and said, "Hannah dear, in order to do that, I will have to have my own Damascus journey."

CHAPTER TEN

I t was snowing lightly on Tuesday morning. The Coopers and Jacob Kates sat down to a warm, hearty breakfast.

The Cooper kitchen was always a cheerful place, and even the heavy gray clouds that filled the sky couldn't put a damper on the happy chatter around the table. Little Eddie, who sat in his high chair between his mother and youngest sister, made everyone laugh when he insisted on feeding himself pancakes cut in small pieces. Syrup was running down his chin, and his tongue was out as far as it could go as he tried to lick every drop. Knowing he was the center of attention, he beamed and clapped his sticky hands together.

When breakfast was over, Jacob helped Hannah and Mary Beth with the kitchen chores while Chris and B. J. were straightening up their room.

Patty Ruth took on the tricky job of washing Eddie's hands and face.

Eddie cooperated fully when Patty Ruth used a warm, wet cloth to wash his hands, but the instant she raised the cloth to wash away the syrup on his face, he started giggling and turning his head quickly from side to side.

Patty Ruth did the best she could, but Hannah saw that it was futile. Moving to the high chair, she said, "Patty Ruth, I think it's going to take a grown-up to get that face clean."

The little redhead sighed in exasperation and willingly handed the cloth to her mother. Eddie continued to squirm and laugh, but Hannah had his face shiny clean in short order.

Soon Chris, Mary Beth, B. J., and Patty Ruth were in their coats and ready to leave for school. They hugged their mother, kissed little Eddie's cheek, and hugged Uncle Jacob.

When the children were gone, Hannah said, "Well, Jacob, it's almost time to open the store. We'd better get down there."

Little Eddie was bundled up quickly, and Jacob carried him as they went carefully down the stairs, which were slowly gathering new snow. Before going to the Cooper apartment for breakfast, Jacob had built a fire in the store's potbellied stove, and a warm, toasty atmosphere welcomed them when they entered through the back door.

While Jacob carried Eddie to the pallet on the floor near the stove, Hannah paused for a moment, and just stood there looking around at the shelves stocked with everything from yard goods to molasses. She glanced at the wooden counter and the large glass jars filled with crackers, candy, flour, and sugar. A satisfied smile lifted her lips, and a prayer of thanks was sent heavenward.

A squeal from Eddie caught her attention. She quickly hung her coat and scarf on a peg by the door and squared her shoulders, ready for the workday to begin.

As Jacob opened the top of the potbellied stove and tossed in another log, he thought again of Mary Beth's words from Sunday night about the price she would be willing to pay to see him saved. Tears filled his eyes. Hannah drew up beside him, and was about to say that she would go prepare the cash drawer when she saw his tears.

Brow furrowed, she said, "Jacob, are you all right?"

Wiping away the tears, the little man sniffed and said, "I'm all right, Hannah. It's just that sweet Mary Beth and her words of love..."

"She is sweet, all right. And she loves her Uncle Jacob very much."

With that, Hannah went behind the counter and began preparing the cash drawer for business while Jacob unlocked the front door of the store and let in the customers who were already waiting.

The day's business began as usual.

At the marshal's office, Dutch Hendrix was standing at his cell door, gripping the bars, when Deputy Jack Bower came into the cell block, carrying a tray of steaming food.

"Here's your breakfast, Dutch," said Bower as he bent over and slid the tray through the space beneath the barred door. "Better enjoy it. You won't have many more."

Marshal Lance Mangum entered the cell block as Hendrix sneered, picked up the tray, and said, "That's what you think, Bower. My men will break me outta this two-bit jail before the law can put a noose around my neck."

Mangum stepped up beside his deputy and said, "Your men will never save you from hanging, Dutch."

Dutch laughed. "You don't know my men, Mangum. They'll break me out, all right. The jail doesn't exist that can hold Dutch Hendrix."

"You'll find out just how wrong you are, you cold-blooded killer," Bower said. "This jail *will* hold you till you take your walk to the gallows in front of the whole town."

Hendrix laughed. "Get outta here and let me eat my breakfast."

Mangum and Bower closed the cell block door and walked into the office.

Jack said, "Is that just a facade, or do you suppose that gang of his would actually make an attempt to free him?"

"I don't know. But we can't afford to guess. We need to

beef up security around here immediately. Let's start with our usual two dozen volunteers. If we have eight well-armed men inside this jail at all times, Dutch's four pals will be well outnumbered. How about you going out and contacting our volunteers and setting up three shifts per twenty-four hours of eight men each?"

"Sure, boss."

"Make sure they understand that this will only last till Hendrix hangs, which will be less than a week."

At the Fort Bridger school, schoolmarm Sundi O'Brien was just inside the door, welcoming her students as they arrived. Some of them slipped and called her Miss Lindgren, quickly correcting themselves. This had been common since Sundi had married Dr. Patrick O'Brien three weeks earlier.

When the Cooper children arrived, Sundi asked how little Eddie was doing, and after B. J. had told her he was doing fine, Patty Ruth stepped up and said, "Do I get my reg'lar hug, Mrs. O'Brien?"

"Of course," said Sundi, and folded her into her arms.

Chris said, "Mrs. O'Brien, would you like for me to shovel the snow off the porch? It's only an inch or so deep, but there'll be that much less of it when school lets out if I clean it off now."

"That would be good, Chris. Thank you."

"Mrs. O'Brien, I sure am looking forward to starting our Saturday classes at the Crow village this week," Mary Beth said. "And just think—this will be the last Saturday I will teach as a thirteen-year-old."

Sundi's eyes widened. "That's right! You're birthday is on the twenty-fifth, isn't it? That's a week from tomorrow."

Mary Beth's eyes sparkled. "Do you think I'll be a better teacher because I'll be fourteen?"

Sundi laughed. "Honey, I don't think you can get any better. More educated, yes, but your dedication to teaching can hardly be improved. I know your big dream is to be a teacher when you grow up, but as far as technique and love for your students, you're already top-notch. And I'm sure all the Crow Indian children in Chief Two Moons's village would agree."

Mary Beth's face brightened. "Thank you, Mrs. O'Brien. This day has hardly begun, and you've made it a beautiful day for me already!"

It was coming up on nine o'clock when Rafe Ketcham, Rex Holt, Durbin Mitchell, and Spike Denny rode casually into Fort Bridger and turned south on Main Street.

Snow was still falling lightly.

Pointing with his chin as they rode four abreast, Rafe said, "The school is at the south end of town. We'll be passin' the marshal's office in a minute. It's on the left two more blocks down."

Spike chuckled, brushing snow from his eyelashes. "If that tin star only knew what he was about to face!"

People along the street glanced at the four strangers, but paid them little mind.

When they drew near the marshal's office and jail, Rafe said, "There it is, boys."

The outlaws eyed each other and grinned.

While they were passing it, Rafe set his gaze on the door and said, "Don't worry, Dutch. We'll have you out of there shortly."

"Yeah," Durbin said. *"Real* shortly."

Sundi O'Brien was standing before her students, teaching a history lesson for the older ones while the younger ones were drawing pictures of birds. She was at the chalkboard behind her desk, writing some historical facts, commenting on them as she went.

"Now, I want you to be sure and get this," she said, "because it will be on the test. Napoleon Bonaparte's first weakness after showing so much strength appeared in the Peninsular War that lasted from 1808 to 1814, and his alliance with Russia was tenuous. When Czar Alexander I rejected the Continental System—"

Sundi's words were cut off by the sound of heavy footsteps on the front porch of the building, and the door burst open. Four mean-looking men stomped in, waving revolvers, and one of them growled, "Everybody stay right where you are! You too, Teach!"

"What do you want?" asked Sundi. Some of the smaller girls began to whimper.

Rafe Ketcham, who had just given the command, moved up the center aisle toward the teacher, most of the children's eyes following him. Rex Holt and Spike Denny moved side by side about halfway up the aisle and stopped, giving the boys and girls harsh looks to keep them fearful.

Durbin Mitchell stayed at the door, leaving it open in spite of the cold air so he could see if anyone was approaching the school.

Terror gripped the students, making their hearts pound as Rafe stepped up to the teacher and said, "You and all these kids are bein' held hostage, lady."

Sundi's lower lip quivered slightly as she said, "Why are you doing this? For what reason are we being held hostage?"

"You'll know shortly," Rafe said, turning to run his gaze over the class. He pointed to a tall, lanky boy and said, "C'mere, kid."

All eyes were now on the boy as he rose from his desk and stepped up to the outlaw.

"How old are you, kid?" asked Rafe.

"Sixteen."

"What's your name?"

"Luke Patterson."

"Well, Luke, I want you to run a little errand for me. I want you to go to the marshal's office and tell him that Dutch Hendrix's gang has your teacher and all of your fellow students at our mercy at the schoolhouse. You tell him that I want Dutch out of that jail immediately. I want him sent back here with you. Have you got that?"

"Y-yes, sir."

"Now, how long will it take you to get to the marshal's office?"

"'Bout five minutes if I run."

"All right, then you run. Tell the marshal if you and Dutch ain't back here in twenty minutes after you get to that jail, we're gonna shoot one person every minute till the two of you get here, startin' with your teacher."

A tumult of moans and cries swept over the children, and Sundi's face lost color.

Running his gaze over them, Rafe shouted, "Shut up! Stop that bellerin'!"

The children tried to stifle their cries. Rex and Spike glared at them, telling them to get quiet in a hurry. The smaller girls were having the hardest time.

Rafe said, "Luke, you tell that marshal that there'd better not be anybody with the two of you when you get back, or we'll shoot your teacher before they can bat an eye. You got that?"

"Yes, sir."

"Now listen good. Tell Mangum that when you and Dutch get back here *alone,* we're gonna ride away, but we're takin' two of the smaller kids with us."

"Oh no!" gasped Sundi. "Please don't—"

"Quiet!" snapped Rafe, giving her a fiery look.

Sundi's hand went to her mouth, her face showing the anguish that was in her heart.

Turning back to Luke, Rafe said, "Tell the marshal if anybody follows us, we'll kill the kids. If we're not followed, we'll leave 'em at some ranch or farm when we're a safe distance away and ride on. You got that?"

"Yes, sir."

"Okay. Repeat it back to me so I know you've got it straight."

The smaller girls were still whimpering as Luke repeated the instructions back to Rafe Ketcham.

"All right," said Rafe. "Now get goin'. And you'd better run fast, boy!"

Not bothering to put on his coat, Luke darted past Durbin and out the door.

Rafe pointed a finger at Sundi and said, "Siddown, Teach!"

Sundi burned him with hot eyes as she eased onto the chair behind her desk.

Rafe looked toward the little girls who were still whimpering and bawled, "Get quiet right now!"

Among the little girls was Patty Ruth Cooper. With tears bubbling from her eyes, she clamped a hand over her mouth and looked toward Chris. Anguish showed on his face as he raised a hand and said, "Sir…"

"What?" barked Rafe.

"Could I go to my little sister? She's one of them that's crying."

"You stay right where you are, kid! She can quiet herself without your help."

Patty Ruth gulped as she swallowed tears, and ran her gaze to B.J., then Mary Beth. Both showed in their expressions that they wanted to go to her, but knew they could not.

Seated next to Patty Ruth was her best friend, Belinda

Fordham, whose father was a captain at the fort. Belinda's face was wet with tears. Looking past the fearsome outlaw, she said in a timorous voice, "M-Mrs. O'Brien, I…I need to go out to the—"

"Shut up, kid!" Ketcham said.

"Please," said Sundi. "Let me take her to the outhouse. You can have one of your men accompany us."

"Neither one of you is goin' nowhere!"

"Rafe," came Durbin's voice from where he stood at the door. "The little girl is scared, and she needs to go out there. I'll go with her and the teacher."

Ketcham shook his head. "We need you at that door."

"Then have one of these other guys take them."

"Oh, all right. Spike, you go with 'em."

Sundi was out of her chair instantly. She dashed to Belinda, picked her up, and said, "Come on, honey. I'll take you."

As Spike moved up beside them, Sundi set her eyes on Durbin and said, "Thank you. It's nice to know that at least one of you has some kindness in him."

At the marshal's office, Lance Mangum was talking to the eight men who had volunteered to help guard the jail, while Deputy Jack Bower was still out lining up men for the other two shifts.

Mangum was standing in front of his desk, arms folded across his chest, and running his gaze over their faces. "I can't tell you how much I appreciate your volunteering, gentlemen. Hendrix's gang are a bad bunch, and I just couldn't take any chances. I'm going to put two of you in the cell block with Dutch, three of you at the back door of the building, and the other three will stay here in the office and keep sharp eyes on the street for any sign of—"

Suddenly the door burst open, and a white-faced Luke

Patterson came in, gasping for breath.

Stepping up to meet him, Mangum said, "Luke, what's wrong? You look scared to death."

"Mar-Marshal, we've got trouble at the school! *Big* trouble!"

Gripping his shoulders, Mangum said, "Catch your breath, Luke. Then you can tell me."

Luke took several gulps of air, then said, "The Dutch Hendrix gang has Mrs. O'Brien and all the students held hostage in the school! They're holding guns on them!"

"How many are there?"

"Four. The guy who seems to be in charge told me to give you a message." Still working at catching his breath, Luke passed Rafe Ketcham's message on to the marshal word for word.

By the time he finished, Lance Mangum's rage had his face beet red. "Those dirty skunks would dare put Sundi and those children in such a position!"

"What are you going to do, Marshal?" asked one of the volunteers.

"I'm thinking," said Mangum. "As desperate as those men are, I have no doubt they will carry out their threats. But even if I would give them Hendrix—"

Mangum's words were cut off by his deputy coming through the door.

Jack was ready to tell the marshal that he had the other volunteers lined up for their shifts, but when he saw the white face of Luke and the red face of his boss, he said, "What's wrong?"

The marshal filled him in quickly, then said, "As I was about to say, even if I would give them Hendrix, they would take some of the children with them as hostages. They're a bunch of killers. Once they felt they were safe and didn't need them, they just might kill them anyway."

Mangum's attention was drawn to three army officers who had paused on the boardwalk to talk to Fort Bridger's mayor, Cade Samuels. "Jack, will you step out there and tell Captains Kirkland and Fordham and Lieutenant Carlin I need to talk to them this instant?"

Jack nodded and headed for the door.

To his eight volunteers, Mangum said, "Time is short. We've got little more than five minutes. Those low-down skunks have left me only one choice, and it's *not* to deliver Hendrix to them."

CHAPTER ELEVEN

When Sundi O'Brien emerged from the outhouse with Belinda Fordham in her arms, the child took one look at Spike Denny and turned her head, putting a powerful grip on Sundi's neck with both arms.

"Please, Mrs. O'Brien," she said in a terrified voice, "don't let the bad man hurt me!"

"Don't be afraid, honey," said the teacher, "the bad man isn't going to hurt you."

"Bad man, eh?" said Spike, as they headed toward the schoolhouse.

"You've earned the title. I hope you're proud of yourself."

Spike did not comment.

"Tell me," said Sundi, "what makes a man want to be an outlaw?"

"Shut up, lady," grumbled Spike.

"Are your parents proud of you?" she said.

"My parents died when I was ten."

"Well, at least they don't have to carry the shame of what their son turned out to be."

"I told you to shut up."

Inside the schoolhouse, many of the younger students were weeping. Chris Cooper turned and looked at Mary Beth. Her features were pale, but she was trying to keep calm. B. J. was doing the same.

Chris's desk sat next to that of his good friend, sixteen-year-old Bob Imler. Bob was a big, strong, husky boy who had been led to Christ a few months earlier by Mary Beth.

When Chris let his eyes run to Bob, he found the big boy looking at him. Rafe Ketcham and Rex Holt were busy trying to get the frightened younger ones to stop wailing.

Glancing back at Durbin Mitchell, Bob saw him looking out the door.

He leaned close to Chris and said in a low tone, "I wish I had a gun in my desk. I'd fix those outlaws good."

"Don't try anything foolish," Chris whispered.

"Somebody's gotta do something. These guys have to be stopped."

"Bob, they're armed. There's nothing we can do. I hate the thought of that Dutch Hendrix getting out of jail, and even more, I hate the thought of them taking two of the smaller children with them, but there's no way we can prevent it."

At that moment the back door came open and Sundi appeared with Belinda in her arms, Spike Denny behind them.

The wailing children cried even louder when they saw their teacher, calling her name and begging her to help them. She carried Belinda to the section where the little girls were and started to set her down at her desk. But Belinda put a death grip on her neck and begged, "Please let me stay with you!"

At the same time, Rafe stepped up to her and said, "Lady, you gotta do somethin' to shut these kids up!"

Still holding Belinda, Sundi said, "It would get very quiet in here if you would let all of them leave, and just hold me hostage."

Rafe frowned. "No way, lady. That's real noble of you, but all of these kids are stayin' here. You just talk to 'em and make 'em shut up."

"Look, you need somebody in here and somebody to take along with you so you'll be sure the marshal will let you and your boss go without interfering. If you had just me, it would be as good as having the children. Let them go."

"I told you nobody's goin'! Now get busy and shut 'em up!"

Sundi moved closer to the wailing group and tried to calm them. But it was to no avail.

Suddenly six-year-old Molly Goodman rose from her desk, clung to Sundi's arm and wailed, "Please, Mrs. O'Brien! Make the bad men go away! I'm scared!"

Rafe gripped the child's shoulder, pinched hard, and said, "Siddown, kid!"

Molly screamed and tried to get loose from his grip. Rafe shoved her to the floor, telling her to stop screaming.

Holding Belinda in one arm, Sundi knelt beside Molly and picked her up. Terror was evident in the little girl's huge eyes, and tears were spilling down her face. "Molly, honey," said the teacher, "are you hurt?"

Molly sobbed, but shook her head.

Sundi talked to her in soothing tones and though the child continued to cry, she cooperated by sitting back down by her desk.

Amid the wailing children, Patty Ruth Cooper was trying her best not to cry, but trying wasn't good enough. Tears rained down her pale cheeks. She wiped them away, but more took their place. No sound was coming from her. She sat still, but her tear-blurred eyes kept darting to Chris, B. J., and Mary Beth, begging silently for help.

Belinda still clung to Sundi's neck as she stood up, faced the outlaw as he continued to demand that she quiet the children, and said, "Don't you understand? There's nothing I can do! Let them all leave, and keep me as hostage."

At the spot where Sundi and Rafe stood, they were just

across the aisle from Bob Imler, who was studying Rafe. The man was holding his revolver loosely.

A few desks away from Chris and Bob, Mary Beth was looking at her petrified little sister. She could stand it no longer. Rising to her feet, she got Rafe's attention, and speaking above the wailing, she said, "Mister, my little sister's over there. Could I please go to her?"

"Yeah, if you can make her shut up, go ahead."

Mary Beth rose from her desk and began weaving her way toward her little sister.

Sundi was finally able to get Belinda to sit back at her desk, and just as she put her down, another little girl began to scream. His temper already hot, Rafe slapped the child across the mouth, telling her to shut up. The blow sent her reeling back from her desk, and when she hit the floor, Sundi saw that the blow had also cut her lip.

Sundi went blind with rage. Rafe's back was toward her, and she leaped on him and clawed at his eyes, screaming, "Leave these children alone, you beast!"

Rex and Spike looked at each other, wondering if they should go to Rafe's rescue while the small woman dug her fingernails into his eyes. They were about to make their move when Rafe used his free hand to throw Sundi over his shoulder. She hit the floor but immediately sprang to her feet.

Rafe swore at her and swung a fist, connecting with her jaw. She went down hard, dazed. The children wailed even louder.

Bob Imler lunged for the loosely held gun in Rafe's hand. Rafe saw him coming, but was not able to keep him from getting hold of the gun. Abruptly they were in a contest for control of the revolver, turning, twisting, grunting. Rafe's breath hissed in and out as he began to get the upper hand. He was able to force the muzzle toward Bob's face, and ear back the hammer.

Bob threw his weight into his opponent and the gun fired.

The bullet struck Mary Beth in the chest and the impact slammed her into a desk. From there, she slid to the floor, lying on her back.

At the same time, Spike Denny cracked Bob on the head with his gun barrel, and the boy collapsed in a heap.

The one-room schoolhouse was a bedlam of wailing and screaming as gun smoke filled the air. Patty Ruth sprang from her desk and knelt beside her sister. "Mary Beth! Mary Beth!"

Chris and B. J. left their desks and bolted toward their sisters. Dizzy from the punch, Sundi staggered toward the spot where Mary Beth lay on the floor.

Rex and Spike stood like statues, looking down at the girl with blood spreading on her dress as Rafe swung toward the rear of the room and said, "Durb...anybody comin?"

"Not yet."

"Well keep a sharp eye!"

Unchecked tears streamed down Patty Ruth's cheeks and dropped on her sister's dress while she cried, "Mary Beth! Mary Beth! Wake up! Please wake up! Oh, please open your eyes!"

B. J. knelt beside Patty Ruth and looked at his big sister, a lump in his throat. Chris quickly dropped to his knees on Mary Beth's other side and focused on the bullet hole. "Oh no! That slug has to be awfully close to her heart!" Biting his lips, he took her limp hands in his own and began rubbing them vigorously, speaking her name over and over.

Gulping sobs to keep them from breaking free, Sundi knelt beside Chris. The tears coming from her eyes blinded her.

When there was no response from Mary Beth, Chris looked hopefully for the rise and fall of her chest, but saw none. Looking up at Rafe Ketcham, he screamed, "You killed my sister! You killed my sister! You'll pay for this, mister!"

B. J.'s gaze was fastened on Mary Beth, and suddenly he became aware of a slight movement of her chest. "Chris, look! She's breathing!"

Chris's head snapped around. "Yes! Oh yes, she *is* breathing, B. J. She *is!*"

Sundi rolled off her knees and sat on the floor, taking Mary Beth's head into her lap. Patty Ruth leaned into her teacher, getting as close as she could to the comfort Mrs. O'Brien offered.

Chris jumped to his feet, saying, "I've got to go after one of the doctors!"

"Nobody's goin' anywhere till Dutch walks through that door," Rafe said. "When we've gone, takin' a couple of kids with us, you can go get the doctor."

"Mister, Mary Beth is shot real bad! She'll die if I don't get a doctor here!"

"You ain't goin' nowhere," Rafe said in a tight voice.

Sundi looked up at the outlaw, eyes blazing. "Have you no human qualities at all?"

"Shut your mouth or I'll punch you again."

B. J. and Patty Ruth had their eyes fixed on their unconscious sister, whose chest was weeping blood.

Suddenly Chris bolted toward the door. Spike Denny moved swiftly and seized him by the arm. "You deaf, kid? Rafe said nobody's goin' anywhere."

"Please, mister. Let me go. My sister needs a doctor."

"I said you ain't goin' anywhere!" gusted Spike, and gave Chris a shove toward the spot where Mary Beth lay.

Maintaining his balance, the boy bolted for the door again. Spike slapped him hard, knocking him to the floor.

Abruptly, Durbin Mitchell slammed the door, headed for Ketcham and said angrily, "Rafe, we've got to let that boy go for a doctor!"

Rafe's eyes flamed. "Get back to that door and watch for Dutch!"

"You promised me that none of these kids would be hurt. That girl's got a bullet in her, and if she don't get medical attention, she'll die!"

Rafe hissed through his teeth, "If the girl dies, too bad." Then pointing to Bob Imler, who lay on the floor unconscious, he said, "That brat there on the floor shouldn't have jumped me. It's his fault she's got a bullet in her."

"I don't care whose fault it is, Rafe! We can't let that girl die!"

Ketcham's features hardened. "Get back to the door."

Durbin's chin jutted. "Not till that boy's on his way to bring a doctor."

At the same moment Ketcham and Mitchell were arguing, Marshal Lance Mangum and Deputy Jack Bower were running toward the schoolhouse from the back, which was its blind side. Flanking them were Captain Dane Kirkland, Captain John Fordham, Lieutenant Dobie Carlin, and the eight volunteers. Every man had his gun drawn.

They had heard the shot that came from the schoolhouse just as they were leaving the marshal's office.

As they neared the school, Jack said, "Marshal, I hope that shot came from somewhere else on this side of town, but I've got a feeling it came from inside that schoolhouse. The twenty minutes isn't up yet. If those dirty skunks have shot somebody…"

"That's enough, Durbin!" Rafe Ketcham said. "I don't want to hear any more about it! Nobody's leavin' this buildin' till Dutch gets here. Once we're gone with the hostages, they can go after all the doctors they want."

"You heartless animal!" screamed Sundi from where she sat on the floor with the unconscious Mary Beth's head in her lap. "This girl did nothing wrong! Why should she have to die? If you have an ounce of decency in you, you'll let Chris go after one of the doctors!"

Ketcham turned and put stony, dispassionate eyes on Sundi. "Shut up, Teach, or there'll be a bullet for you, too."

Mitchell took two steps back and whipped out his gun, cocked it, and aimed it straight at Ketcham's nose. "Don't test me on this, Rafe," he said with gravel in his voice. "The boy is goin' after the doctor right now. I ain't lettin' that girl die if I can help it! Go, boy!"

Chris started toward the door, but was caught by Rex Holt. "You ain't leavin, kid. Rafe said so."

"Let him go, Rex!" barked Mitchell. "I mean it! Let him go, or I'll drop Rafe where he stands!"

"Drop the gun, Durbin!" came a voice filled with anger.

Durbin held the gun steady, keeping his eyes focused on Ketcham.

"Spike, I thought maybe you had some decency in you."

Standing at an angle where his gun was pointed at Mitchell's back, Spike said, "We gotta stay unified in this, Durb. Drop the gun, and I'll try to get Rafe to forgive you."

As he spoke, Spike moved to a spot where his gun was now lined on Mitchell's chest. Durbin couldn't resist glancing at him, and in that split second that his eyes were off of him, Rafe grabbed Mitchell's gun and tried to wrest it from his grasp. The gun fired, sending a bullet into the ceiling.

The children screamed louder than ever.

B. J. wrapped his arms around Patty Ruth as she screamed and held her tight.

Sundi jerked from the sharp sound as she was tearing part of her petticoat off at the bottom to use as a compress on Mary Beth's wound. When she regained control of her nerves, she went back to work on the petticoat.

On the floor, Bob Imler was just barely beginning to move his head and his hands.

As the two outlaws struggled for supremacy, Mitchell's strength surprised Ketcham. He yanked his gun from Ketcham and was thumbing back the hammer when Spike Denny's revolver roared, and Durbin Mitchell dropped like a poleaxed steer.

The high-pitched screams increased in volume.

At the same instant, the back door flew open and Marshal Lance Mangum charged in, holding his gun in ready position, and shouting, "Drop those guns and get your hands in the air!"

On his heels were his deputy, the three army officers, and the eight men who accompanied them.

Deputy Jack Bower shouted, "All boys and girls drop to the floor, fast!" His eyes were searching for the teacher, and as the students obeyed his command, he saw Sundi on the floor, holding Mary Beth's head in her lap.

The three outlaws looked at each other with defeat on their faces, and let their guns fall with a clatter to the floor.

Sundi called out, "Lance, Mary Beth has been shot! She's still alive but needs medical attention immediately!"

Quickly, the children whose fathers were in the group ran to them, and were gathered in their arms, including Ryan, Will, and Belinda Fordham and Travis Carlin.

Captain Dane Kirkland moved to Rafe Ketcham, Spike Denny, and Rex Holt, holding his gun on them, and said, "You boys will rue the day you ever walked into this schoolhouse. I guarantee it. Put your hands on top of your heads and lace your fingers together."

When it was done, Kirkland called for two of the volunteers to hold their guns on them till they were ready to go. He then headed for the spot where Mary Beth was being held by the teacher.

The marshal moved up first and hunkered down beside the wounded girl. "Looks bad."

"Yes," said Sundi.

Chris was there and said, "I'll go get one of the doctors."

"I think it would be better if we take her to the clinic," said Mangum.

Captain Kirkland had drawn up. "I'll carry her."

Mangum gave him a grateful nod. "Good. I'll put these no-goods in jail, then I'll come to the clinic."

Mangum helped Sundi to her feet. As Kirkland and the Cooper children headed for the door, Sundi called after them, "I'll be there in a few minutes!"

As they moved past the three outlaws who were being held at gunpoint, Patty Ruth paused, made a face at them, and stuck out her tongue; then she hurried to catch up with the others. When they moved outside, Kirkland walked as fast as he could, doing his best to keep from jostling the wounded girl. Chris, B. J., and Patty Ruth followed, almost running to keep up with him.

"Boys," said the captain, "fill me in on all the details, will you?"

Back in the schoolhouse, one of the volunteers said, "Marshal, we've got a fella over here on the floor who's been shot. Looks to be in bad shape."

"That's one of the outlaws," said Sundi. "He showed some decency when Mary Beth was shot. He tried to get the others to let Chris go after one of the doctors for her, and got himself shot for it."

Sundi looked toward Bob Imler, who was now sitting up, rubbing his head in a daze. "Bob may be hurt too, Lance. They cracked him on the head when he tried to get a gun from one of them so he could stop this whole thing."

"So which one of them shot Mary Beth?" Mangum asked.

Sundi pointed at Rafe Ketcham. "That one."

"Whattaya mean?" bellowed Ketcham. "I didn't shoot her deliberately!"

"And just what is that supposed to mean?" asked Mangum, moving toward him.

Pointing at Bob Imler with his chin, Ketcham said, "That kid tried to get my gun away from me, and while we were strugglin', the gun went off and hit the girl. It's his fault, Marshal."

Bob was struggling to his feet with the help of one of the men. Holding a hand over the bleeding gash on his head, he said with slurred tongue, "If you hadn' been here holding guns on us, there wouldn' have been a reason for me to try to get your gun."

"Yeah, but if you hadn't jumped me, kid, that girl wouldn't have a bullet in her now. It's your fault."

The marshal's temper showed as he fixed Ketcham with steely eyes and snapped, "It's *not* his fault! If you hadn't been here holding guns on this teacher and her students, Mary Beth wouldn't have a bullet in her chest!" He drew a deep breath. "And let me tell you something. All three of you are going to pay for what happened here today. You're going to wish you'd never seen Fort Bridger, much less ever dared to come into this school and threatened the lives of these children and their teacher."

Rafe swallowed hard but remained silent. Spike and Rex exchanged glum glances.

Sundi turned to the deputy and said, "Jack, I need to get to the clinic. Will you see that all of these children get home?"

"I'll take care of it," said Jack. He turned to the volunteers. "Maybe some of you gentlemen would help me." All agreed to do so.

"I need four of you men without children to pick up the wounded outlaw and Bob Imler and carry them to the clinic," said Mangum. "The rest of you can help Bob get all of these children home."

The marshal then turned to the outlaws, who were still under the guns of some of the volunteers, pulled his own weapon, said, "Okay, gang, now you can join your boss behind bars. Let's go."

Chapter Twelve

A t the clinic, Dr. Patrick O'Brien was examining elderly Clarence Prewitt on one table while his father was working on a feverish ten-month-old baby boy on the other.

While Patrick was probing carefully about Clarence's ribs, Clarence said, "Those gunshots definitely came from the south side of town. I can't imagine—oh!"

"Sorry," said the young doctor. "Didn't mean to hurt you."

"It's all right, Doctor. You can't know how bad I banged up those ribs without putting some pressure on them."

Looking over at Clarence, the older Dr. O'Brien said, "What were you going to say?"

"Hmm?"

"You were about to say there was something you couldn't imagine."

"Oh. I can't imagine it having been a shootout—you know—between a couple of gunfighters. That doesn't happen back in the neighborhood somewhere. They always shoot it out right on Main Street so they can make a spectacle of themselves."

"A bit early too," said Doc, sponging the baby with cool water. "They don't usually slap leather till the saloons and the business places have been open for at least an hour and there are plenty of potential spectators moving about on the board-walks. And, as you said, they do it on Main Street to get all the attention they can so the guy who walks away can be noticed by as many people as possible."

Clarence winced as Patrick touched the sorest spot once more, then said, "As far as I know, there aren't any neighbors in this town feuding with each other, so I don't think it could have been something like that."

"I'd say it might have been somebody shooting a raccoon who got into their trash bin," said Patrick, "but the sequence of the shots would rule that out. If whoever was shooting at the varmint had missed with the first shot, the second would have come immediately. And if there had to be a third, it would have come quickly too."

"Right," said Doc, spooning a dark liquid into the baby's mouth, accompanied by sounds of extreme protest. "The sequence was odd. One shot, then several minutes passing before the second shot, then the third shot in a minute or so. I can't imagine what it was."

"Well," said Patrick, "if somebody was hit, we'll soon know it."

"So what's the verdict, Doctor?" said Clarence as Patrick stopped probing.

"Well, Mr. Prewitt, you're going to be fine. Those ribs are bruised, but none are broken."

Clarence smiled. "I don't understand how you can know whether they're broken or just bruised."

Patrick chuckled. "If they were broken, I would know because when I touched them, you'd have been screaming your head off."

Patrick helped Clarence sit up, then aided him in buttoning up his long johns.

"Well, Jesse Ferguson Jr.," said Doc to the baby, "you're going to be fine, too. Let's get you dressed, and your mother can take you home."

In the clinic office, Edie O'Brien sat at her desk, talking to Earline Prewitt and Carol Ferguson. The door to the examining and operating room opened, and Doc came out, carrying little Jesse. Carol rose from her chair, waiting to hear the doctor's diagnosis.

"It's just because he's teething, Carol. He'll be fine. I gave him a good dose of the same medicine I've prescribed for you to pick up from Fort Bridger's pharmacist. The dosage will be written right on the label on the bottle."

"Thank you, Dr. O'Brien," Carol said with a smile as she took the baby. "I'm glad it wasn't something serious."

As Carol was bundling the baby in a heavy blanket, Patrick and Clarence came out of the back room. Bending some to favor his sore side, Clarence said, "No broken ribs, honey."

"Oh, I'm so glad!" said Earline.

Carol gave Edie a smile and a wave, and moved outside, closing the door quietly.

"He's going to be sore for a few days yet, Earline," said Patrick. "Keep some salicylic acid handy."

"I've got plenty, Dr. Patrick. Thank you."

Patrick helped Clarence into his overcoat and placed his hat on his head. "There you go, partner. No more climbing on ladders, understand?"

Clarence dipped his head. "I just hate to bother the neighbors when I need help."

"I know every neighbor you have, Mr. Clarence," Patrick said, tilting his head down. "The men are all a great deal younger than you, and any one of them would be happy to give you a helping hand when you need it. No more ladders. Next time it could very well be broken ribs...or worse. Am I getting through?"

Clarence grinned shyly. "Yes, Doctor. You are."

"Good!" said Earline. "I haven't been able to get through for twenty years!"

The O'Briens laughed.

Earline slipped an arm around her husband's waist. "Come on, honey. Let's go home so you can rest."

As they headed out the door, Clarence looked over his shoulder. "Thank you, Dr. Patrick. We'll pay you the first of the month."

"That's fine," said Patrick. "Take care of yourself."

Earline's attention had been drawn up the street. Looking back through the door, she said, "Doc, a soldier is coming this way, carrying a young girl! I think she's unconscious!"

Doc and Patrick moved out onto the boardwalk. Both saw Captain Dane Kirkland coming hastily but carefully with the limp form of Mary Beth Cooper in his arms. Chris and B. J. were hurrying along beside the captain, each gripping a hand of Patty Ruth's. Her feet were scarcely touching the ground.

Patrick bolted off the boardwalk, slipping some on the snow, and ran hard to meet Kirkland in the street. When Kirkland drew up, Patrick saw the blood on the front of the girl's dress.

"She's been shot, Doctor!" Kirkland said.

"Let's get her inside," said Patrick, running in front of them.

When they reached the clinic, Doc was holding the door open. As they filed inside, Edie was at the door of the back room, anxiety on her face. Patrick led Kirkland into the back room, and as Doc moved past Edie, he said, "What happened, Captain?"

"A shooting at the school," Kirkland replied with strain in his voice. "Outlaws took the place over."

"Is Sundi all right?"

"Yes. One of the outlaws hit her and knocked her down,

but she's all right. She's upset, of course, but she's fine."

"You're sure she isn't hurt?"

"She seemed to be fine."

Patrick nodded. "There were three shots fired. Anybody else get shot?"

"Yes. One of the outlaws. They'll be bringing him in a couple of minutes. One of the boys took a whack on the head. What's his name, Chris?"

"Bob Imler. They'll be bringing him too, Dr. Patrick."

"Captain," said Patrick as they drew up to the examining table, "what were outlaws doing taking over the school?"

"I'll let Chris tell you, Doctor. He filled me in some, but there wasn't time for me to get the whole picture."

"Let's get her on the table, first," said Patrick. "Bring Chris in so he can tell us about it while we go to work on her."

"Will you need me, son?" asked Edie.

Without looking back at her, Patrick replied, "Probably not, as long as I've got Dad, Mom."

"I'll stay out here with B. J. and Patty Ruth, then. Let me know if you need me."

"Will do."

Chris stopped short by several feet of the examining table as Kirkland carefully laid Mary Beth on it. He then stepped back and put an arm around the pale-faced boy. Doc rushed to the medicine cupboard, saying, "I'll get everything we need, son, while you cut her dress away so we can get to the wound."

"Right," said Patrick, picking up a pair of scissors from a small cart next to the table. Using his body to block the view of Mary Beth's wound, he started cutting the bloody dress and said, "Who shot her, Chris?"

"You know that outlaw they have in the jail?"

"Dutch Hendrix."

"Well, his gang came barging into the school with their guns drawn. They sent Luke Patterson to the marshal's office to tell Marshal Mangum they wanted their boss let out of jail immediately, and if it didn't happen, they'd start shooting us."

"Tell me just one more thing," said Patrick, "then you can go. Dad and I want to hear it all, but it'll have to be later. Right now, Mary Beth's life is our primary concern. Why did they shoot her?"

"It was really sort of an accident. Bob Imler tried to take one of the outlaws' gun away from him, and when they were struggling over it, the gun went off and hit Mary Beth." Chris's features were pinched. "Will she be all right?"

Patrick licked his lips. "It's just too early to tell. We'll know more when we get to the wound."

"I'm going home to tell Mama," said Chris. "Please take good care of Mary Beth."

"We'll do everything we can, Chris," said the older doctor.

As he stepped into the office and waiting room, Chris said, "Grandma, I'm going home to tell Mama about Mary Beth. Can B. J. and Patty Ruth stay here?"

"Of course, honey. You go on. Did Grandpa or Dr. Patrick say how she is?"

"They really don't know, yet. I'll be back with Mama in a few minutes."

In the back room, Captain Kirkland looked on from a short distance while the doctors poured antiseptic on each other's hands. "She's critical, isn't she?"

"Yes," said Patrick. "I'm concerned that the slug is lodged dangerously close to her heart."

Kirkland grimaced. "I know you want me out of here. I'll be in the waiting room."

When the door closed behind the captain, Patrick picked up a pair of forceps, looked at the wound, and said, "Dad, this is going to be touchy."

Edie appeared at the door. "Son, I just wanted to let you know that Sundi is here."

"And she's all right? Captain Kirkland said one of the outlaws hit her and knocked her down."

"Her jaw is swollen some, but she's okay. I'll put a cold, wet cloth on it. She says to tell you she loves you and has been praying for Mary Beth."

"Tell her I love her, too, Mom. And the more prayer for this girl, the better. We're about to go after the slug."

When the door closed, Doc said, "Son, we'd better pray ourselves before we go after the slug."

Edie was trying to calm B. J. and Patty Ruth with Dane Kirkland's help when two townsmen came through the door, carrying Durbin Mitchell. Two more followed, bearing a groggy Bob Imler with a bandanna wrapped around his head.

Edie moved to them and said, "We've got another examining table back there. You can put this wounded man on it, and there's a cot you can lie down on, Bob. Doc and Patrick are taking the slug out of Mary Beth's chest right now. Let me step in and tell them you're here."

Opening the door, Edie said, "Dad, Patrick, that wounded outlaw is here. He's unconscious. We'll put him on the other table, and I'll have Bob Imler lie down on the cot."

"They'll have to wait their turn, Mom," Patrick said. "Right now, Mary Beth takes precedence over all else."

"Of course, son," said Edie. "We'll bring them on in."

At Cooper's General Store, several customers were standing in line at the counter while others were moving among the aisles, picking up items to purchase. Among them were Glenda Williams and Mandy Carver. Hannah and Jacob were hurriedly totaling bills and sacking goods while everybody was talking about the gunshots they had heard coming from the south side of town.

Little Eddie was sitting in a high chair behind the counter, playing with his toy horse.

Dan Bledsoe, who owned the clothing store next door, said so all could hear, "I saw Marshal Mangum and Deputy Bower running that way a little while ago with three army officers and a bunch of men. A couple minutes or so after that, I heard the first shot. The other two shots came a few minutes after that. Whatever it was, they must have taken care of it. There haven't been any more shots."

Suddenly the door burst open, jingling the bell loudly, and Chris came running in, eyes wide, face pallid. He threaded his way quickly through the customers and pushed his way up to the counter. "Mama! Mary Beth's been shot! She's at the clinic!"

Hannah's head bobbed. Starting around the end of the counter, she asked, "How bad, Chris?"

"Real bad."

"O dear God…" Hannah paused at the end of the counter and looked anxiously at Glenda Williams and Mandy Carver. "Could one of you take over in my place, and the other take Eddie home with you?"

Before either could reply, Jacob said, "Hannah, I'm going with you. If Glenda or Mandy can take care of these people, they can then just close the store. We'll take Eddie with us."

Having exchanged glances, both women started to speak at once. Glenda nodded at Mandy, who looked at Hannah and said, "Honey, you and Jacob go on. Glenda and I will handle things here. We'll keep the store open, and we'll take care of Eddie. Let us know as soon as you can how that sweet girl is."

Hannah felt as if her heart had stopped the moment the words had come out of Chris's mouth. She had to concentrate hard to keep from sinking into a heap on the floor. "I will," she said, nodding.

Jacob grabbed Hannah's coat and his own, saying, "Come on, Chris," and hustled them out the door.

The cold air slapped Hannah's face, clearing her mind as they headed down the street with Chris helping her into her coat. She began questioning Chris as to what had happened. The explanation came rapidly from his mouth.

Tears gushed down her cheeks and her voice broke as she said, "But all you know is that she was hit in the chest. You don't know what Grandpa and Dr. Patrick think about her chances of making it?"

"They really couldn't say yet, Mama. They were just getting started on her when I left."

Trying valiantly to stem the flow of tears, Hannah kept walking—almost running—toward the clinic with Jacob and Chris flanking her. Each was holding one of her hands. All the while, a prayer was being sent to the heavenly Father.

At the Fort Bridger jail, a sour-faced Dutch Hendrix was sitting on one of the cots in his cell, wondering why his men hadn't learned where he was by now and broken him out.

He was also wondering what was going on with the marshal. He had heard several voices in the office a few minutes ago, but couldn't make out what they were saying. They seemed excited about something as they filed out the door. Then all was silent.

The cell block was on the back side of the building, and with the windows closed against the cold, he could barely hear any sounds from the street.

A half hour or so had passed since the men in the office had left.

Dutch adjusted his position on the cot and sighed as he

put his elbows on his knees and rested his chin in his hands. Suddenly his head came up as he heard loud voices out on the street. Seconds later, he heard the office door come open. He could make out the marshal's voice punctuated with the shuffle of feet, but his words were indistinct.

Dutch tensed as he heard the door of the office come open, then more footsteps in the corridor between the office and the cell block. He rose from the cot and moved to the barred door of the cell.

When the cell block door came open, Dutch Hendrix couldn't believe his eyes. His countenance fell and went gray as he saw Rafe Ketcham, Rex Holt, and Spike Denny being ushered into the cell block at gunpoint by Marshal Lance Mangum, hands on top of their heads and fingers laced together. His men avoided eye contact with him, their faces reflecting the dismal feeling inside them.

His throat tight with shock, Dutch asked, "What happened, boys?"

Still none would meet his gaze.

"They can tell you all about it," Mangum said. "You've got maybe three or four days before you'll face Judge Hankins and take your walk to the gallows."

For a moment, Dutch was speechless. He watched as Mangum opened the adjacent cell, pushed Holt and Denny inside, slammed the steel-barred door with a clank, and locked it.

Inserting the key in the door of Dutch's cell, the marshal unlocked it, pulled it open, and still holding his cocked revolver, said, "There you go, Rafe."

Rafe gave him a hateful glare, hesitating.

Mangum scowled. "Well, now, you can walk into the cell under your own power with no knot on your head...or you can go in while you're out cold *with* a knot on your head. Choice is yours."

"I'd like to have you all to myself with no badge on your chest, Mangum. We'd see who had a knot on his head."

"You're a dreamer, Ketcham," Mangum said. "Which way is it going to be? Like I said, the choice is yours."

Rafe held the marshal's gaze for a long moment, then moved inside the cell.

Mangum slammed it shut, ran his eyes over all four, and said, "You'll all face Judge Hankins. And I have a feeling you'll all take that long walk together to the gallows."

There was dead silence.

Finally Dutch broke it when he looked at Rafe and said, "Where's Durb?"

Rafe turned away.

Features reddening, the gang leader swung his gaze to the next cell. "Rex, where's Durb?"

Rex was sitting on a cot, staring at the floor. He did not look up, nor did he reply.

Getting angrier by the minute, Dutch roared, "Spike, where's Durb?"

Spike was seated on the other cot, his face turned away from the adjacent cell. He didn't move.

"These guys are angry at Durbin Mitchell, Dutch," said Mangum, holstering his gun. "He stepped out of the role as a bad guy and did something decent. He went against these other three and tried to keep them from being so rough and unfeeling with the schoolmarm and the children…and got himself shot for it."

Dutch's mouth fell open. "Schoolmarm? Children? What were you guys doin' at the school?"

Still, none of Dutch's men would answer him.

"Which one of you shot Durb?" demanded Dutch.

"It was Denny," said Mangum.

Dutch glared through the bars at Spike. "What did you do that for?"

"Durb put a gun on me, Dutch!" said Rafe, moving up close to his boss. "Spike did the right thing. He shot him."

Dutch looked at the marshal. "How bad is he?"

"I'm not sure if he'll make it. He was shot in the chest. He didn't look good when he was carried away from the school toward the clinic."

Looking around at the three again, Dutch bawled, "I asked what you guys were doin' at the school!"

In the silence that prevailed, Mangum said, "They did something really stupid."

Fixing Ketcham with hot eyes, Dutch said, "I want to hear it from you! What were you doin' at that school?"

"Tryin' to work a way so we could get you out of here," said Rafe. "We figured holdin' the teacher and the brats hostage, we could call the shots and make this tin star let you outta jail. That's what we were doin'."

"You really bungled it up good, you fools!" Dutch bellowed. "Now we're all in this rotten jail, and we gotta figure out a way to escape before that judge gets to town!"

Rafe turned and sat down on his cot, putting his face in his hands. All three men sat in silence.

Hendrix unleashed a string of profanity on his men, calling them every vile name he could think of.

The marshal wheeled and headed for the door.

Dutch took his attention off his men, moved to the barred door of his cell, and shouted, "Mangum, this jail still can't hold me! These fools bungled it, but I'll break outta here some way!"

Mangum stopped, turned around and said, "You have more gang members out there somewhere, Dutch? Bring them on. We'll see about that!"

Dutch was swearing at his men again as Lance Mangum walked the corridor, stepped into the office, and closed the door behind him.

CHAPTER THIRTEEN

As Hannah Cooper and Jacob Kates hurried along the street with Chris, the boy was filling them in on the details of the incident at the school.

"Those men were so mean," he said. "Especially the one called Rafe. He kept yelling at Mrs. O'Brien to make the little children stop crying. The little girls were scared the worst, and were really crying loud. At one point, Molly Goodman became so frightened, she left her desk, clung to Mrs. O'Brien, and begged her to make the bad men go away."

"Bless her heart," said Hannah.

"The one called Rafe grabbed Molly and threw her on the floor, yelling at her to stop screaming. And then a couple minutes later, little Bessie Lou Markham got so scared that she began screaming at the top of her voice. That mean ol' Rafe slapped her face real hard. Knocked her off her desk and split her lip."

"Oh my," said Hannah.

"That's when Mrs. O'Brien got real, real mad. She jumped on Rafe's back and was clawing at his eyes. He flipped her over his shoulder. She got up in a hurry and went after him again. He punched her this time and knocked her down. Stunned her pretty bad."

"That low-down skunk needs his plow cleaned," said Jacob.

They were nearing the clinic. Chris hurriedly told his mother and Jacob about the outlaw named Durbin getting shot by one of the others because he wanted to let him go after a doctor for Mary Beth.

"And Mama," said Chris, "guess who it was that carried Mary Beth all the way from the school to the clinic."

"Who, honey?"

"Captain Kirkland. He was really careful, too. B. J., Patty Ruth, and I were with him. I think he's probably still at the clinic."

"I'll have to thank him," said Hannah. "After I see my Mary Beth."

Tension was high in Hannah as they stepped out of the street onto the boardwalk, and Chris hurried ahead and opened the door. The instant Hannah was through the door, she found B. J. and Patty Ruth running toward her, arms open. Both began to cry as Hannah folded them into her arms.

"Mama!" said Patty Ruth. "Oh, Mama! Mary Beth is hurt bad!"

"I know, honey," said Hannah, looking toward Dane Kirkland, who was standing close by. "Dane, how is she?"

"She's still alive," he said, the strain of the moment showing in his face. "Both doctors are working on her."

Moving toward the back room door, Hannah said, "I've got to go see Mary Beth."

Laying a hand on her shoulder, Dane said, "Doc asked that you stay out here."

Looking at him askance, she said, "That's my daughter they're working on back there!"

"That's just the point," Dane said softly. "Doc said they can work much better without family members in there asking questions. He emphasized that they are not to be disturbed. Mary Beth's life is at stake, Hannah."

Tears misted the anxious mother's dark brown eyes. "I

know. That's why I wanted to go back there. I want to see her. I want to know what they can tell me about her chances of living. Isn't Sundi here? Where's Edie?"

"Did Chris tell you about the outlaw who was shot?"

"Yes."

"Well, Edie is back there trying to keep him alive till the doctors can get to him, and Sundi's back there with Bob Imler. He's got a pretty deep gash on his head."

Hannah nodded, wiped a hand over her face. "Dane, I have to know how serious Mary Beth's wound is."

"I won't lie to you," said Dane. "Doc told me she is critical. But he also said that he and Patrick will do everything they can for her." He touched her arm. "Come over here and sit down, okay?"

Hannah took a deep breath, sighed, and said, "All right."

"Let's get your coat off."

While Dane was hanging up her coat, Hannah sat down on one of the wooden chairs in the waiting area, next to Jacob. Chris, B. J., and Patty Ruth began crowding close to her. Jacob slid over to the next chair to allow the children full access to their mother.

Hannah picked up Patty Ruth and placed her on her lap. With an arm around her, she looked up at the captain and said, "Dane, Chris told me you carried Mary Beth here from the school. I want to thank you for that."

"There isn't anything I wouldn't do for the Cooper family," Dane said.

Clinging to her mother, Patty Ruth said, "Mama, is Mary Beth going to die?"

Hannah's throat tightened. She tried to speak, but the stricture in her throat prevented it.

Dane laid a hand on Patty Ruth's shoulder. "Honey, remember that we prayed together while Chris was on his way to bring your mother?"

The child looked up at him and nodded.

"We asked the Lord to spare Mary Beth's life, didn't we?"

Patty Ruth nodded again. "Yes, sir."

"Then we must trust her to God's hands and believe that Mary Beth is going to live."

Patty Ruth's lips quivered as she said, "Could we pray again, now that Chris and Mama and Uncle Jacob are here?"

"We sure can, honey," said the captain, dropping to one knee while keeping his hand on the child's shoulder.

Heads were bowed and eyes were closed as Dane Kirkland led them in prayer for Mary Beth's life. While the captain was praying, Jacob had his head bowed and his eyes closed like the others. After several minutes, he opened his eyes and looked at Hannah. She held her children close to her and made tiny assenting sounds as Dane prayed. Jacob's heart felt like it was going to shatter in his chest. He closed his eyes, bit his lips, and wiped away the tears that were spilling down his cheeks.

At that moment, Dane said his heartfelt amen, and every eye turned to the door of the back room as it opened and Sundi O'Brien came out, closing the door behind her.

Hannah stiffened and said, "How is she?"

"I can't really tell you, Hannah, dear. I dare not ask any questions while the doctors are working on her. They are quite intent on what they are doing."

"You've not heard them say anything to each other that would give any indication how it's going?"

"Nothing I could understand. They've said a few things, but it's been in barely more than a whisper."

"Captain Kirkland said you've been taking care of Bob."

"Yes."

"And he's all right?"

"I believe so. He's going to need some stitches to close up the gash. Edie put a temporary bandage on him, and the blood flow is minimal. He's developing a monstrous headache, though. He's resting as well as can be expected."

"So how's the wounded outlaw doing? Edie's taking care of him, I understand."

"Well, she's doing what she can for him, but like Mary Beth, he got hit in the chest. There's not a lot Edie can do but try to stay the flow of blood till the doctors can get to him."

Hannah's voice trembled as she said, "Sundi, I have to know if they think Mary Beth is going to make it. What, in their opinion, are her chances? We've prayed, and I'm trying to let the Lord give me His peace, but it wouldn't hurt if I knew what Doc and Patrick think. Maybe they've said something to Edie. Can I go in and ask her what she knows?"

Giving the distressed mother a compassionate look, Sundi said, "Edie hasn't heard any more than I have. She couldn't tell you, either. It would have to come from Doc or Patrick."

Hannah nodded. "I understand. Thank you."

"Hannah," said Sundi, "I need to get back to Bob. Is there anything I can get you before I go? Some water, maybe?"

Hannah indeed found her mouth dry. "That would be nice."

"I can get it for her, Mrs. O'Brien," said Dane, running his gaze to a pitcher and several cups on a small table next to Edie's desk.

Sundi gave him a thin smile. "All right. If anyone else wants water, please help yourself." Sundi started back toward the door, paused, and said, "Hannah, if I hear or see anything significant, I'll come and tell you."

Hannah nodded. "Thank you, dear."

Dane hurried to the table, poured a cup full of water, and while he was heading back for Hannah, the rest of the group went for water.

By the time Hannah had emptied her cup, Patty Ruth was back on her lap, and Chris and B.J. were on the chairs beside her. Dane sat down next to Jacob, patted his shoulder and said, "I appreciate your being such a friend to this family."

"It was they who took me in when I was desperate, Captain. How could I be anything but a friend to them? These are the easiest people to love I've ever met."

Kirkland grinned. "I know what you mean."

Hannah laid her head on Patty Ruth's red locks and closed her eyes. She thought of Mary Beth in the operating room, hovering between life and death, and her mind went back to October 25, 1857…

It was a beautiful fall day in Missouri. Hannah's labor pains were coming one after the other as Dr. Roy Gleason and his nurse, Dora Jennings, stood over the bed in the Cooper home, making preparation for the second Cooper child to come into the world.

Dora was dabbing perspiration from Hannah's brow when there was a tap on the bedroom door.

"Yes, Solomon?" said the doctor, while pressing experienced fingers on Hannah's swollen middle.

Hannah heard the door open, and opened her eyes to see her husband's handsome face. "How soon, now?" asked Solomon.

"Very soon," replied Gleason. "We'll let you know. Now go take care of Christopher and keep your mind occupied."

Solomon's gaze met Hannah's. "I love you, sweetheart."

In the midst of a sharp pain, Hannah nodded, and was able to squeak out, "Me too."

Before Hannah knew it, she heard Dr. Gleason urging her to take tiny breaths and push. She could feel Dora's hand gripping her own, and could barely hear her saying words of encouragement.

Suddenly, a wave of dizziness swept over her. She heard

the doctor say, "It's a girl, Hannah! She's got two arms, two legs, and ten little fingers and ten little toes. She's perfect!"

Instantly there was a sharp slapping sound, followed by a loud, shrill wail.

"Oh, praise the Lord!" Hannah gasped. "Praise the Lord!"

Dora let go of Hannah's hand, took the crying baby from the doctor, and hurried to a table nearby.

The silver-haired physician covered Hannah's legs and smiled. "I'm glad to report that mother is doing fine, too. I'll be right back to finish up here, but Solomon needs to hear that he's got a beautiful baby daughter."

"Yes!" said the weary mother.

Hannah watched as Gleason opened the door and found Solomon standing there, a look of expectancy on his face. He had little twenty-month-old Christopher in his arms. "I heard the cry, Doctor. What—"

"A girl! She's fine, and so is her mother. You can come in shortly."

Solomon nodded, sent a glance to Hannah, and smiling broadly, said, "We got our little Mary Beth, darlin'."

"Yes!" she said, feeling the weakness brought on by four hours of labor. "Our little Mary Beth…"

Patty Ruth squirmed on Hannah's lap, bringing her back to the present.

"Our little Mary Beth," she said in the same soft tone she had said it almost fourteen years ago.

Patty Ruth looked into her eyes. "She is our Mary Beth, isn't she, Mama?"

"Yes, honey," replied Hannah, sending a glance at the closed door to the back room. "She belongs to all of us."

Hannah closed her eyes again. Patty Ruth snuggled in her arms and laid her head on Hannah's breast.

Hannah recalled many precious memories of Mary Beth's life in the next few years. Even as a three-year-old, she had shown a trait of unselfishness and concern for others. With each passing year, that trait grew with her.

Hannah thought of the day when Mary Beth was six, and one wintry day came home from school without her coat. Chris was in bed with a cold, which meant Mary Beth had gone to school without her usual escort. When a concerned Hannah asked her shivering daughter what happened to her coat, Mary Beth confessed that she had given it to her little friend, Francie Tomkins. Hannah knew Francie's father had died of pneumonia the previous year, and the mother was in extreme poverty, trying to provide for her four children. Mary Beth had explained that Francie's old coat was tattered and didn't keep her warm anymore, so she gave her coat to Francie.

Many other incidents of selflessness on Mary Beth's part drifted through Hannah's mind, even those that had taken place the past fourteen months they had been in Fort Bridger.

She also recalled the day Mary Beth received Jesus into her heart just before she turned seven...and of how she quickly developed a concern for lost souls. She let her mind drift across the years and lay hold on many memories of people Mary Beth had witnessed to, and of some she had led to the Lord. She thought of Bob Imler lying on a cot in the back room of the clinic, whom Mary Beth had led to Christ only a few months ago.

Hannah then thought of Jacob, and how burdened Mary Beth was for him. Often at prayer and Bible reading time, the sweet girl had broken down of late, weeping over Uncle Jacob's lost condition.

Dane and Jacob were talking in low tones, as were Chris and B. J.

Hannah could hear Patty Ruth's even breathing as her head lay on her breast. She had fallen asleep in her mother's arms.

Hannah looked toward the closed door of the back room once more and pictured her oldest daughter on the operating table. A lump formed in her throat. "Oh, dear Lord," she said in a whisper, barely moving her lips, "You took my precious husband from me. Are you going to take Mary Beth, too?"

Doubts and fears assailed her, and she asked the Lord to forgive her for doubting Him. "Lord, You understand what I'm going through. I didn't want Solomon to die, either, but You took him. I…I know You never do wrong, but…I'm having an awful time thinking that You might decide to take my Mary Beth from me, too. Help me, Lord Jesus. Help me to trust You, and not to get in Your way. But I…I'm asking You to please let Mary Beth live. Please, Lord. Please."

The desperate mother swallowed hard and said again in the same soundless whisper, "Dear Lord, I don't mean to be selfish. Please help me. I…I want Your will to be done. And…and—" Something lodged in her throat momentarily. She swallowed with difficulty. "Dear God, this is very hard for me to say…but if You can get more glory to Your name by taking her home than by sparing her life…I want You to have the glory. Help this poor servant of Yours to accept Your will. I love You, Lord Jesus, and—"

Hannah's prayer was interrupted by the sound of the front door opening. She opened her eyes to see Marshal Lance Mangum and Deputy Jack Bower enter.

Patty Ruth stirred and came awake as both Jacob and Dane stood up.

Mangum set his gaze on Hannah and asked, "How's Mary Beth?"

At the same moment, the back room door came open, and Sundi came out, closing the door behind her.

"Maybe Sundi can tell you more than I can, Lance," said Hannah.

Drawing up, Sundi said, "Patrick and Doc aren't saying

much, but I came out to tell you, Hannah, that they got the slug out. I heard Patrick drop it in a pail. They're working at getting the bleeding stopped, but I don't know as yet what the prognosis might be."

"Well, praise the Lord she's still alive," said Lance.

"Yes," said Jack. "I'm so glad to know that." Then he said to Sundi, "I saw to it that all the children got home; even those who live in the country."

"Thank you," she said. "I hope none of them have nightmares."

"Sundi, what about Bob Imler?" Mangum said.

"He's doing all right. The doctors will have to take some stitches in his head as soon as they can."

"And what about Durbin Mitchell? He still alive?"

"Yes. Edie's watching over him as best she can until the doctors are finished with Mary Beth."

Mangum nodded. "The other three gang members have joined their leader in jail and will face the circuit judge in a few days."

"I hope the law sees to it that they get what they deserve," said Jacob.

"They're all wanted for murder," Mangum said. "They'll face the gallows."

"Well, I have to get back," said Sundi.

As she pivoted and headed toward the door, Hannah called after her, "Thank you for letting me know the bullet is out."

Sundi gave her a little wave and said, "I'll keep you posted," and moved through the door.

B. J. moved to his mother, took hold of her hand, and said with pinched face, "Mama, I'm scared. I'm afraid Mary Beth is going to die just like Papa did."

Tears were misting Chris's eyes. "That's what B. J. and I were talking about, Mama. We want to believe that God is going to keep Mary Beth alive, but...but He let Papa die. Maybe He will let Mary Beth die, too."

Patty Ruth flung her arms around Hannah's neck and said with a quaver in her voice, "I'm afraid too, Mama!"

Hannah bit her lips. "We...we have to trust the Lord, children. We have to. He is the one who holds Mary Beth's life in His hands."

Dane Kirkland hunkered down in front of Hannah. "Let's pray some more for Mary Beth, okay?"

"Oh, yes...please," Hannah said with tears welling up in her eyes.

The lawmen removed their hats and bowed their heads with the others as Dane began praying.

CHAPTER FOURTEEN

While Captain Dane Kirkland was leading the group in prayer, Jacob Kates's mind strayed to the Scriptures Hannah and Mary Beth had shown him about the Messiah, and how Jesus Christ had met the prophecies perfectly.

This had troubled him immensely. Since so many of the prophecies Hannah showed him had to do with Christ's crucifixion, Jacob went into the store one night and took Hannah's Bible from under the counter. In his quarters, he read the crucifixion account in all four gospels. In reading John's account, he found that in order to kill the three men who were crucified that day so they could get them buried before sundown, the Roman soldiers had broken the legs of the two thieves, but when they came to Jesus, He was already dead so they didn't break his legs.

As Jacob read on, the next four verses captured his attention:

> But one of the soldiers with a spear pierced his side, and forthwith came there out blood and water. And he that saw it bare record, and his record is true: and he knoweth that he saith true, that ye might believe. For these things were done, that the scripture should be fulfilled, A bone of him shall not be broken. And

again another scripture saith, They shall look on him whom they pierced.

Jacob had found a cross-reference at John 19:36, directing him to Psalm 34:20. He quickly turned to that verse in his own Hebrew Bible and found that, indeed, it said that not one bone of Messiah's would be broken. Another cross-reference pointed him to Zechariah 12:10, which he knew well. Jehovah had promised in the previous verse that He would destroy all the nations that had come against Jerusalem...and then He said in verse 10: "And I will pour upon the house of David, and upon the inhabitants of Jerusalem, the spirit of grace and of supplications: and they shall look upon me whom they have pierced."

Jacob had been so disturbed over these Scriptures, seeing them fulfilled in Jesus Christ, that he had not been sleeping well.

As Dane wept and prayed for Mary Beth, Jacob asked himself if he had been deceived all along. Was it possible that all the rabbis he had sat under were actually blind to the truth? Had they never studied the New Testament to learn what it said about Jesus Christ being in the earthly line of David? Had they never looked to see the prophecies that had been fulfilled by Jesus Christ? Had they never considered the possibility that Jesus was more than just a good Jewish man? How could they not see those things Hannah and Mary Beth had shown him?

The name Mary Beth came from Kirkland's lips as he prayed on, and penetrated Jacob's thoughts.

Mary Beth. Suddenly her heart-gripping words so lovingly spoken to him a few days ago echoed through his mind: *I love you so much that if giving up my life would cause you to call on Jesus and be saved, I would do it.*

Jacob clenched his hands into fists and bit down so hard it lanced pain through his jaws.

As Captain Kirkland continued to pray, there was a slight sound of the front door opening and someone entering, but the captain kept on praying and no one but Jacob looked up to see who had come in. It was Pastor and Mrs. Kelly.

The Kellys stopped just inside the door, closed it quietly, and waited. The pastor already had his hat in his hand. He glanced at Jacob, who now had his head bowed and his eyes closed.

After a few more minutes, Kirkland closed his prayer, and when heads came up, Rebecca Kelly rushed to Hannah and put her arms around her.

"Hello, Pastor," said the marshal. "I'm glad you've come."

"We came as soon as we were told what happened," said Kelly. He looked at Kirkland. "Other than what we learned while you were praying, what can you tell us?"

"I'll tell you as much as we know, Pastor," Hannah said.

While she gave the Kellys what information she could, it was all Jacob could do to sit still. As soon as Hannah had finished her brief account about Mary Beth, Jacob stood up, put on his coat and hat, stepped to Hannah, and said, "I need to get some fresh air. I'll be right outside."

"Jacob, dear," she said in a tender tone, "I can't tell you what it means to me that you care so much about Mary Beth."

The little man thumbed tears from his eyes as he ran his gaze over the faces of the three Cooper children in the room, and sniffing, said, "Hannah, I love Chris, B. J., Patty Ruth, and little Eddie too, but I...I just can't bear the thought of sweet Mary Beth not making it. As I said, I'll be right outside."

Stepping out into the brisk fall air, Jacob pulled his coat collar up close to his chin while pacing the boardwalk in front of the clinic. Speaking aloud, he said, "God, is this what Mary Beth's getting shot is all about? She loves me so much that she is willing to die if that's what it takes for me to become a Christian. God, have I been stubbornly blind to the truth? Saul of Tarsus was a Hebrew of the Hebrews. Like me, as I understand it, he was fighting to hang on to his religion. But from what Hannah showed me, he took that journey to Damascus, and if what it says there in the New Testament is true…he found out, indeed, that Jesus Christ is the true Messiah.

"God, I was always taught that the New Testament wasn't inspired by You…that it was only a collection of writings made by men who wanted to shine a bright light on Jesus Christ. But…somehow, as Hannah and Mary Beth have read it to me—and I have read some of it for myself—I can't shake the impression that it is true."

A ranch wagon was passing by. The driver called Jacob's name and waved to him. Jacob stopped pacing, forced a smile, and waved back.

Resuming the pacing, he said, "Dear God, can this be? Is Jesus Christ really Your Son…the Messiah…the Saviour? Can it be that all these years, I have looked for Messiah to come, and I have been wrong? That He has already come? And…and that He died as our Passover Lamb as Hannah once told me?"

Once again Jacob's mind went to the crucifixion of Jesus Christ, then to Zechariah 12:10. The words seemed to sear into his brain: *They shall look upon me whom they have pierced.*

The battle that raged inside Jacob Kates grew more intense as he continued to pace the boardwalk.

Inside the office, Chris Cooper said, "Pastor, did anyone tell you about that outlaw who's lying back there with a bullet in his chest?"

"Yes, though not much in the way of details. I think Mrs. Kelly and I have the story straight on Bob's getting hit on the head, but we really weren't told much about—what's his name?"

"Durbin Mitchell. He got shot because he didn't like it that his pals wouldn't let me run and get one of the doctors when Mary Beth was shot. He put his gun on the one named

Rafe Ketcham and told him to let me go, that he wasn't letting Mary Beth die if he could help it. Then one of the other outlaws shot him."

"Well," said Kelly, "at least he has some decency to him. That's more than you can say for most outlaws."

"Most of them have no conscience," said Jack Bower. "Seems they're like those people Paul wrote to Timothy about. You know, the ones whose conscience had been, as it were, seared with a hot iron."

"Yes," said Mangum. "Most of them are like that. Since this Durbin Mitchell took a bullet in an attempt to help Mary Beth, I'll bring up his deed if he lives to face the judge."

The door opened and Jacob came back into the office, his eyes red and swollen.

When he had closed the door, Hannah said, "Jacob, are you all right?"

The little man shook his head. "I won't be all right, Hannah, until I know Mary Beth is going to live."

Suddenly the door to the back room opened, and Doc O'Brien came out, his face gray and grim.

Everyone tensed up. Hannah's heart leaped in her chest. Sundi came out, too, closing the door behind her. The group uniformly held its breath, waiting for the doctor to speak.

Doc swung his tired gaze to the marshal and sighed. "Lance, you know about this Durbin Mitchell, and what he did, I assume."

"Yes."

"Well, Edie did everything she could for him while Patrick and I have been working on Mary Beth. I appreciate what the man did to try to help Mary Beth, and I wish we could have saved him, but he just died."

Mangum's head lowered a little. "Too bad. I was going to do what I could for him when he stood before the judge."

Breathing hard with her children clinging to her, Hannah

said, "Doc, what about Mary Beth?"

Every eye was on the silver-haired physician as he said, "The slug is out. Patrick is closing up the wound with Edie's help. But...but—"

Hannah's back arched. "But what?"

Doc rubbed his jaw. "Hannah, I have to be honest with you. The slug was dangerously close to her heart. So close that it was impossible for us to accurately assess the damage. I...can't tell you that she's going to live. Right now, she is very close to death."

The room went silent as a tomb.

Doc took hold of Hannah's hand. "Patrick and I will do everything that is humanly possible for Mary Beth, but her life is in God's hands. One of us will be with her at all times, Hannah, I promise you that."

Hannah's lips quivered. Nodding, she said, "I know you will both give her the best care possible."

Patting her hand, Doc said, "Now, you should take these children and go home. It could be a long time before we know anything. I will let you know as soon as I can tell you anything definite."

Doc turned to look at the others, and didn't see Hannah begin to shake her head. "The rest of you should go back to whatever you were doing before. When there is any significant change, I'll see that you are informed."

Hannah rose to her feet, Patty Ruth and B. J. clinging to her. "Doc, I'm not leaving. I can't. I've got to stay here with her."

"But you're already tired, Hannah," protested Doc. "You need some rest."

"Not as much as I need to stay close to my daughter."

Seeing the stubborn look in Hannah's eyes, Kelly said, "Tell you what, Hannah. Rebecca and I will take these three to your apartment and stay with them until you feel you can come home. We'd be glad to take them to our home, but they'll be more comfortable in their own surroundings. Where's Eddie?"

"He's with Glenda and Mandy, Pastor. They're watching over the store at the moment, too."

"We'll take Eddie up to the apartment, too," said Rebecca. "And don't you worry, honey. Pastor and I will see that they're taken care of."

"Mama," said Chris, "I'll stay here with you."

Hannah gave him a soft, appreciative look. "It will help me more, Chris, if I know you're there at home to help Pastor and Mrs. Kelly with B. J. and Patty Ruth."

"All right," said Chris.

Jacob said, "Hannah, would you like for me to stay here with you?"

"Your presence would of course be a comfort, Jacob, but it would help me most if I knew you were back at the store, and Glenda and Mandy could go home."

"All right. And please let me know of any change in my little Mary Beth's condition, won't you?"

"Of course."

"Hannah," said Captain Kirkland, "is it all right if I stay here with you? I've already sent a message to Colonel Bateman, informing him that I might not be back to the fort until much later."

Hannah tried to form a smile on her lips. "Of course, Dane. I appreciate your kindness."

Mangum looked at his deputy. "Well, Jack, we'd better get back to the office. Dutch and his bunch might be trying to rip the bars out."

"I wouldn't put it past them," said Jack. "Dutch was so sure our jail couldn't hold him. And now, with his boys locked up too, he's probably desperate enough to try anything."

Pastor Kelly said, "Kids, give your mother a hug, and we'll take you home."

Suddenly the door to the back room opened, and Edie

came out, leaving it open behind her. Her face was drawn and gray, and there were tears in her eyes. Everyone looked at her, their hearts almost stopping.

Hannah felt a sharp pang shoot across her chest as Edie looked at her, and with trembling lips, said, "We...we lost her. I'm so sorry, Hannah. We couldn't save her."

Doc stood speechless, eyes wide. Chris blinked in disbelief. B. J.'s facial features seemed frozen. Patty Ruth closed her eyes, bowed her head, and gripped her mother's hand.

Jacob and the others stood in shock.

Hannah's knees went watery. The pulse in her temples throbbed. She felt herself threatening to split apart in little pieces.

Doc was trying to think of something to say while Rebecca and Sundi put their arms around Hannah.

The pastor stepped close to Hannah, and was about to say something when suddenly Patrick's voice came loud and clear through the open door behind Edie, "Mom, wait! I've got a pulse, here! She's alive! Dad, come help me!"

As Doc hastily brushed past Edie through the door, Hannah gently broke loose from Rebecca and Sundi, let go of Patty Ruth's hand, and dashed into the back room, breaking into sobs of relief.

Sundi and Rebecca grasped Chris, B. J., and Patty Ruth, who started to follow. "Please," said Sundi, "it's best if you stay here for now."

Edie hurried behind Hannah as she drew up to the operating table beside Doc. Patrick was on the other side of the table, relief evident on his face as he gently massaged the sides of Mary Beth's neck. She was breathing heavily, and her closed eyelids were fluttering.

"Oh, thank You, Lord!" cried Hannah. "Thank You! She's alive!"

Doc began rubbing the girl's hands.

Mary Beth's eyelids fluttered rapidly, then she opened her eyes, staring blankly at the ceiling. Hannah drew in a sharp breath, bent low over her, and said, "Mary Beth, it's Mama. Can you see me, honey?"

Mary Beth turned her head in Hannah's direction. Her mouth opened slightly, then sagged as her eyes closed and her head went limp.

"Oh no!" Hannah gasped. "No!"

"She's just passed out again, Hannah," said Patrick. "She's still breathing."

Hannah's hand went to her mouth. Tears filled her eyes. "Doc, Patrick, she's going to make it, isn't she?"

Father and son looked at each other, then Doc said, "We can't give you anything definite at this point, Hannah. But she rallied from what Patrick and Mom thought was death, and that is a plenty good sign. We'll stay with her, Hannah. She will not be alone for a minute."

Hannah looked down at her precious daughter. She stroked the blond locks back off her moist brow and ran a trembling hand along her ashen cheek. As she bent down and kissed the same cheek, she said, "I love you, sweetheart. I love you."

Edie touched her arm. "Come, Hannah. We've got to let Doc and Patrick care for her."

Hannah nodded, reluctantly stepped back from the table, and with lagging steps, headed for the door with Edie at her side. When they reached the door, Hannah stopped, looked back over her shoulder, and said, "Please, Lord…please…"

When Hannah and Edie entered the office, they found Pastor Andy Kelly leading the group in prayer. Hannah moved up to her three children and put arms around them. They gripped her hard, looking up long enough to glimpse her, then bowed their heads again.

When Kelly closed his prayer, all eyes turned to Hannah and Edie.

"Is she going to be all right, Mama?" asked B. J.

"Grandpa and Patrick can't say for sure, yet, but she did open her eyes for a few seconds. That's at least a good sign."

"Let's get you kids home," said the pastor.

"The rest of us better go, too," said the marshal.

As the group was filing out the door, coats on and buttoned, Edie said, "We'll see that all of you hear if there's any significant change."

"Thank you," said Jacob. Then to Hannah he said, "Please sit down and rest."

She managed a thin smile and nodded. Then taking a step toward the door, she called, "Chris…!"

The boy appeared quickly. "Yes, Mama?"

"Would you go tell Grandma and Grandpa about Mary Beth, please? I'm sure they haven't heard anything about her being shot, or they would be here."

"Sure will," said the boy.

"And honey…tell them not to come here. If they want to come to the apartment, that will be fine. Once I know Mary Beth is stabilized, I'll come home."

"Okay, Mama. I'll tell them."

Sundi headed for the back room, saying, "I'd better go see how Bob is doing."

When the door was closed by Jack Bower, who was the last one out, Edie said, "Now, Hannah, do as Jacob told you. Sit down. I'm going back to see if there's anything I can do to help my men."

"Thank you for everything you've done, Edie," said Hannah. "You've been so good to us."

"Just doing what I should, sweetie," said the woman as she headed for the back room.

When the door clicked behind Edie, Dane took hold of Hannah's arm and guided her to a chair, saying, "Let's obey Jacob and get you seated."

Hannah said, "Okay. Jacob gets kind of bossy at times. Strange, isn't it? I'm his boss, yet he bosses me."

"Well, in a case like this," Dane said, "I'm glad he does."

Hannah settled on one of the chairs, then Dane sat down beside her. Patting her arm, he said, "Hannah, Mary Beth is going to make it. I feel so strongly in my heart that the Lord is going to spare her life."

Hannah tried to smile. "Thank you for the encouragement, Dane. I appreciate your care and concern."

The back room door opened. Patrick said, "Hannah, she's coming around again. Why don't you come in, in case she comes fully awake?"

"May I come in, too, Doctor?" asked Kirkland.

"I'd like to let you, Captain, but it's best that only one visitor be in here at a time. I hope you understand."

"Of course. I'll be right here, Hannah, if you need me."

"Thank you, Dane," she said, giving him another thin smile.

As the three Cooper children, the Kellys, and Jacob made their way along the boardwalk toward the general store, people on the street who had heard about Mary Beth being shot stopped and asked about her condition. Jacob and the Kellys told them Mary Beth was still alive, and that the doctors were watching her closely. Each person spoke to the children, trying to encourage them about their sister.

As they neared the store, Chris said, "I'll go on over to the hotel and tell Grandma and Grandpa about Mary Beth. I know they'll want to come to the apartment, so we'll be there shortly."

"Fine," said the pastor.

B. J., Patty Ruth, and the Kellys had barely entered the apartment when the sound of footsteps was heard on the stairs outside. B. J. hurried to the door and opened it just as Mandy and Glenda drew up. Glenda was carrying the baby and had him wrapped in his heavy blanket.

Glenda said, "Pastor, Mandy has to get on home to her children, but I'll stay here if you and Rebecca need to get back to the church."

"We're okay on that," said Rebecca. "I'm sure Abby could use the motherly touch. You go on home to her."

"You're sure? I'll be glad to stay."

"We're sure," said the pastor. "Thank you, Glenda, for the offer."

As the two women headed for the door, Glenda said, "Jacob told us that Captain Kirkland is staying at the clinic with Hannah. If you should learn that he has to return to the fort while Hannah's still at the clinic, would you send Chris or B. J. for me? I'll go stay with her."

"Hopefully Hannah will get to come home in a short while," said Kelly, "but if not, I'm sure Captain Kirkland would come by here before going to the fort. We'll let you know if you're needed."

"My family and I will be praying for Mary Beth," said Mandy.

"Us, too," put in Glenda.

"Thank you," said the pastor. "We must all pray for her earnestly and fervently."

"Yes," said Rebecca, putting an arm around Patty Ruth. "This precious family has had so many heartaches in the loss of husband and father. We don't want them to suffer the same thing in the loss of Mary Beth. The Lord said in Jeremiah 33:3, 'Call unto me, and I will answer thee, and shew thee great and mighty things, which thou knowest not.' Let's all trust the Lord for a great and mighty thing in the saving of Mary Beth's life."

CHAPTER FIFTEEN

Hannah Cooper stood over Mary Beth, whose eyes were about half open. They were glazed, but she was trying to focus on the face that hovered over her.

Dr. Patrick O'Brien stood slightly aloof, wanting Mary Beth to see only her mother if she did regain consciousness. Edie was once again in the office, and Sundi was standing beside Bob Imler where he lay on the other examining table while the older physician was bandaging his head after stitching up the wound.

Bending low, Hannah said, "Mary Beth, can you see me, sweetheart? It's Mama. Can you hear me?"

Mary Beth's mouth opened. Her tongue touched her lips, and her languid eyes leveled on Hannah for several seconds, but they still did not come clear and focus. Her eyelids fluttered and closed.

"Honey, please," said Hannah. "Please wake up. I need to see you awake."

A gentle hand touched Hannah's shoulder. "She's under again," said Patrick. "But at least she seems to be rallying."

Hannah heard Doc speaking softly to Bob Imler and glanced that direction. Doc and Sundi were helping the boy make his way back to the cot.

A moment later, the silver-haired physician stepped up,

and Patrick said, "She almost came out of it, Dad. She looked a bit more alert than before. Kept her eyes open a bit longer. Even moved her mouth a little."

Doc nodded. "Glad to hear it."

"So this is a good sign," said Hannah.

"Positively," said Doc. "One of these times, she'll open those big blue eyes and she'll be able to look at us and actually see us."

"I want to be here when she does," Hannah said.

"There's no way to know when that might happen. You look awfully tired. Why don't you go home and get some rest? When she rallies again, Patrick will run and get you."

"One of us will be right here with her every minute," Patrick said. "If she should come out of it anytime during the night, and I'm on duty, I'll wake Dad so he can watch her while I come and bang on your door. He'll be sleeping right over here on the cot. And that's where I'll sleep when he's on duty."

Hannah sent a glance to the cot where Bob lay once again, with Sundi sitting at his side. "But, then, where will Bob be sleeping?"

"At home," said Patrick. "I sent a couple of Bob's friends from school to ride out to the Imler farm and tell his parents what happened to him, and to bring a wagon and pick him up."

"Oh. I'm glad to know he can go home."

Doc bent his head down, looked at Hannah over the tops of his spectacles, and said, "Now, that's what I want you to do too. Go home."

"Do you both think she's at the point where she's out of danger?"

"We didn't say that, Hannah," spoke up Doc. "But this rallying gives us more hope than we've had so far. When I spoke a moment ago about her opening her eyes one of these times and being able to see us, it's this hope I was basing it on. We've got to keep a positive attitude."

"In all honesty," said Patrick, "her vital signs are very weak, and her heartbeat is erratic. She has a long way to go, and she's not out of danger. But Dad and I both want you to go home and rest. First, Mary Beth is in God's hands, and second, she is in our hands. Please keep this in mind as you go home."

Hannah gave them both a grim smile. "All right. But whenever she rallies again, I have your solemn promise that you'll come and get me, no matter what time it is...day or night."

"You sure do," said Patrick.

Hannah nodded, turned back, and bent over her daughter. She kissed her forehead and said in a low voice, "I love you, precious Mary Beth. Please come back to me real soon."

Both doctors had misty eyes as Hannah turned back, thanked them for what they were doing for her daughter, and moved toward the cot. As she drew up, Sundi smiled. Bob's features were solemn as he looked up at her. His face tinted a bit as he said, "Mrs. Cooper, I'm so sorry. It's my fault that Mary Beth got shot."

Leaning over him, Hannah said, "Don't call it a fault, Bob. Chris told me all about it. You did a very brave thing by trying to stop the outlaws from brutalizing your teacher and your fellow students. You certainly didn't intend for Mary Beth to get shot."

Tears welled up in the boy's eyes. "Thank you for saying that, Mrs. Cooper. Mary Beth means very much to me. She's been such a good friend, and most of all, she led me to the Lord. I feel so bad that she was hit by that bullet." He sniffed, blinked tears onto his cheeks, and said, "I want to tell her how bad I feel about it."

"You'll get your chance to do that," said Hannah. "Mary Beth is going to come through this. I'm trusting the Lord to bring her through it. You just pray hard for her, won't you?"

"Yes, ma'am. I have been and I will be. Mrs. O'Brien and I

have prayed together for her, too."

"I appreciate that," said Hannah. "Well, those two doctors over there are sending me home, so I guess I'd better be going."

As Hannah stepped into the office, the sound of a wagon rolling to a stop outside the front door met her ears. Dane Kirkland rose to his feet to meet her. Before Dane could ask about Mary Beth, Edie looked out the window and said, "It's Bob's father."

Big Rufe Imler hopped out of the wagon and stomped heavily across the boardwalk. Bowling his way through the door, he ran his hot gaze over the faces of Hannah and Dane, then looked at Edie and said, "Where's my boy?"

"He's in the back," replied Edie, rising from the desk. "I'll tell the doctors you're here."

"I'll just come back there and get him," Rufe said.

"You wait here," said Edie. "Mary Beth Cooper is back there, and she is not to be disturbed."

"I'm goin' to my boy!" Rufe said as he headed toward the back room door.

Dane blocked his way. Rufe looked the captain up and down. "Get outta my way," he grunted.

"Didn't you hear what Mrs. O'Brien said? Mary Beth is back there hanging on to life by a thread. Your presence in the room could be detrimental. Bob's teacher is back there with him. I'll stick my head in and tell her you're here."

Rufe sighed, nodded, and said, "I…I'm sorry Mary Beth was shot. I admire that girl for her spunk. I sure hope she'll be all right."

"We're praying she will be, Mr. Imler," said Hannah.

Dane opened the back room door and found Sundi already walking beside Bob, heading toward him. "We heard Mr. Imler's voice," said Sundi.

When they came into the office, Rufe glanced at the bandage on his son's head and with a scowl said, "Bob, that was a foolish thing to do, you know that, don't you? You had no business tryin' to take on those outlaws."

"They were being mean to Mrs. O'Brien and some of the kids," Bob said. "I had to try to stop them."

Rufe shook his head, then put his harsh gaze on Edie. "Don't look to me to pay for this bandage and all. Let the school board pay the bill. They should have the school better protected. Let's go, boy."

As they started out the door, Bob paused, looked back, and said, "Thank you for taking care of me. And Mrs. Cooper, thank you for not hating me."

"I could never hate you, Bob," Hannah said.

When Rufe and Bob were out the door and climbing into the wagon, Hannah said to the others, "Well, at least Rufe showed some concern about Mary Beth."

"What did he mean, he admires Mary Beth for her spunk?" asked Dane.

"That's because she witnessed to him about the Lord and he couldn't back her down. It was Mary Beth who led Bob to Jesus. She also convinced Rufe to let Bob be baptized and attend church when at first he said he would never allow it."

Dane shook his head in wonderment. "There aren't many girls like Mary Beth. She's one in a million."

When Hannah and Dane entered the apartment, Ben and Esther Singleton were already weeping over their granddaughter. They wept harder when they saw Hannah, and both of them put their arms around her.

When the emotions settled down, little Eddie was in B. J.'s arms, and reached for his mother. Hannah took him and folded him close to her heart.

"How's she doing?" asked Pastor Kelly.

Hannah said, "There's a little bit of encouragement. Let's

sit down and I'll tell you about it."

Everyone listened intently as Hannah told them about Mary Beth rallying slightly twice. She explained what the doctors said about it, and made sure they understood that Mary Beth was still not out of danger. When she finished, Hannah said, "Chris, will you go down and tell Uncle Jacob this latest bit of information, please? I told him I would keep him up to date."

"Sure, Mama," said Chris.

During the next hour, Ben and Esther brought up memories of Mary Beth in days gone by. This stimulated the boys and Patty Ruth to bring up their own memories of their sister.

The sun had set, and twilight was coming on when Jacob knocked on the door. When he came in, he thanked Hannah for sending Chris down to give him the latest information, then said, "Hannah, word about Mary Beth is all over town and fort. People have told me to give you their love, and they want you to know they will be praying."

"Thank you for telling me, Jacob," Hannah said. She ran her eyes over the group. "I'll fix supper now."

"Not for me," said Ben. "All of this about our girl has stolen my appetite."

Everyone else said they had no appetite, either.

"Well, I know Eddie does," said Hannah. "I'll feed him while the rest of you just relax as best as you can."

Patty Ruth sat at the kitchen table while her mother prepared food for Eddie, and held Biggie on her lap while little brother was being fed. When Hannah and Patty Ruth returned to the others, Pastor Kelly said, "How about us having prayer together for Mary Beth once more?"

"Yes," said Hannah. "Let's do that."

While the pastor led them in heartfelt prayer, Jacob kept his head bowed and eyes closed. He was touched by the way these Christians seemed to have a hold on God that he had never known. Again, some of the Scriptures Hannah and Mary Beth had shown him ran through his mind, as well as those he had read on his own.

When the pastor closed his prayer, Hannah said, "It's almost 7:30. I want to go back over to the clinic and see Mary Beth for a little while."

"That would be good," said Rebecca. "You'll rest better if you've seen her one more time this evening."

"I'll walk you there," said the captain.

"Can we go too, Mama?" asked B. J.

"No, honey. The doctors will only allow one person in the room at a time and then, only adults. It's best that you stay here."

"Hannah," said Jacob, "would you care if I run on ahead of you and Captain Kirkland and just spend a couple minutes with Mary Beth?"

"I wouldn't mind at all."

"Thank you." He took his coat off a hook and hurried outside.

"Mama, would you give Mary Beth a kiss for me?" asked Patty Ruth.

"Of course," Hannah said, rising.

"Give her one for me too, Mama," said Chris.

"And me," said B. J.

Dane was helping Hannah into her coat.

"Better do it for all of us," said Esther.

"I will," Hannah assured her. "We'll be back in a little while."

As Hannah and Dane walked down the dimly lit street, he said, "I am feeling more confident all the time that Mary Beth is going to pull through this, Hannah."

They were passing under a street lamp, and Dane saw Hannah's lips quivering. She nodded, but a lump in her throat kept her from commenting. He ventured an arm around her shoulder. "You just keep believing. From what I've learned about that girl tonight, I can see she's got grit. A lot of times, that makes a big difference in whether a person makes it or not when their life is on the line."

Biting her lips, Hannah nodded again. As they neared the clinic, the lump in her throat had gone. She looked up at him and said, "I don't know how to thank you, Dane. You are such a good friend."

"No thanks is needed. Thank you for the privilege of being a friend to you and your precious children."

When they stepped up to the door of the clinic, it came open. Edie said, "Jacob told me you would be here."

Edie embraced Hannah and said, "Mary Beth is still unconscious, and there have been no more rallies. I'll go tell Jacob you're here."

"It's all right, Edie," Hannah said. "Let Jacob stay in there a few more minutes. He loves Mary Beth so much."

The three of them sat down, and Hannah said, "Mary Beth has faithfully witnessed to him, wanting so desperately to win him to the Lord."

Edie said, "Bless her heart. If God could use anybody to bring Jacob to Jesus, it surely could be Mary Beth."

At that moment, the door to the back room came open and Jacob came out, wiping tears. When Hannah's eyes touched him, he said quickly, "I heard your voices and knew you'd want to get in there with her. She's still unconscious."

Hannah nodded. "Thank you for coming to see her, Jacob."

"I'll go on back to the apartment and tell everyone there is no change."

There was a tap on the front door. Edie moved swiftly, unlocked it, and found Colonel Ross Bateman and his wife standing there.

"Come in, folks," said Edie.

As they stepped into the office, Sylvia rushed to Hannah and embraced her. "How is she, Hannah?"

"She's still unconscious. We've had a couple of encouraging things happen. She almost woke up twice."

"Hannah," said the colonel, "I had to come over here and make sure Captain Kirkland was all right, which I see he is. And I wanted to check on Mary Beth, anyway. When I told Sylvia I was going to the clinic, she said she was coming with me. I'm glad there is some encouragement."

"I'll be back at the fort after I escort Hannah home, Colonel," said Kirkland. "She was about to go in now and see Mary Beth."

"Well, we'll move on," said Bateman.

"Hannah," said Sylvia, "everyone at the fort is pulling for Mary Beth. And, honey, if there is anything I or we can do, please let us know."

"I appreciate that," said Hannah. "And I will."

Sylvia hugged Hannah one more time and hastened out the door with her husband. Hannah turned to Jacob and said, "I'll not be long."

Both doctors were hovering over their patient as Hannah came into the room. Doc was listening to Mary Beth's heart with a stethoscope. They both looked at Hannah and gave her weak smiles.

"No rally yet?" she said, looking at Patrick.

"No. Not even a glimmer of one. But her pulse is a bit stronger."

"Really?"

"Yes."

"Oh, praise the Lord!"

Doc took the stethoscope from his ears and said, "More good news, Hannah. Her heartbeat is no longer erratic. It sounds quite normal."

Hannah's eyes lit up. "Wonderful! Thank You, Lord! Oh, thank You!"

Running her gaze between the doctors, Hannah said, "Any speculation as to when she might regain consciousness?"

Both shook their heads as Patrick said, "None at all. I wish we could be more positive for you. She could stay in this state for some time yet. Or she could come out of it any minute."

"At least we have a little more hope now," said Doc. "She's not out of the woods by any means, but we are more optimistic than we were two hours ago."

Hannah rubbed her temples for a moment, eyes cast toward the floor, then looked at them again. "Would you tell me something?"

"Sure," said Patrick.

"Did the bullet damage her heart?"

"It was close, but it missed the heart by a fraction of an inch. No damage to the heart."

"Yes," Doc breathed with a sigh, "thank the Lord."

"Our biggest concern before beginning the removal of the slug," said Patrick, "was that I might damage the heart getting it out."

"But," said Doc, "he was able to get it without having to touch her heart."

Hannah bit her lips, took hold of Mary Beth's hand, and said, "Much praise to the Lord."

"Son," said Doc, "we should let Hannah have a few minutes alone with Mary Beth."

"We'll be in the office," said Patrick. "If there's any change, please let us know."

When the door closed behind the doctors, Hannah bent over and kissed a wan cheek. "This is from me, sweetheart," she said. Then she kissed her once for each person back at the apartment, naming them as she did it. She turned and pulled up a stool and lowered her exhausted body down on it, then again took her daughter's hand. Tears filled her eyes and began to spill down her cheeks. Stemming the flow with a hanky, she said softly, "My sweet Mary Beth, I know your papa would love to have you with him in heaven, but he also knows how much we need you with us. Besides, you have so much to live for here on earth, yet. You've dreamed for years of becoming a teacher. Now that you're fourteen, your dream is closer than ever to being realized."

Hannah dabbed at her tears again, still holding Mary Beth's hand.

"Don't give up, my precious girl. You're a fighter. Fight this battle through. Just think…Eddie is just getting to know you, and he would miss you so much if you weren't here to be with him. He loves the attention you give him, and I think he'd rather you gave him his baths all the time. He giggles and splashes more when you're bathing him."

Hannah went on and on as if the girl could hear her, and intermittently stopped talking to Mary Beth and prayed for her.

Sometimes it was hard to tell where one stopped and the other began. The tears also came and went as if of their own free will, and her mind went to David when he said to God, "Put thou my tears into thy bottle."

The ghost of a smile flitted across her face as she said, "Lord, my bottle must be a big one. I've certainly shed a lot of tears. Especially the past fourteen months."

Hannah wiped tears once more and looked down at her daughter's face. Mary Beth was no longer a little girl. There was maturity in her features that her mother had not noticed until now. She thought of how Mary Beth had reminded her recently that she was probably no more than five years from marriage.

How could this be? It seemed like only yesterday that she was changing her diapers. And time passed so quickly. Mary Beth seemed to go from the crib to her first year of school in no time at all.

Hannah raised the hand she was holding and kissed it. A sigh escaped her lips as she said, "Please, Lord Jesus. Spare this precious child. Give her back to us. Please…"

A still, small voice seemed to say, "Mary Beth is in My care. Trust Me."

A deep peace made its home in Hannah's heart, and she felt a complete rest in God's care, under His sheltering arm.

CHAPTER SIXTEEN

J acob Kates left the clinic and headed toward the store and the Cooper apartment. The full moon was lucent and pure against the deep blackness of the night. The crisp air slightly stung his face as he moved briskly down Main Street. An occasional tremor ran the length of his body at the thought of losing the sweet girl. A dreadful heaviness weighed him down, a feeling that his blood had turned to liquid lead. "Dear God," he said aloud, "please don't let her die. Please."

Jacob took a deep breath. "And dear God, this troubling issue that Hannah and Mary Beth have been pressing me with about Jesus Christ. Have I been blinded to the truth all along? I need Your help. I've got to know."

The moon's stark glare caused the shadows along the street to appear deep and clear-edged. Voices seemed to whisper to him from those shadows, saying that Jesus Christ loved him enough to go to the cross for him. They told him that Jesus fit every prophetic description of Messiah, including the love Messiah would have, not only for His own people of Israel, but for all the people of the world.

Jacob thought again about Saul of Tarsus. He relived the scene as the prime persecutor of Christians journeyed toward Damascus with papers in his possession from the high priest in Jerusalem, giving him the authority to capture the followers of Jesus Christ and take them to Jerusalem to be punished.

Jacob pictured the bright light that suddenly shone down from heaven, causing Saul to fall to the ground and how that bright light pierced all the way into his soul when he heard the voice of Jesus Christ and acknowledged Him as his Messiah and Lord.

Once again in his mind, Jacob heard Hannah ask him, "What could your Messiah do or be that would make him different than Jesus Christ?" He vividly recalled that he had no answer.

Then once again, he heard Hannah ask him if he would put his faith in Jesus to save him like Saul of Tarsus did, and his own words to her came back to him: *Hannah, dear, in order to do that, I will have to have my own Damascus journey.*

At the Imler farm, Cordelia was pouring gravy into a bowl at the stove when Rufe came in from the barn, carrying a bucket of milk. He stepped to the end of the cupboard and poured the milk through a strainer into a milk can.

Turning toward him, Cordelia said, "Supper will be ready in about three minutes, Rufe."

He gave her a nod, set the empty bucket on the cupboard, then removed his hat and coat while crossing the kitchen to the hooks by the back door. Returning to the cupboard, he began washing his hands at the water pump.

While her husband was washing up for supper, Cordelia went to the parlor where her fifteen-year-old son was lying on the couch. Bob's eyes followed her as she came into the room. She bent over him, checked the bandage that encircled his head, stroked his cheek lovingly and said, "Supper is just about ready, honey."

Bob looked up at her with sad eyes and said, "I'm not hungry, Mom."

"Honey, you must eat in order to keep up your strength."

Tears misted his eyes. "Mom, I can't eat with Mary Beth lying there in the clinic so close to death." He sniffed. "In fact, she might be dead already. And...and it's all my fault."

Suddenly Bob closed his eyes, and a low guttural sigh issued from his mouth as tears spilled down his cheeks. A cry started deep in his soul...in the depths where the pain had lain the longest. Unleashed now, it clawed his throat in an outpouring of torment as he broke into heavy sobs. "It's my fault, Mom! It's all my fault! Mary Beth is going to die—or has already died—and I'm the one who caused it!"

Rufe appeared at the parlor door.

Cordelia knelt beside the couch, took Bob into her arms, and raising her voice above the loud sobs, said, "Son, listen to me! When your father brought you home, you told me you tried to take on the outlaws because they were being mean to your teacher and some of the other students. Don't blame yourself that the gun went off and hit Mary Beth. It was not your fault."

"That's right, Bob," spoke up Rufe, moving into the room, "Mary Beth's bein' shot wasn't your fault. I've thought this over, and I want to say that I'm proud of you. You did the right thing to try to stop those low-down outlaws."

The boy's head lay against his mother's shoulder. He choked on a sob, cleared his throat and cried, "But...if Mary Beth dies, she'll die because of me. If I hadn't grabbed that outlaw's gun, Mary Beth wouldn't be lying in the clinic at the edge of death! If she dies, I'll never be able to forgive myself."

Kneeling beside his wife, Rufe said, "She's not gonna die, Bob. God won't let her die."

Bob's head came up. A frown touched his brow. "Do you really think so, Pa? God won't let her die?"

Rufe tenderly patted the side of Bob's head just beneath the bandage and said, "I'm sure God won't let her die. She's too important to God for Him to let her die."

While Bob stared at his father through his tears, Cordelia said, "I want to hear why you believe this, Rufe, but I would like to hear it at the table. I have supper ready."

"C'mon, son. You've got to eat so you don't get all weak and puny."

When the Imler family was seated at the supper table, Rufe began loading his plate in preparation to wolf down the meal, when he saw his son bow his head to pray over the food. Ever since Bob had been saved, the boy had bowed his head to silently pray, and even though Cordelia had always waited for Bob to finish praying before she began eating, Rufe had always dug in.

This time, however, Rufe said, "Uh...son..."

Bob opened his eyes and looked up. "Yes, Pa?"

"How 'bout prayin' out loud?"

Bob smiled weakly. "Sure, Pa."

This time, both parents bowed their heads and closed their eyes as Bob prayed, "Heavenly Father, I ask You please to do as Pa said, and not let Mary Beth die. Pa's going to tell us why she is too important to You to let her die, but Mom and I haven't heard it yet. So I'm just asking that You keep her alive. Thank You for this food. Give us strength with it. In Jesus' name I pray. Amen."

When the food was dished up and on the plates, Cordelia said, "All right, Rufe. Tell us what you meant when you said Mary Beth's too important to God for Him to let her die."

Rufe swallowed a mouthful of mashed potatoes and said, "Well, right after Bob got saved, I went to the Cooper apartment to chew Mary Beth out for makin' my son a religious fanatic. You know me. I tried to scare her good." Rufe shook his head. "But that little gal wasn't scared of me. She picked up a Bible and preached to me. I was surprised to hear that kind of thing comin' from this here little female...especially one who is barely in her teens. She took my term 'religious fanatic' and showed me right from the Bible that bein' saved was different from bein' religious. She convinced me that Bob had not gotten 'religion' but had come to know Jesus Christ and had all of his sins washed away and forgiven, which religious people don't have. She told me all about why Jesus had gone to the cross, shed His blood and died, and rose from the grave so He could provide salvation for sinners."

A smile spread over young Bob Imler's face.

Rufe chuckled and said, "When that perky little thing told me if I didn't get saved like Bob did, I'd go to hell, I told her I didn't believe in hell. Then she reminded me that when I was bawlin' her out for makin' a fanatic outta Bob, I used the word *hell* three times. If I didn't believe in hell, why did I use the word so much?" Rufe chuckled another time. "That little blue-eyed blond was not only not afraid of me, but she done put me in a corner."

Cornelia said, "Come to think of it, Rufe, I don't think I've heard you use the word *hell* since that day."

The big man cleared his throat. "Well, I've slipped and used it a couple of times since then, but not on purpose. I decided not to use it anymore."

"Then you now believe in hell, Pa, just like the Bible says?" Bob said.

Rufe cleared his throat again. "I do...I sure do, boy."

Eyes brightening, Bob said, "So it was what Mary Beth showed you in the Bible that changed your mind?"

"That, and the way she preached it to me. I have to say that the things she preached to me have stuck in my mind, and I've thought a lot about them ever since. She didn't bat an eye when I stormed at her for makin' a religious fanatic outta you. I mean, here I am a man six feet tall, weighin' right at three hundred and twenty pounds...and she's a girl not more'n five-feet-two and ninety pounds, yet she didn't back up a step when I lit into her. I like that girl."

"Me too, Pa."

"I told that little Jewish guy who manages the Cooper store that if Mary Beth was a boy, I'm sure she would grow up to be a preacher. And I meant one of those hellfire-and-brimstone preachers who don't back down from nobody. She's a special girl and determined to serve God with everything that's in her. That's plain and clear. That's why I said what I did about her bein' too important to God for Him to let her die. Certainly with a servant like that, God wouldn't let her life be cut short."

"Pa, you said you've thought a lot about the things Mary Beth preached to you since then. Have you...thought about becoming a Christian so you won't go to that awful place called hell?"

Rufe frowned, chewed the food in his mouth, and said, "I've thought about it a little."

"Well, I've thought about it a lot," spoke up Cordelia, "ever since you became a Christian, son."

"Really, Mom?" said the boy, a smile spreading across his face.

"Yes. Really."

"Pastor Kelly would be glad to come out and talk to you about it."

"I would have asked him to come, Bob, but—" Cordelia turned her eyes on Rufe, and keeping them there, said, "I was afraid of what your pa might do."

Rufe frowned. "What do you mean?"

"Well, do you remember right after we moved here, Pastor Kelly came to make a friendly call? Remember?"

Rufe's face tinted slightly. "Yeah."

"You quite rudely told him to leave and never come back."

"Well, now, Cordelia, if you really want to talk to the preacher 'bout bein' saved, it's all right with me."

"It...it's really all right? You wouldn't mind if I have Bob stop by the parsonage on his way to school in the morning and ask Pastor Kelly to come out and talk to me?"

"Yeah. That would be all right. That is if Bob feels like goin' to school tomorrow."

"I'll be fine, Pa. I was already planning on riding into town early in the morning so I could go to the clinic and check on Mary Beth before I went to school. I have to know if she's all right."

"Of course," said Rufe. "I would expect you to do that."

"Pa, I—I—"

"What, boy?"

"Well, I've been scared to talk to you about my being saved, but I really need to tell you that I want you and Mom to be saved. I want both of you in heaven with me forever and ever."

Rufe was sipping coffee. He swallowed, set the cup down, and said, "We both appreciate that, son. Maybe I'll sit in on your mother's conversation with the pastor when he comes."

Bob's eyes widened. "Really? Would you really do that, Pa?"

"Well, I might. I just might."

Later, at bedtime, Cordelia left Rufe in their room, saying she was going to Bob's room to kiss him goodnight.

When she tapped on Bob's door, asking if she could come in, there was a lengthy silence, then she heard his voice.

"Sure," came the soft reply.

When she opened the door, Cordelia was surprised to see her son still fully dressed, sitting on the edge of his bed. His shoulders were slumped. Tears were coursing down his cheeks, dripping off his chin onto his folded hands that rested in his lap. He turned sad eyes toward her.

Sitting down on the bed beside him, Cordelia put an arm around his shoulder, squeezed tight, and said, "Honey, I know you're under this load of guilt, and I wish I could help you. Do you suppose you could find some verses in your Bible that would help you?"

The husky boy sniffed, wiped tears from his cheeks with a palm, and said, "I don't know it real good yet, Mom. But maybe I could find some Scriptures Pastor Kelly has preached from recently that would help."

As he spoke, Bob looked toward the small table that stood beside his bed. He frowned and stood up. Stepping to the table, he opened the single drawer, found it empty, and turned toward his mother with a puzzled look on his face. "I...I don't know where my Bible is, Mom. I always keep it right here on the table. Except when I take it to church with me, of course."

"Well, honey, it couldn't just get up and walk away. You didn't leave it at church Sunday, did you?"

"No. It was here this morning. I read from it before going to school. Pastor Kelly says we should read God's Word every morning to start our day off right."

"It has to be around here somewhere," said Cordelia.

"I'll find it, Mom...but right now what I need is to ride into town and see about Mary Beth. I have to know if she's all right."

Rising to her feet, she put her arms around the son who was already taller than she and said, "I understand, Bob, but you need to get a good night's rest, then you can check on Mary Beth in the morning. She's probably still unconscious."

"But I need to know. I need...well, I just need to see her and be with her, even if she is still unconscious."

"I know it would help you just to know. It's not knowing what's happening that's worst of all. But you really need to get in that bed and rest. You'll feel more like riding into town in the morning."

Tears flowed as Bob eased back in his mother's arms, looked into her worried eyes and said, "But, Mom, what if she dies? I know I didn't purposely cause that outlaw's gun to go off and hit her, but I won't be able to sleep unless I know she's still alive and what the doctors say about her condition. No matter how you look at it, it's still my fault she got shot. And…and if she dies, it'll be my fault. I have to go and see how she is doing."

"But, son, you shouldn't be riding your horse yet. You need a good night's rest, first."

Bob's face pinched. "I have to go now, Mom. I have to know how she is."

Suddenly big Rufe's voice came from the open bedroom door. "Tell you what, son, I don't think I'm gonna be able to sleep, either, and I doubt that your mother is. Let's just get in the wagon and go to town. I want to know about Mary Beth, too, and I want to talk to that preacher tonight. You think he'll talk to Mom and me, even if it's late? Even if we get him out of bed?"

"I know he will, Pa. Pastor Kelly cares about people and wants to see them saved. He always—"

Bob's words cut off when he saw what was in his father's hand.

Cordelia's eyes widened as Rufe raised the black Book up and said, "I…uh…borrowed your Bible this afternoon. I was tryin' to find some of those places that Mary Beth read to me about Jesus on the cross, and…and about hell. Sorry. I forgot to put it back."

"It's all right, Pa," Bob said, letting a smile curve his lips. "You're welcome to read my Bible anytime."

Rufe stepped to the table and laid the Bible where he had found it.

Running his gaze from Cordelia to Bob, he said, "I haven't really been honest. I said at the supper table this evenin' that I've been thinkin' about becomin' a Christian a little. That was a lie. I've been thinkin' about it a whole lot."

"Oh, Pa," Bob said, wiping the last of the tears from his cheeks. "I'm so glad to hear this! Let's go to town. You can let me off at the clinic while you go and talk to Pastor Kelly."

"While *we* talk to Pastor Kelly," put in Cordelia. "I'm going to get this salvation business settled, too."

"I'll go hitch up the team," Rufe said, and hurried out the door.

Pausing in the kitchen, the big man put on his hat and shouldered into his heavy coat. After buttoning it all the way up to the collar, he went to a small table by the door where a lantern waited. He lit the lantern, adjusted the wick, and stepped out onto the back porch.

As he lumbered his way in the circle of light toward the barn and corral, Rufe said, "God, I can't stand this misery anymore. Ever since that sweet little gal preached to me, I've been scared to death of goin' to hell. There's a lot I don't know about all of this, but one thing I do know: I don't want to burn in hell. Mary Beth showed me that Your Son died on the cross to pay for my sins, and that bein' forgiven and cleansed and goin' to heaven was open even to a no-good, low-down sinner like me. Please help me to understand it when the preacher shows it to me, and help Cordelia to grasp it, too. And God…I know I don't have the right to ask this of You, but please don't let that wonderful little gal die."

Inside the house, Cordelia was fussing over Bob, making sure he was dressed warm enough. She tied a scarf around his neck while he was buttoning his coat. When the scarf was in place, she pulled his coat collar up under his chin, then checked the bandage on his head.

"I think you should wear one of your stocking caps instead of your hat," she said, adjusting the collar one more time. "It might push on your gash. I don't want you to—"

Smiling, Bob took her hands in his and said, "Mom, I'm fine. I just need to see Mary Beth. And…and I'm so encouraged because you and Pa want to talk to Pastor Kelly about being saved. I didn't think this would ever happen. My...well, my faith has been so weak. I could picture you getting saved, but it was hard to believe it could happen to Pa. But even though my faith hasn't been very strong, I have been praying. I really have."

"I know you have, son," said Cordelia. "And don't stop now."

"Oh, I won't."

They heard the wagon pull up to the back porch. Bob helped his mother into her coat, and as she was tying the scarf on her head, he put his stocking cap on and said, "I love you, Mom."

"I love you too, son," she said, giving him a tender look.

Moments later, the Imler wagon bounded along the country road in the moonlight, heading for Fort Bridger.

CHAPTER SEVENTEEN

At the clinic, Drs. Frank and Patrick O'Brien sat with Captain Dane Kirkland in the waiting area of the office while Edie was working on patient files at her desk. Kirkland was telling the doctors about some of his experiences in fighting Indians.

While the captain was relating an incident in which he had to battle two Sioux warriors in hand-to-hand combat at the same time, Doc let his line of sight trail to the clock on the wall. When Kirkland finished his tale, Patrick shook his head in wonderment and said, "It's a miracle you're still alive, Captain."

"You used the right word, Doctor. Miracle. Only by the miraculous hand of God on me was I able to survive with only a slight gash in my left arm."

Patrick smiled. "Aren't you glad the Lord watches over His born-again children as He does?"

"Amen to that," said Kirkland.

Doc looked at the clock again. "Hannah's been in there alone with Mary Beth for almost an hour. Maybe I'd better go check on her."

"I'll go," said Edie, pushing her chair back and rising to her feet. "You men go on with your conversation."

As Edie entered the back room, she found Hannah bending over her unconscious daughter, talking to her in low tones while stroking the hair that fell down over the girl's forehead. Hearing

Edie come in, Hannah straightened up, set soft eyes on the woman and said, "You might think I'm a bit off balance mentally, but I need to talk to her even though I know she can't hear me."

"Not at all, Hannah," said Edie. "It helps you. I understand that. Frank was run down by a team of frightened horses several years ago and was unconscious for four hours. I talked to him just like you're talking to Mary Beth now."

"Then you know how it helps."

"I sure do. Any change at all? Her breathing or anything else?"

"No. She's just the same."

"I really think you should go home, Hannah, and get yourself a good night's rest."

"In a little while. Is it all right if I stay just a little longer?"

"Sure. I know Doc and Patrick want to check her heart and pulse within another half hour or so. I'll tell them you'll be leaving soon."

Hannah nodded. "I'll be out before then."

Edie went to the door. Pausing before opening it, she looked over her shoulder and said, "Lots of people are praying for her, honey. Don't give up."

"I won't. The Lord gave me a sweet peace in my heart a little while ago. I feel much better about her now."

"Good. Just keep looking to Jesus, dear."

When the door clicked shut, Hannah turned back to Mary Beth, whose face was void of color. She lovingly caressed a cheek, then took hold of a limp hand and said, "My precious Mary Beth, I love you more than you could ever know. You have been such a bright spot in my life. From the day I knew you were in my womb, I felt an exceptional bond between us. As the months passed, and I felt you move within me, it was like the Lord was telling me He was giving me a very special child. And my thoughts were right, sweetheart. You are indeed a very special child."

Once again, tears flooded Hannah's eyes, and as they trickled down her cheeks, she said, "The Lord gave me a sweet peace a little while ago when I was standing here praying for you. He spoke to my heart and told me I am to trust Him... that you are in His care. And, sweetheart, I'm trusting Him to do what is best for you. He holds your life in His hands.

"Of course, I want you back. But Mary Beth, after that peace settled in my heart, I told Jesus if He can get more glory by taking you home to be with Him, that I would understand and let you go without becoming bitter. I...I know your papa would love to have you with him in heaven, and that would be a precious and wonderful reunion. You and Papa were so close. But...I guess I'm a bit selfish. In my heart of hearts, I want to keep you here with me. Jesus understands that, Mary Beth. I know He does. And He wouldn't want me to feel any other way about it."

Still holding the limp hand, Hannah closed her eyes and said, "Dear Lord, though it was hard to say earlier, and it's still hard to say at this moment...if You can be glorified in a greater way by taking—" She choked up, bit her lips, and cleared her throat. "If You can be glorified in a greater way by taking my sweet Mary Beth home, then...I will understand. But...but if by letting her live, You can get more glory to Your name, then please let her live."

Both doctors and Edie had started into the room as Hannah was praying, but quietly waited until she was through.

She saw them at the door as she wiped tears and said, "Oh, my. Did I stay too long?"

"No," said Patrick, moving toward her with his parents following, "but Dad and I feel we should check her vital signs right away."

Edie put an arm around Hannah's waist and said softly, "You must go home now and get some rest."

Hannah clung to Edie. "Maybe I should stay. Out in the

office, I mean. I really should be close by. My parents, the Kellys, and Jacob are with the other children. I know my mother will put them to bed. I really—"

"No, Hannah," Edie said firmly. "You need to go to bed, yourself. You'll be doing Mary Beth a favor if you go home and get some rest."

Hannah hugged her, then smiled as she looked her in the eye and said, "You know, Edie, I can almost hear Mary Beth saying the same thing. That's the kind of girl she is. She mothers me a lot. She really did so when I was carrying Eddie."

"I know. So do as Mary Beth would tell you if she was conscious. Go home."

Doc looked at Hannah and said, "As we told you, Hannah, Patrick and I will be right here in this room all night."

Hannah managed another smile. "And like you said earlier, if there is any significant change, I will be notified immediately, no matter what time it is. Right?"

"Right," said Patrick. "I'll be the very guy to knock on your door."

Hannah nodded, then bent down and kissed her daughter's brow and said, "I love you, Mary Beth. I'm going home to get some sleep—as I know you would tell me to do. I'll be back in the morning."

"If you want to wait just a moment, Hannah," said Doc, "we can tell you about her vital signs."

"Of course."

Edie stood beside Hannah while they watched the doctors do their work. After a minute or so, Doc took the earpieces of the stethoscope from his ears and said, "Her heartbeat is still steady and normal."

"Thank You, Lord," said Hannah, looking heavenward.

Captain Dane Kirkland was on his feet as the women came in. "How's she doing?"

Hannah reported what the doctors had just told her, and

as he gave praise to the Lord, Dane picked up Hannah's coat and helped her into it.

Edie tied Hannah's scarf on for her, then kissed her cheek and said, "Sleep tight."

"I will," said Hannah, "and Edie, dear, it's time you were getting to bed, too."

"I will pretty soon."

"Promise?"

"Promise."

Edie was telling them both good night when Dane and Hannah stepped out into the cold night air. They heard the latch on the door click as they started down the boardwalk.

Hannah drew in a deep breath. After the stuffiness in the back room and the cloying odor of ether, the biting night air was refreshing. She raised her eyes heavenward. The stars twinkled brightly and the moon cast its soft glow on the snow that had been piled along the edge of the boardwalk, turning it into a million shining diamonds.

"Beautiful night," Hannah said.

"I'll say. I'm so glad Mary Beth is showing some improvement," Dane said, offering his arm as they stepped off the boardwalk to cross the street.

"Yes. Praise the Lord. Right now, any encouragement at all is a help. Thank you, Dane, for staying at the clinic this evening. It meant a lot to know you were out there in the office. And thank you for the wonderful support you've been to my whole family."

They reached the boardwalk on the other side of the street, and as Dane assisted her in stepping up onto it, he said, "I'm so glad the Lord has given me the opportunity to know you and those marvelous children. Biggie, too."

"Oh, yes…Biggie. Are you aware that 'Biggie' is only his nickname?"

"No. So what's his real name?"

"Big Enough Cooper."

Dane chuckled. "Well, I guess he's big enough to handle the job as watchdog and protector of the family."

"That he is."

They had two blocks to go and still were walking quite slow.

After a silent moment, Hannah said, "You know, Dane, when Solomon was taken from me, I thought nothing could ever hurt so bad. But I was wrong. The pain I've experienced in this ordeal with Mary Beth is as great as that was."

"All I can say, Hannah, is the pain I went through in losing Mary and Donnie was more than I could have imagined. At least they were both already dead when I returned to the fort. I didn't have to watch them linger at the point of death and wonder if they were going to live or die. I can only try to imagine how it's been for you with Mary Beth hanging on the edge. I know it's got to be tough, but you are a good soldier. You're handling it well."

"Part of that is because of the strength you've given me, Dane…and others, too. But mostly, it's the grace of God. In His infinite wisdom, He knows just how much I can bear. And just as His grace was sufficient for my trial and grief over Solomon, God's grace and God Himself are the same for me, now. He is the same yesterday, and today, and forever, and not only does He never change, but His compassions fail not. What would I ever do without the love and care of my best Friend, my blessed Saviour?"

"What would either of us do? He's been so good to us."

"Yes, and He has especially blessed me by giving me such faithful friends like the O'Briens, the Williamses, the Kellys… and now you. Your own grief and heartache is still fresh, and here you are going out of your way to help me."

They were crossing the street, heading for the next boardwalk.

Patting the hand that held onto his arm, Dane brought them to a halt. "Please. To be of help to you, Hannah, is not going out of my way. It is what I want to do, and it is a pleasure. Not for one minute do I consider it an inconvenience. Do I make myself clear?"

Dane and Hannah found themselves standing in clear moonlight. She looked up into his eyes and sensed a compassion beyond measure in this man who had so quickly become her friend.

"Yes," she said softly, "you make yourself quite clear. Thank you, Dane. I appreciate you more than I could ever put into words."

As they moved on and stepped up onto the boardwalk, Dane said, "I'm so glad Colonel Hammer arranged my transfer here to Fort Bridger. Otherwise I would never have met you."

She looked up at him and smiled.

"And talk about helping someone, please forgive me for saying it probably for the dozenth time, but you have been such a help to me in the loss of Mary and Donnie. No wonder your kids are such special children. They get it from their mother."

Hannah chuckled lightly and said, "I'm sure glad I have you fooled."

"Oh, I'm not fooled, dear lady."

"You're not?"

"No, ma'am. The Lord has given me excellent insight into people, and it tells me that Hannah Cooper is the very best."

Lord, Hannah said in her heart, *it seems that You knew Dane and I needed each other at this very time in our lives. Thank You for sending him here. And...since You are already aware that I'm far from the best of anything, let's just keep it between us, okay? We'll just let him think what he wants to about me.*

They walked on in silence, with Hannah hanging onto Dane's arm, and soon crossed the last side street before entering the block where Cooper's General Store was located just three doors down.

As they were nearing the store, they saw a wagon coming from the south end of town. Paying it no mind, they moved between the general store and Bledsoe's Clothing Store and headed down the narrow passageway toward the alley.

Rufe Imler guided the wagon to a halt in front of the clinic. He hopped down from the seat and turned to look up at his wife, raising a hand to help her down. Bob could hardly believe his eyes when he saw what his father was doing.

Looking a bit shocked, Cordelia gave her hand to Rufe and allowed him to assist her down.

The Imlers moved up to the office door, and as expected, they found it locked with a Closed sign in the window.

"I know at least one of the doctors is in the back room with Mary Beth," said Bob. "If we knock loud enough, he'll hear it."

"We shouldn't knock loud, son," said Cordelia. "This little sign in the window says if there is an emergency, Dr. Frank O'Brien lives in the apartment above. The stairs are right over there. Maybe we should go up and knock on the apartment door."

Rufe put his face close to the window, shading his eyes from the side. "I can see light at the bottom of the door that leads to the back room. I'll go ahead and knock, but only loud enough to get their attention."

In the cell block at the Fort Bridger jail, a single lantern burned from a small table near the door that led to the office.

Rex Holt and Spike Denny were on their feet in the adjacent cell, looking through the bars at Dutch Hendrix, whose face was thunder black as he growled at Rafe Ketcham, "You shut your mouth, Rafe! I don't wanna hear any more of your insults, y'hear me?"

Rafe's eyes were narrowed and his lips were pressed together until they had no color. Showing no fear, Rafe squared his shoulders. "You're the one who's been shootin' off his mouth about no jail that exists can hold the great Dutch Hendrix! Well, let's see some action! That judge is comin' to town real soonlike, and every one of us is gonna stretch a rope if we're still behind these bars when he gets here!"

"I've been thinkin' on it!"

"Yeah? Well while you've been thinkin' on it, time is passin', and the noose gets closer. I joined up with you 'cause you persuaded me that you were this hotshot gang leader who'd make me rich and never let the law catch up to the gang. Well, you were stupid enough to let Mo Froggate get away with a pile of money—part of which was mine—so I ain't rich, and I'm behind bars because you were so stupid when you came to this town to have your revenge on Mo, you got yourself caught by the law! These boys and I shouldn't have had to take over that schoolhouse in the first place. And we wouldn't have, if you'd used your head. But, no…you had to go and stab Mo right there in the store. You're nothin' but a big blowhard!"

Dutch aimed a big fist for Rafe's jaw, but Rafe dodged it and chopped Dutch with a smashing blow to the mouth. Dutch shook his head, growled like an angry grizzly, and threw his weight against Rafe, driving him hard against the bars. Rafe sent a powerful blow to Dutch's belly, and for an instant, Dutch bent over, the breath whooshing out of him. Rafe cracked him on the side of the head, but Dutch shook it off as if it were nothing and drove a shoulder into Rafe, slamming him once more against the bars.

They fought and heaved and wrestled around the small cell with the other two outlaws looking on. Suddenly both combatants went down on Rafe's cot, smashing it flat, with wood splinters scattering across the floor. Dutch sprang to his feet and sent a swift kick into Rafe's ribs. Rafe let out a yelp, but rolled to his knees and made a dive for Dutch's legs.

Dutch's weight came down on him, flattening him face down on the floor. Rafe managed to roll onto his back, and clawed at Dutch's face, but Dutch brought his hands down on Rafe's throat, closing his fingers around it in a viselike grip.

"Dutch!" shouted Rex Holt. "Don't kill him!"

Dutch Hendrix squeezed down hard on Rafe's throat. Rafe fought and struggled, his face turning blue.

Deputy Jack Bower was whistling a gospel tune as he unlocked the office door at the boardwalk and stepped inside. A lantern had been left burning low in the office. Moving through its soft glow, Jack went to the door that led to the cell block. Opening it, he headed down the narrow, dark corridor. Just before he reached the cell block door, he heard a scuffling sound. When he opened the door, he saw Dutch on his knees, straddling Rafe, a death grip on his throat with both hands. Rafe was kicking, struggling to free Dutch's hands from his throat.

Rushing to the cell door, Jack shouted, "Let go of him, Dutch! Get off him!"

Hendrix looked up at the deputy with wild, furious eyes, then turned back to Rafe and continued choking him. Rafe's face was purple.

Jack whipped out his revolver, cocked the hammer, and aimed it through the bars. "I said let go of him, Dutch!"

Without looking up again, Dutch growled, "He dies, Deputy!"

"If he dies, you die, mister! I said let go of him!"

"Hah! You ain't gonna shoot me! You want to see me hang real bad!"

"Right now, Dutch! Let go of him, or you get a bullet in the leg! I mean it!"

Hendrix looked up at the deputy, focused on the black muzzle of the gun, and a look of resignation formed on his face. He released his hold on Rafe, and stood up. Rafe was gagging and choking, grasping his throat. Dutch stood over him, breathing hard, and said through his teeth, "I'll get to you later."

Still holding his gun on Hendrix, Jack said, "Not unless you can chew your way through steel bars, you won't." As he spoke, he inserted the key in the lock, slid the food tray aside with his foot, and opened the door. "Out, Dutch."

Fixing steely eyes on the deputy, Hendrix moved slowly out the cell door. Bower kept the muzzle of the gun trained on him and pointed to the farthest empty cell. "In there."

The deputy locked Ketcham's cell, then waved the gun at Hendrix. "I said in there, Dutch."

Reluctantly, Hendrix obeyed. When Bower was turning the key in the lock, Dutch glared at him with hate-filled eyes.

Jack grinned at him through the bars. "Don't look at me like that, Dutch. You wouldn't be in here facing the noose if you hadn't chosen to be a killer and an outlaw. There's nobody to blame but yourself."

Turning back, he walked to the other cell. Rafe Ketcham was now on his feet. His eyes were watery as he kept trying to clear his throat.

"You all right, Rafe?" asked the deputy.

The outlaw nodded and squeaked out an affirmative reply.

Jack holstered his gun, picked up the food trays, and said, "Everybody get a good night's sleep." He snuffed the lantern and said, "Remember what I said, Dutch. There's nobody to blame but yourself. Life is made up of choices. You made the wrong ones."

In the back room at the clinic, Drs. Frank and Patrick O'Brien were standing over Mary Beth, who was still unconscious. Doc was listening to her heart again, while Patrick was once more checking her pulse. Edie had gone upstairs for the night.

Doc was just removing the earpieces from his ears when they heard a knock at the clinic's front door.

"Her pulse is fine, Dad," said Patrick, releasing the girl's wrist. "I'll go see who it is."

There was a second knock as Patrick entered the office. Fumbling for the lantern that sat on a table, he called toward the door, "Just a minute!" and lit the lantern. Then carrying the lantern to the door, he turned the lock and opened it. "Oh, the Imlers. Come on in."

"Doctor," said Rufe as they stepped inside, "we want to know how Mary Beth is doing."

"Well, she's still unconscious and still considered critical, but her vital signs have shown some improvement."

"Good," said Rufe.

"Dr. O'Brien," said Bob, "my parents have to go talk to someone here in town for a while. I was wondering if I could stay back there near Mary Beth for that time."

"Well, it's getting rather late, and we're about to settle down for the night. I understand your anxiety over Mary Beth, and I can take you back to see her for a few minutes, but we've really got to make ready for the night."

"I understand, sir," said Bob. "I'll just go back with you for a few minutes, then. Would you and Mom wait for me, Pa?"

"Sure," said Rufe. "You go ahead."

As the doctor and the boy entered the back room together, Patrick laid a hand on his shoulder and said, "Bob, don't let your guilt over this destroy you. I know you were trying to do the right thing when you went after that outlaw's gun. You were trying to protect your fellow students, and you were trying to protect my wife. I deeply appreciate that. It certainly was not your fault that the bullet hit Mary Beth."

Doc looked up and smiled at Bob as the two drew near, then stopped a few feet from the table.

Tears filled Bob's eyes. "But Dr. O'Brien, if I hadn't jumped that outlaw, Mary Beth wouldn't be hanging on the edge of death right now."

"I can't argue with that, son," said Patrick, "but from what I've been told, those skunks were going to start killing students any minute; that is, after they killed my wife. You might very well have saved Mrs. O'Brien's life and the lives of your fellow students by what you did."

Bob wiped the tears from his eyes and said, "Really, Dr. O'Brien? Do you really think maybe I did save lives by what I did?"

"I sure do."

CHAPTER EIGHTEEN

Dr. Frank O'Brien smiled at Bob Imler as Patrick guided him up to Mary Beth's side.

"How's your head feeling, Bob?" asked Doc.

"It's fine, sir," Bob replied in a low tone, fixing his eyes on the girl. "I came to see Mary Beth. Dr. Patrick said I could come in for a few minutes."

"Bob's parents are in the office, Dad," said Patrick. "They're going to see someone in town tonight. Bob wanted to stay while his parents made the visit, but I explained that we need to get things settled in for the night, so I offered to let him come and see her briefly."

"I really appreciate it too, Dr. Patrick," Bob said, keeping his gaze on the girl.

"Dad, we both know the load this boy has been carrying over the way Mary Beth was shot," said Patrick. "I think it helped him to realize he just might have saved lives by what he did."

Bob looked up at Patrick. "Thank you for putting it to me that way, Dr. Patrick. It really does make me feel better. Only...I'd feel a whole lot better if I knew Mary Beth was going to make it."

"We're doing all we can, son," said Doc. "Her life is in God's hands."

"Yes, sir," said Bob, his voice cracking. He studied Mary Beth for a moment, swallowed hard, and sniffed. "Mary Beth is the one who led me to the Lord. She means an awful lot to me. She is going to live, isn't she? Please tell me she's going to live."

Doc laid a steady hand on the boy's shoulder. "Her condition has improved some, Bob, but at this point, we can't say that she is going to make it."

Bob bit his lips while tears coursed down his cheeks and dripped off his chin. "She just has to make it, Dr. O'Brien. She just has to. She's the best friend I have in this world."

"A lot of prayer has gone to the throne of grace for her, Bob," said Patrick. "We're trusting the Lord to spare her life."

Bob sniffed, glanced up at Patrick, then looking at the face that was as white as the pillowcase she lay on, he said, "Mary Beth, please don't die. Please come back to us. I…I love you, and I so very much want you to live."

Mary Beth lay motionless, but breathing steadily.

Bob bent close to her, sniffed again and said, "I'm going now, Mary Beth, but I'll be back tomorrow. Please be here."

"I'll walk you back to the office, Bob," said Patrick.

Together, they moved toward the door. When they entered the office, Rufe and Cordelia left their chairs.

Patrick said, "I hope your visit here in town won't take too long. This boy is tired. He needs to get to bed pretty soon."

"We'll get him home as soon as we can, Doctor," said Rufe, putting on his coat. "I might as well tell you…we're goin' to the parsonage to talk to Pastor Kelly."

"Oh," said Patrick, a bit surprised. "Well, you might go by the Cooper apartment first. The last I knew, Pastor and Mrs. Kelly were there."

Dane and Hannah climbed the stairs toward the apartment, and when Dane opened the door, the aroma of fresh coffee greeted them. Hannah saw Glenda Williams standing in the kitchen in front of the stove. Everyone else was in the parlor area. Glenda made a dash for Hannah and threw her arms around her.

"Glenda, I'm glad to see you," said Hannah, "but what are you doing here?"

Glenda gave her an extra squeeze. "I came over to stay the night, so these other people can get to their beds. I've already got Eddie bedded down. Tell us about our sweet girl."

By this time, the others had gathered around. All eyes were fixed on Hannah.

"Well, Mary Beth's condition is still critical. She's still unconscious, but I'm glad to be able to tell you that her heartbeat is no longer erratic and her pulse is a bit stronger."

"Praise the Lord for this much good news," said Ben. "At least there's some improvement."

"She's going to make it," said Dane. "I just know it."

"That's what we've been praying for," said Andy Kelly.

"And we'll continue to do so," Rebecca said, a brightness in her eyes.

"I've got coffee on the stove for the grown-ups and hot chocolate for the kids," said Glenda. "If everybody will find a seat in the parlor, I'll serve you."

"Not by yourself, you won't," Hannah said. "I'll help you."

"Oh no, you won't," said Esther. "I'll help her. You go sit down, Hannah, dear."

"I really need to be going," Dane said.

"Now, Captain," said Glenda, "a few more minutes won't matter to the United States Army. You and Hannah must both be chilled from your walk. Sit down. I'll serve you two first. There's just something comforting about hot coffee."

"Aunt Glenda..." Patty Ruth said. "Is hot chocolate **as** comforting as hot coffee?"

"Well...I never thought about it."

"If it's not, how come us kids have to drink hot chocolate instead of havin' coffee?"

Ben laid a hand on Patty Ruth's head. "Coffee will stunt your growth, sweetie pie. The reason only grown-ups drink it is because they've reached their full growth. You wouldn't want to stay the same size you are now, would you?"

Patty Ruth thought on it. "I guess not, Grandpa."

Leaning down close to her ear, Ben said, "Hot chocolate is comforting too."

The child showed her two new upper teeth in a wide grin. "If you say so, Grandpa." Turning to her brothers, she said, "Let's get comforted, boys."

Moments later, when Glenda and Esther came into the parlor area together, they noticed that Captain Kirkland had seated himself on the love seat next to Hannah. A tiny smile creased the corners of Glenda's mouth, and she threw a quick glance at Esther. Hannah's mother returned the smile, and they started pouring coffee.

Mary Beth remained the topic of conversation over coffee and hot chocolate.

When the drinks had been consumed, Glenda said, "I can make more if anybody wants it."

"Not for us," said the pastor. "I'm going to take Rebecca home, then spend the night in the waiting room at the clinic."

"Pastor, I appreciate your wanting to do that," said Hannah, "but it's best that you go on home and get your rest."

"But if there's a change in our Mary Beth's condition, I want to be there so I can come and let you know."

"Dr. Patrick has already volunteered to do that," said Hannah. "Thank you so much for offering, but there really isn't any need for you to stay there all night."

Kelly stood up and gave his hand to Rebecca to help her off the couch. "If there should be a significant change, you will let me know, won't you, Hannah?" he asked.

"Of course, Pastor," said Hannah, also rising. "Papa, Mama, I want you to go on back to the hotel and get to bed. If there's any significant change, I'll let you know."

At that moment, footsteps were heard on the stairs.

"I'll go to the door, Mama," said Chris, heading that way.

The knock came just as Chris laid his hand on the knob. He opened the door and said over his shoulder, "Mama, it's Mr. and Mrs. Imler and Bob."

Hannah headed toward them. "Hello," she said warmly. "Please come in. Bob, how are you feeling?"

"Better, ma'am, thank you."

Every eye was on the Imler family as they stepped inside. Rufe removed his hat and said, "Mrs. Cooper, we were just at the clinic to check on Mary Beth. Bob, especially, has been very concerned about her. And we were glad when the doctors told us she's shown at least a little improvement."

"So very glad," said Cordelia. "She's such a lovely girl."

"Thank you," Hannah said.

Rufe looked at the preacher. "Pastor Kelly, as we were about to leave the clinic, I told Dr. Patrick we were going to the parsonage to talk to you. He said the last he knew, you and Mrs. Kelly were here, so we should come here first. Would you have time to talk to us tonight?"

Kelly stepped closer. "Of course. What about?"

Rufe cleared his throat, glanced at Cordelia, and said, "It's…uh…something very important, Pastor. We'll explain it when we sit down to talk."

"All right. Mrs. Kelly and I were about to head for home. You follow us, and we'll talk at the parsonage."

"Thank you," said Rufe. "We'll do that."

The Kellys put on their wraps and bid everyone good night.

Only a couple of minutes after the Imlers and the Kellys had left, Ben and Esther hugged their daughter and grandchildren and headed for the hotel.

Dane shouldered into his coat and put on his campaign

hat. The Cooper children thanked him for being so kind to their mother and caring so much for their sister. Hannah walked him to the door and expressed her appreciation once again for being such a good friend to her family.

When the captain was gone, Hannah turned and said, "Chris, B. J., and Patty Ruth, it's time for you to get to bed. Tell your Aunt Glenda good night, and your Uncle Jacob, too."

Quickly, the trio hugged Glenda, then Jacob, and hurried off to their rooms. Hannah called after them, "I'll be there shortly to tuck you in!"

Glenda was in the kitchen, washing cups, saucers, and silverware.

Jacob said, "Hannah, I...ah—"

"What is it, dear Jacob?" she asked.

"Well, I know you're tired. But...but can I talk to you after you tuck the children in?"

"Why, of course. In the meantime, you can go chat with Glenda if you wish."

Glenda chuckled. "If he comes over here, I'll put him to work drying dishes."

"Be glad to," said Jacob, and headed for the kitchen.

Glenda said, "Hannah, you might want to check on Eddie before you tuck the other children in. He was pretty fussy earlier, and it took me quite a while to get him to sleep. It wasn't his tummy, I'm sure. I think it's just the strain everyone's feeling over Mary Beth."

"I'm sure that's it," said Hannah. "Even though he's just a baby, he senses that something's wrong. I'll look in on him right now."

Moving down the hall, Hannah entered her bedroom, quietly tiptoed to the crib, and looked down at little Eddie, who was sleeping soundly. "What a little angel you are," she whispered as she gently stroked his downy head, then ran her finger over his cheek, which was rosy with sleep.

She pulled Eddie's blanket up tight under his double chin, and he snuggled down in it a little deeper. A tender smile pulled at his soft baby lips, and Hannah's sore heart felt a measure of ease.

"You look so much like your papa, Eddie," she whispered. "Thank You, Lord, for this wonderful little blessing. You knew exactly what I would need in Solomon's absence. This little boy is such a precious gift to me."

Hannah leaned over and placed a feather kiss on his cheek, and his sweet smile deepened.

When Hannah opened the door to the girls' room, she looked first at Patty Ruth's bed, which was closest to the door, but found it unoccupied. In the soft glow of the lantern that sat on the dresser, she saw the child in Mary Beth's bed. The covers were pulled up to her chin.

Moving toward her, Hannah said, "What's this?"

Wiggling beneath the covers, the little girl said, "I feel closer to my big sister bein' in her bed, Mama."

Hannah bent down and kissed her forehead. "You sweet thing. I love you so much."

"I love you so much too, Mama," said Patty Ruth. "You're the bestest Mama in all the world."

"And you're the bestest little redheaded girl in all the world." With her face so close to Patty Ruth's, Hannah saw tear streaks on her cheeks and unshed tears on her long lashes. "Honey, you've been crying, haven't you?"

Patty Ruth sniffed and nodded. "Yes, Mama. I asked Jesus to make it soon that Mary Beth would be back here with us and sleeping in her own bed. I couldn't help but cry when I was talkin' to Him."

"Poor baby. This has been a very upsetting day for you, and you've been so good through it all." As she spoke, she smoothed back some curls from her little daughter's forehead. "I want you to get to sleep now, okay?"

"I will, Mama."

Hannah kissed her freckled cheek. "Good night, sweetheart."

Patty Ruth's arms came out from under the covers. She reached up, and Hannah bent down so she could wrap them around her neck. The child squeezed her mother's neck and kissed her cheek. "Good night, Mama."

Hannah doused the lantern on the dresser and headed for the door. Just as she reached it, Patty Ruth said, "Mama…"

Hannah stopped and turned around. "Yes, honey?"

"If…if Mary Beth should die, she'll be in heaven with Jesus and Papa real quick, won't she?"

Hannah swallowed hard. "Yes. Real quick. The Bible says for a Christian, to be absent from the body is to be present with the Lord. So whenever one of God's born-again children dies, he or she is instantly in heaven with Jesus, the angels, and all the saved people who have gone on before…like Papa did."

Patty Ruth nodded, satisfied with her mother's answer to her question.

Moving into the hall, Hannah left the door open a few inches and headed for the boys' room. "Thank You, dear Lord, for my Patty Ruth. Thank You for her very recent salvation. Help her in her own little girl way to lean on You through this difficult time."

Hannah opened the door of the boys' room, and smiled as she saw that B. J. was in Chris's bed with him. Her motherly heart went out to her sons.

"I'll get in my own bed in a few minutes, Mama," said B. J. "I just needed to be close to Chris right now."

"That's fine, son," said Hannah, drawing up to the bed, "as long as your big brother doesn't mind."

"It's okay with me, Mama," Chris said. "I sort of need some company, too."

Hannah sat down on the edge of the bed next to B. J.,

took each boy's hand in one of her own, and said, "I know this is a troubling time for all of us, but we must remember that the Lord is in control. We don't know why this happened to Mary Beth, but we want God's will to be done, don't we?"

Both boys nodded their agreement.

"We must trust the Lord to take us through this, as He has promised. You've both heard me say many times…and claim it before God many times…that in every valley He takes us, He gives a special blessing. He won't fail us, boys. There is some kind of special blessing awaiting us because of all that's happened."

"I know you're right, Mama," said Chris, "but it's so hard to find that blessing right now."

Squeezing the hands she was holding, Hannah said, "Then let's pray for Mary Beth right now and ask God to help us find that special blessing. B. J., you pray first, then Chris. And I'll close."

Both boys prayed, begging God to make their sister well, and to help them find the blessing He had prepared for them. Both boys also prayed for their mother, knowing the burden she was carrying.

Hannah's tender heart was touched as she listened to her sons pray so earnestly. When Chris finished his prayer, Hannah was so choked up, she could hardly speak.

Both boys opened their eyes, and Chris said, "Mama, are you all right?"

Hannah cleared her throat gently, nodded, and said, "I'm fine, honey. It's just that…well, there are many emotions running through me right now. Give me just a minute, here."

She swallowed hard a couple of times, cleared her throat again, and said, "All right. Let's bow our heads again. I'll pray, now."

Gripping her sons' hands again, Hannah said, "Precious Father, You have been so good to us. We can never thank You enough for all Your kindnesses. As we trust You with Mary

Beth's life, please keep us aware of how You have blessed us in days gone by and help us to recognize the special blessing You will give us in this time of testing. And Lord, most importantly, help us to give You all the praise and all the glory that is due Your wonderful name."

Hannah went on to pray for Mary Beth once again, then for each of her children. When she finished praying, B. J. wrapped his arms around her neck and gave her a big kiss on one cheek then the other. "Thank you, Mama, I feel lots better. Guess I'll get in my own bed now."

While B. J. was going to his own bed, Hannah hugged her oldest, and said, "Thank you, Chris, for watching out for your little brother."

A serious look captured the boy's young features. "Mama, since Papa's been gone, I've tried to sort of fill in for him. I know what it would mean to both B. J. and me if we had Papa here to hold us close. I just wanted to sort of be Papa to my little brother."

From his bed a few feet away, the nine-year-old said, "You make a good papa, big brother."

"Yes, he does, B. J.," said Hannah. Then to Chris she said, "Many has been the time since the Lord took your papa home that you've filled in marvelously, Chris." She kissed his forehead and stood up. Going to the other bed, she bent down, kissed B. J.'s forehead, then walked toward the dresser where the lantern stood, giving off its light. Dousing it, she said, "You boys get to sleep now."

"We will, Mama," they said in chorus.

When she reached the door, Hannah put her hand on the knob, looked back and said, "I love my boys. Good night."

"We love you too, Mama," they said.

Hannah smiled to herself, stepped into the hall, and leaving the door partially open, headed back toward the front of the apartment.

CHAPTER NINETEEN

Corporals Lenny Binder and Carson Ford were in the tower at the fort's main gate, looking out across the moonlit land that rolled toward the Uintah Mountains when they heard the sound of footsteps coming from the deep shadows off to their left.

Both gripped their carbines and waited as the sounds grew louder. Only seconds had passed when they saw a man emerge from the shadows into the moonlight. They looked at each other and grinned. Ford pivoted and hurried toward the stairs.

Bending over the railing, Corporal Binder said, "Good evening, Captain Kirkland. Carson's on his way down to open the gate for you. How's the Cooper girl doing?"

Looking up at the corporal, Kirkland said, "She hasn't regained consciousness since she was shot, Lenny, but since the doctors removed the slug several hours ago, they say her vital signs have shown slight improvement."

"I'm glad for that, sir. I sure hope she's going to be all right."

The gate squeaked open, and Corporal Ford said, "I heard what you said about Mary Beth, Captain. I'm glad she's still alive. From what Colonel Bateman told me, it didn't look too good for her."

"She's still critical, but at least there's been some improvement. I'll see you later, gentlemen. I'll be back in a little while after I talk to the colonel."

The gate clicked shut and Ford looked up at his partner. They gave each other a quizzical look, then Ford headed back up the stairs.

Sylvia Bateman opened the door in response to Kirkland's knock and said, "Hello, Captain. Did you want to see my husband?"

"Yes, ma'am. It will only take a minute."

"Please come in. I'll get him for you. How's Mary Beth?"

"She's holding her own at present, ma'am. The doctors still consider her critical, but her improvement has been encouraging."

Footsteps were heard at the back of the house. The colonel called, "We have company, Sylvia?"

"Yes, dear. It's Captain Kirkland."

At that moment, Bateman appeared. "Hello, Captain. What can you tell us about Mary Beth?"

Dane repeated his report of Mary Beth's condition to Bateman, then said, "Sir, I've come to ask your permission to spend the night at the clinic. I just feel I should be there."

The colonel smiled. "You've taken a liking to that girl, haven't you?"

"I have, sir. In fact I've taken a liking to that whole family. Hannah's gone home for the night, and both doctors are going to trade off staying awake to watch over Mary Beth, but I would like to be there. They'll have me in the office, but at least I'll be close."

Bateman frowned. "Aren't you scheduled to lead your patrol out at dawn?"

"Yes, sir. But I thought perhaps you could send Captain Ron Phillips in my place. I just think it would mean a lot to Hannah to find me at the clinic in the morning and to learn that I was there all night."

Sylvia smiled as her husband pulled at his ear. Nodding, he said, "I guess it would mean a lot to Hannah. And I'm sure since you've gotten yourself involved with Mary Beth's being shot, it would make you feel better to be right there near her."

"Yes, sir. It would."

"All right. I'll assign Captain Phillips to your dawn patrol. You go do what you have to do."

"Thank you, Colonel," said Kirkland, smiling broadly. "I appreciate this very much."

"But try to get a little sleep too, will you?"

"Yes, sir."

"And report back here by nine o'clock in the morning. That is, unless Mary Beth has taken a turn for the worse. Then I'll expect you to send word to me in that event. Understood?"

"Absolutely, sir."

"Fine. Then be on your way."

Kirkland thanked the colonel, told both of them good night, and headed back across the compound toward the main gate. As he drew near, he looked up to the corporals in the tower and said, "I need out now."

The captain gave the guards a brief explanation about his plans for the night, and hurried into town at a brisk pace. When he neared the clinic, he saw three paint horses tied at the hitching rail, and a small group of people on the boardwalk in front of the clinic door. Drawing closer, he recognized Adam and Theresa Cooper and Chief Two Moons. There were two Crow braves with the chief.

"Everything all right, here?" Dane asked.

"Yes," said Patrick O'Brien from the clinic doorway. "Adam and Theresa were in Green River most of the day and didn't learn about Mary Beth being shot until they returned home a few minutes ago. Carrie Wright told them. I let them go in and see her."

"We didn't want to go to Hannah's apartment this late and disturb her," said Adam. "So we just came here to see what we could learn from the doctors about Mary Beth's condition."

"Captain Kirkland," spoke up Two Moons, "I arrive here at clinic with these two braves at same time Adam Cooper and his squaw arrive. Dr. Patrick O'Brien allow Two Moons to go in and look at Mary Beth Cooper. I pray the Lord Jesus to make her well."

Kirkland smiled. "We're all praying the same thing, Chief."

Two Moons nodded, the night breeze toying with the feathers in his headdress. "We go, now. Dr. Patrick O'Brien, you will tell Hannah Cooper Two Moons was here."

"I sure will," said Patrick.

"And you will tell her Two Moons and Sweet Blossom will be praying for Mary Beth be well real soon."

"I'll tell her."

"Two Moons will be back soon to see how prayers being answered."

"You come back anytime you want," said Patrick.

The Indians mounted and rode away.

Adam said, "Well, Theresa, we might as well get on back home. Thank you, Doctor, for letting us see Mary Beth."

When the Coopers faded into the shadows, Patrick looked at the captain and said, "Let me guess why you're back. You're going to spend the night here."

A shy grin captured Kirkland's mouth. "If it's all right with you. I'll stay out of the way, I promise."

Patrick clapped a hand on Kirkland's back. "Come on in. It's getting cold out here."

The Imler wagon pulled up behind the Kelly buggy in the yard of the parsonage, and as the pastor was helping Rebecca down, she whispered, "I think maybe Rufe and Cordelia are wanting to talk to you about being saved. I just have this feeling in my heart. If I'm right...I want to sit in on it."

"I wouldn't have it any other way," he assured her.

As the Kellys were leading the Imlers into the parlor, the pastor looked at the boy and asked, "Are you having any pain, Bob?"

"Just a slight headache, Pastor. It's really not bad."

"I want to commend you for your act of courage at the school today. That was a brave thing to do."

"Thank you, Pastor," Bob replied in a humble tone.

The Imlers were invited to sit on the couch, and pastor and wife sat on overstuffed chairs, facing them.

Running his gaze to Rufe, Kelly said, "Now, what can I do for you?"

Rufe scrubbed a palm across his mouth and cleared his throat. "Well…uh…first, Pastor Kelly, I need forgiveness for the rude way I treated you that day several months ago when you came to our place to visit us and invite us to church. I told you to get off my property and never come back. Can you find it in your heart to forgive me for that?"

With a wave of his hand, Kelly said, "You're forgiven, Rufe. Now, what else can I do for you?"

"I…need some more forgiveness."

"Oh? What for?"

"Aw, you know. That day on the street here in town when I was cussin' Bob's teacher for discipline she had put on him, and you came along. You remember. Well, Pastor Kelly, you were right to interfere. I was way out of line. I'm really sorry."

Cordelia glanced at her husband and nodded.

Kelly smiled. "I forgive you, Rufe. But you really should go to Sundi O'Brien and make your apologies to her."

"I'll do that."

There was dead silence.

Kelly then said, "Is there anything else, Rufe?"

"Uh…yes, Pastor. There is. I…uh…well, that is…" Rufe twisted and turned on the couch, clearing his throat. Finally, he choked on the first word, then started over. "Pastor, I want to be saved. And so does Cordelia."

Rebecca bit her lips as tears surfaced.

Bob's face lit up with joy.

Smiling, Kelly rose from his chair and said, "We can take care of that immediately, folks. I'll be right back."

Cordelia reached over and patted her husband's hand. "I'm so glad we came here, Rufe."

The preacher was back in seconds, carrying two Bibles in addition to his own. Handing one to each of them, he sat back down and opened his Bible.

Before Kelly could speak, Rufe said, "Pastor, right after Bob was led to the Lord by Mary Beth Cooper, I went to the Cooper apartment, found her there alone, and chewed her out royally for makin' a religious fanatic out of my son. You…you should've seen how that girl handled herself. Or maybe I should say how she handled me. I've never gotten over the fact that as much as I tried to bully her, she showed absolutely no fear of me at all.

"I've never gotten over the kind of love she showed me. That girl preached to me right out of her Bible, and I haven't been able to get the Scriptures she showed me out of my mind…especially those on hell. I've lost a lot of sleep, I'll tell you."

"I've lost some sleep, myself," Cordelia said. "Ever since Bob got saved, he has urged me several times to come to the Lord…but I didn't do it because I was afraid of what Rufe would do if I did."

Rufe's features tinted, and his eyes lowered toward the floor.

"Rufe…" said the preacher.

The big man raised his eyes to meet Kelly's.

"If you mean business with the Lord tonight, Rufe, your wife won't ever have to be afraid of you again. Born-again men do not beat and mistreat their wives. Do you understand?"

"Yes. I understand."

Inching forward in his chair, Kelly said, "Rufe, you are known to be a brute to your wife and son, and you are known to be a foul-mouthed bully to anyone you feel you can intimidate. A saved man doesn't beat his wife, nor mistreat his son. A saved man isn't foul-mouthed, and isn't a bully. A saved man will be a gentleman to the ladies, and will treat men right, too.

"Rufe, a saved man isn't perfect. He still has an old sinful nature. But because the Spirit of Christ lives in his heart, he will be different than he was before. Do you understand what I'm saying?"

Rufe rubbed his temples and nodded. "Yes, sir. I understand. I've been a no-good, low-down, dirty skunk, and I know it. I was raisin' my son to be just like me, and he was takin' on my traits real fast. Then he got saved." He shook his head. "Pastor, when Bob got saved, he did a real turnaround. He was like a different person."

"Well, in one sense he is a new person, Rufe. When a person becomes a genuine child of God, he is a new creature in Christ, the Bible says, and old things are passed away and all things have become new. Nobody's ever the same after the Lord Jesus moves into their heart."

"I know what you're telling me, Pastor. I've seen enough change in Bob's life to know what God expects of me when I become a Christian." He turned to Cordelia and took hold of her hand. "And it's gonna be different between us from now on. You saw me do a gentlemanly thing for you this evening that I haven't done in sixteen years."

Tears were misting Cordelia's eyes. "Yes, Rufe, and it was wonderful."

Rufe squeezed the hand he was holding. "I assure you, it's going to be a whole lot different around our house now." Then looking at the preacher, he said, "All right, Pastor Kelly, let's see

what you want to show us in the Bible. This dirty, hell-deservin'
sinner wants to get saved."

When Hannah Cooper returned to the front of the apartment,
she found Glenda and Jacob just about to sit down in the parlor. They both paused, looking at her.

"Was Eddie still asleep, Hannah?" asked Glenda.

"Sure was."

"Do you think Patty Ruth is asleep, yet?"

"I doubt it. She's still pretty much on edge about her sister."

"Well, I know you and Jacob want to talk, so I'll just
meander back there to P. R.'s room and talk her to sleep. A lot
of times, I talk Gary to sleep."

Hannah smiled. "Well, I won't be surprised if the tables
turn and little Miss P. R. talks you to sleep."

Glenda chuckled. "Well, we'll see who talks whom to
sleep. You can come check on us when you're through."

When Glenda had left the room, Hannah said, "Sit down,
Jacob."

The little Jewish man looked troubled as he eased onto
the couch. Hannah sat down on the love seat, facing him.

"What's wrong, Jacob? What can I do for you?"

"Hannah, it's my fault Mary Beth is lying at the edge of
death right now!"

"Why, Jacob, how could it be your fault?"

His hands trembled as he clasped them together and
leaned forward. "Hannah, you have talked to me many, many
times since I came to Fort Bridger about my need to know the
true Messiah."

"Because I love you, Jacob, and I care about where you
spend eternity."

Shaky fingers tugged at an earlobe. "Recently you showed
me the prophecies about Messiah in the Old Testament, then

showed me how Jesus Christ had fulfilled them to the letter. You asked me what my Messiah could do or be that would make him different than Jesus Christ. Remember?"

"Yes, I remember."

"I'm sure you recall that I had no answer to your question."

Hannah nodded and smiled. "You said you had to think about it."

Jacob choked a bit, and said, "It was that very night when the light began to pierce my darkness. I've been blind, Hannah. I've been so blind."

Hannah's heart pounded so hard, she was struggling to breathe. "Jacob, in Romans 10 and 11, the apostle Paul—you know, the Jew who took the Damascus journey and met up with the true Messiah—wrote about Israel's rejection of Jesus Christ as their Messiah, and of God's having passed judgment on the nation for doing so. And part of that judgment was His sending blindness to their spiritual eyes."

Picking up the Bible that lay on the small table next to her, Hannah prayed in her heart, *Please, Lord, don't let the powers of darkness intervene. Keep them away by the power of the blood of the Lamb of God!* To Jacob she said, "Let me read just a portion of it to you."

Rising from the love seat, she sat down beside him on the couch and opened the Bible to Romans 11. Holding the Bible so Jacob could get a full view of the pages, she said, "Look here at the last verse in chapter 10, Jacob. It's talking about God's dealings with your people of Israel. 'But to Israel he saith, All day long I have stretched forth my hands unto a disobedient and gainsaying people.' Now, look at 11:1: 'I say, then, Hath God cast away his people? God forbid. For I also am an Israelite, of the seed of Abraham, of the tribe of Benjamin.' That's your tribe, Jacob."

"Yes. It sure is."

Then Jacob followed as Hannah read verse 8 to him.

"'(According as it is written, God hath given them the spirit of slumber, eyes that they should not see, and ears that they should not hear;) unto this day.' Now, look at verse 25. Under the inspiration of God's Holy Spirit, Paul wrote, 'For I would not, brethren, that ye should be ignorant of this mystery, lest ye should be wise in your own conceits; that blindness in part is happened to Israel, until the fulness of the Gentiles is come in.' So you see, Jacob, you were correct in saying you had been blind."

The little man closed his eyes and shook his head. "So very, very blind."

"And now you see why. The time of the fullness of the Gentiles is yet future. But please take note of the words God told Paul to write, Jacob. 'Blindness in part is happened to Israel.' Because God's chosen earthly nation rejected His Son, the Lord Jesus Christ as their true Messiah and Saviour, He had to bring judgment on them. God gave the people of Israel eyes that they should not see, and ears that they should not hear. But He tells us that the blindness is only in part. Do you understand? Only in part."

Jacob was wiping tears. "Yes. I understand. Only in part."

"So individual Jews can be saved. And many Jews have been saved, Jacob. Saul of Tarsus was one of them. And even in our day, many more Jews will be saved. Not the majority, but a few."

Jacob sniffed, thumbed tears from his eyes, and said, "I want to be one of those few, Hannah."

Hannah felt as if her heart were going to burst.

Chapter Twenty

J acob Kates pulled a handkerchief from his hip pocket, wiped the tears spilling down his cheeks, and wept. Choking on his words, he said, "Oh, Hannah...I've been so blind."

"But now there's light breaking through, isn't there?" said Hannah, fighting to maintain her own composure.

"Yes. Yes, light. Sweet light."

"Jacob, what did you mean when you said it's your fault Mary Beth is lying at the edge of death right now?"

The little man sniffed, wiped his nose, and said, "I haven't ever told you about this, but shortly after you and I had that conversation we just talked about, Mary Beth came to my quarters one night. She had her Bible with her, and she showed me the prophecy Jesus Christ made about Jerusalem's forthcoming destruction because they had rejected Him. She explained how it was fulfilled less than forty years later, in the year 70.

"Hannah, from my school days as a boy, I have known about the destruction of Jerusalem and the temple by Titus Vespasianus and his army. I knew that not one stone was left upon another. Not only did my teachers emphasize this, but so did many a rabbi in our synagogues. The thing that bothers me, is that no one ever told me that Jesus Christ had prophesied it."

"Yes, He did. Perfectly."

Jacob wiped tears again. "Mary Beth did her best to get me saved that night. She wept, telling me she wanted me to be saved."

"She loves you, Jacob. Very, very much. She wants you in heaven with her."

Suddenly Jacob broke down and sobbed. Hannah laid a hand on his shoulder, asking God to give her wisdom.

Finally able to speak, though still weeping, Jacob looked at Hannah through a film of tears and said, "That precious little girl, she—she said to me, 'I love you so much that if giving up my life would cause you to call on Jesus and be saved, I would do it.'"

Hannah had to struggle against breaking down. Her thoughts flashed to Mary Beth, and Hannah found her love for her growing deeper and stronger. *O dear God,* she prayed in her heart, *please let that wonderful girl live!*

As the tears spilled down Jacob's cheeks, he said, "Hannah, God let Mary Beth get shot because of me! If I hadn't been so stubborn, and had admitted that Jesus Christ is the true Messiah and had received Him as my Saviour, God wouldn't have had to let this horrible thing happen in order to get my attention. So this whole thing is my fault!" He gulped on the lump in his throat, swallowed with difficulty, and cried, "It's all my fault!"

Hannah started to say something, but Jacob held up a palm and said, "Please, let me finish." He dabbed at his wet face and cleared his throat. "Hannah, when Saul of Tarsus was on his Damascus journey, Jesus stopped him dead in his tracks and got his attention in a hurry. Do you remember I told you that in order to put my faith in Jesus like Saul of Tarsus did, I would have to have my own Damascus journey?"

"Yes. I remember."

"Well, when God let Mary Beth get shot, I started my Damascus journey, though I didn't know it yet."

Hannah's hand went to her mouth, and fresh tears bubbled up.

"But it wasn't long after my feet were walking that Damascus road that I learned that Mary Beth might die. That's when Jesus stopped me. He had my attention. He has it right now, dear Hannah. Will you help me? I want to be saved."

Hannah took a hankie from her dress pocket, dabbed at her nose and her eyes, and said, "Jacob, of course I'll help you, but I...I have to be sure of something. It's very important."

He nodded, holding her gaze.

"You aren't trying to bargain with God, are you? I mean, saying you want to be saved just so He might let Mary Beth live?"

Jacob shook his head vigorously. "No, no! When I say I want to be saved, I mean it! Yes, I want Mary Beth to live, Hannah, but whether God spares her life or decides to take her to heaven, I know Jesus Christ is the true Messiah and Saviour, and without Him I have no hope. I really do want to be saved."

"That's what I wanted to hear," she said. Wadding the handkerchief in one hand, Hannah opened the Bible with the other, and turned to the book of Mark.

"Jacob, I showed you, one day there in the store, where Jesus said, 'Except a man be born again, he cannot see the kingdom of God.' Do you remember?"

"I do. You showed me from the Bible that we should be born again because we were born spiritually dead the first time. Spiritual life is given to us when we receive Jesus into our hearts as our personal Saviour. It's when we receive Him that we become the children of God."

"I'm glad that's still fresh in your mind. Now, look at what Jesus said in the latter part of Mark 1:15. 'Repent ye, and believe the gospel.' Repentance isn't hard to understand. Children Patty Ruth's age can grasp it. It means to acknowledge to God that you are a sinner—that your sin is against Him and

His Word—and in deep regret for it, you turn from your sin to Him. When Peter was preaching to a crowd of unbelievers in Acts chapter 3, he told them, 'Repent, therefore, and be converted, that your sins may be blotted out.' Without repentance, Jacob, there is no salvation."

"I see that."

"Now Jesus said we are to repent and believe something. What are we to believe?"

"The gospel."

"And what is the gospel?"

"Well, you showed me god's definition of the gospel in 1 Corinthians. I think it was chapter 15."

"And do you remember what that passage says the gospel is?"

"Christ died for our sins, He was buried, and he rose again the third day according to the Scriptures."

"Donderful! You remembered!"

Jacob grinned at her. "How could I forget, the way you drove it into my mind?"

Hannah smiled. "I did, didn't I?"

"Yes, but I understand why, too."

"Good. Jacob, the gospel is strictly the marvelous work of the Saviour in His death, burial, and resurrection…nothing more, nothing less. Now let me whow you one more thing." Flipping pages, she said, "I want you to see that believing the gospel is the same as believing in the Christ of the gospel. Look here at John 3, verse 18. 'He that believeth on him is not condemned: but he that believeth not is condemned already, because he hat not believed in the name of the only begotten Son of God.' It is a person's refusal to put his faith in the Christ of the gospel that condemns him to hell. Do you see it, Jacob?"

"I sure do."

"Do you believe the gospel?"

"Yes!"

"Are you willing to turn from your sin and receive the Lord Jesus into your heart?"

"Oh, yest!"

"Then Romans 10:13 says that whosover shall call upon the name of the Lord shall be saved. Are you ready to call on Him and ask Him to save you?"

"I sure am."

Down the hall in the girls' room, Glenda Williams was lying on Patty Ruth's bed. The six-year-old was fast asleep in Mary Beth's bed. Glenda had been able to pick up some of what was being said in the parlor and knew that Hannah was carefully guiding Jacob through the Scriptures. Intermittently Glenda prayed, asking the Lord to let nothing keep Jacob from being saved.

Glenda sat up on the bed when suddenly she heard the little Jewish man loudly calling on the Lord to save him. He was crying out to God, admitting he had been stubborn and blind about the true Messiah, and asking Jesus to come into his heart and save him.

Leaving the bed, Glenda moved down the hall and stopped at the edge of the kitchen. Her heart was pounding with joy as Hannah was now praying aloud, asking the Lord to be close to Jacob, to help him in his Christian life, and to bless him as he took his stand for Christ in the baptismal waters on Sunday.

When Hannah finished praying, she and Jacob stood up. Hannah embraced him, saying, "Oh, Jacob, I'm so happy! What a blessing to see you open your heart to Jesus!"

Jacob was weeping with relief. When he gained control of his emotions, he looked into Hannah's tear-dimmed eyes and said, "Now that I'm a child of God, and I now have an audience with my heavenly Father, could we pray together and ask Him to let Mary Beth live?"

"Of course," said Hannah.

Both of them were surprised when they heard a feminine voice. "Would you mind if I join you?"

Their heads whipped around to see Glenda coming toward Jacob with open arms. Embracing him, she said, "Oh, Jacob, I'm so happy that you got saved, just like Saul of Tarsus did!"

"We both had our Damascus journey, that's for sure!"

When they let go of each other, Glenda glanced at Hannah, then back at Jacob, and said, "Please forgive me for eavesdropping. I...I really couldn't help but hear what was going on."

"I sure don't mind, Glenda," said Jacob. "You don't have to apologize to me. I'm just glad that you and I are now related, since we're both in the family of God."

Glenda hugged him again. "Thank You, Lord! Jacob is now my brother in Christ. Gary is going to be so thrilled about this!"

Suddenly the grandfather clock in the parlor struck a single chime, telling them it was one o'clock in the morning.

"Well, since the Lord slumbers not," said Hannah, "let's have our prayer time for Mary Beth."

Together, Hannah, Glenda, and the newborn child of God knelt at the couch. When Jacob prayed, he said, "Dear Lord, I...I really don't know how to thank You. I...just can't find the proper words. But I'll say it the best I know how. Thank You for saving this hardheaded sinner. Thank You, Lord Jesus, for going to the cross and dying for my sins. And...and thank You for dear Hannah. She talked to me so many times, trying to get me to believe the truth about You. Bless her for that, Lord. I was such a stubborn mule."

He was crying again. He was kneeling between the women, and both laid a hand on a shoulder.

"And dear God," Jacob went on, "I thank You for sweet little

Mary Beth and her concern for my soul. You were listening that night when she—" He had to stop and steel himself against breaking down again. After a moment, Jacob drew a shuddering breath and said, "Lord, You heard that precious little thing say that she would be willing to give up her life if it meant I would be saved as a result of it." He paused, collecting himself again, and after a moment, said, "Lord, it was Mary Beth's being shot that brought me to the point where I would believe the truth and surrender to You. But, please…please don't let her die! She means more to me than I could ever say. I beg of You, let her live. Give her back to us. Let her live to hear me tell her that her prayers have been answered. Her blind, stubborn Uncle Jacob has gotten saved."

At the O'Brien clinic, the back room was hushed and dim with only one lantern casting its soft glow over the worn Bible that Patrick held on his lap. He was sitting on a straight-backed chair beside the table where the unconscious Mary Beth lay.

Across the room, Doc lay on the cot asleep.

Since his father had gone to sleep at about 10:30, Patrick was on his feet every twenty minutes or so to check Mary Beth's heartbeat, pulse, and respiration. When he found them holding steady, he sat back down and returned to his Bible.

Patrick's ears were alert to Mary Beth's breathing and any movement she might make. Going from one promise in the Word to another, he paused periodically to pray and claim the promises…all of them related in his mind to Mary Beth's fragile grasp on life.

Patrick glanced up at the clock on the wall and noted that it was almost 2:00 A.M. Laying his Bible aside, he rose from the chair, picked up the stethoscope, and listened carefully to her heart. After checking it at different spots, a smile spread over his lips. Looking down at Mary Beth, he spoke as if she were looking up at him. "Hey, sweetie…it's sounding stronger."

He then checked her lungs with the stethoscope, and smiled again.

"You're breathing easier, too. Let's see about your pulse."

Pressing fingers on Mary Beth's wrist, Patrick held it firmly, and another smile broke over his face. "Lord, I think You're going to—"

Suddenly Mary Beth's head began rolling slowly from side to side, accompanied with a weak moan. Patrick's own pulse quickened and his eyes widened.

There was another moan…this time, louder. She rolled her head back and forth a little faster, and moaned louder yet. Patrick's heart was pounding with elation. Another moan, and suddenly her eyes came open. She frowned, closed them quickly, the lids fluttering, then opened them again.

Bending down close, the doctor said, "Mary Beth…can you see me, honey?"

The lids fluttered once more, and the eyes went closed.

"Mary Beth," said Patrick, moving his lips close to her ear, "can you hear me?"

She ejected another moan, rolled her head back and forth again, and made a weak nod, followed with a moan that was almost, "Mm-hmm." Her eyes came open again, and she tried to speak.

"Honey, can you see me?" he said, moving only inches from her face.

Nodding again, Mary Beth ran a dry tongue over equally dry lips and muttered, "Doc-tor Pat-rick."

Patrick reached to the cart near the head of the table and picked up a cup of water. "Here, Mary Beth," he said, his voice quavering, "let me give you some water."

When she had taken a couple of small sips, she tried again to focus her eyes on his face. She worked her mouth again and said, "Thank you."

"You're so welcome, sweetie," he said, almost wanting to shout. "Here. Take some more. Slowly."

It took some five minutes for Mary Beth to drain the cup. She thanked him again, and he smiled when her eyes clearly drew him into focus. "Dr. Patrick, where…where am I?"

"You're at the clinic, honey."

"What happened?"

"I'll explain later. You must rest now."

"I…I feel so tired."

"Mary Beth, I have to step away for just a few seconds. I'll be right back, okay?"

She nodded.

Hurrying to the cot, Patrick shook his father. "Dad! Dad, wake up!"

Frank O'Brien came awake instantly. Drowsy eyes fastened on his son. "What's wrong?"

"Nothing. Mary Beth's awake! Go get Mom and Sundi!"

As Doc sat up, rubbing his eyes, Patrick hurried to the office, and finding Captain Dane Kirkland asleep, stretched out on the long line of hard chairs, touched his shoulder. Before Patrick could speak, Dane was awake, and sat up, blinking. "What is it, Doctor?"

"Mary Beth's regained consciousness!"

Dashing to the back room while the captain was getting himself up, Patrick found his father standing over Mary Beth, whose eyes were closed. He had a grip on her hand, and was calling her name.

Her eyes came open again.

"Oh, wonderful!" gasped Doc, looking at Patrick. "At first I thought maybe I was dreaming."

"No dream, Dad. She's awake."

"I'll go get Mom and Sundi. They'll want to be down here."

Doc was almost to the door that led to the apartment

stairs when Dane came in and rushed up to the table.

By this time, Mary Beth's eyes were closed again. He looked at Patrick and said, "Are you sure she's regained consciousness?"

Patrick grinned, bent over the girl, and said, "Mary Beth, it's Dr. Patrick. Captain Kirkland is here. Open your eyes."

Instantly, the girl was looking at both men, running her eyes between them.

"Praise the Lord!" Dane said, his features lighting up. "Did she just come out of it?"

"A few minutes ago. I've been giving her water."

Rapid footsteps could be heard on the stairs, growing louder. Doc burst through the door and hurried back to the table. "Mom and Sundi will be down in a minute," he said, taking hold of Mary Beth's hand. "Honey, can you see me?"

Mary Beth squinted and set her eyes on Doc. "Grandpa?"

"Yes, sweetheart, it's Grandpa. Grandma and your teacher will be here in a minute."

Mary Beth's lips showed a weak smile. "Is Mama here?"

"Not at the moment, but—"

"I want to see Mama, Grandpa."

"I'll go get her right now," the captain said.

"Not by yourself, you won't," said Patrick. "I told her I'd come and knock on her door if this happened."

"Okay, so we'll both go."

"I'll keep an eye on my little gal, here," said Doc.

At that moment, light footsteps tapped on the stairs, and the two women hurried in, wearing their robes. They quickly drew up to the side of the table. Mary Beth turned and looked up at them. "Hello, Grandma. Hello, Mrs. O'Brien."

Edie smiled at the girl, tears bubbling up in her eyes. "Oh, glory to God! Glory to God!"

Sundi broke into tears. "Oh, I'm so glad I decided to stay here tonight! Hello, sweet Mary Beth. Yes, glory to God!"

"I'm not the least bit sleepy," said Glenda. "Hannah, you go on to bed. I'll sit up in case Dr. Patrick comes."

"I'm not sleepy, either," said Hannah.

"Me, neither," said Jacob.

Hannah smiled. "Well then, is anybody hungry?"

"Not I," said Jacob.

"Nor I," said Glenda.

"Well, I'm not either," Hannah said with a sigh. "How about some tea?"

"Now, I could use some of that," Jacob said.

"Then follow me to the kitchen," Hannah said. "Glenda, if you'll measure out the tea, I'll fill the kettle. Jacob, dear, there are still some coals burning in the stove. Would you stoke it up and toss in another log, please?"

"Consider it done," said the little man, and went to work.

Soon the fire was roaring, and the teapot was full of water. Glenda measured the tea into the teapot. They sat down at the table, waiting for the water to boil.

"This is the greatest night of my life," Jacob said, shaking his head in wonderment. "Just think, Hannah, if you and Mary Beth hadn't cared enough to stick with me about Jesus being the true Messiah, I'd have died lost."

Hannah smiled. "Well, you're saved now. And if I recollect correctly, there are three more Coopers who tried to get you saved, too."

"It wasn't very long ago that little Patty Ruth laid it on me good. God bless her. And those boys preached to me a lot, too."

Glenda set soft eyes on the little man. "There are a lot of people in our church who have prayed for your salvation since you first came here."

"Well, God bless them too, Glenda…and you and Gary.

Thank you for caring about this Hebrew of the Hebrews."

Just as the teapot started to whistle, footsteps were heard on the stairs outside.

Hannah jumped to her feet. Quickly the other two followed, exchanging glances. Hannah took a step, but Jacob touched her arm, saying, "I'll get it."

As Jacob started toward the door, Glenda saw Hannah's face lose color and took hold of her hand.

Hannah gripped Glenda's hand tight and stood mute, staring at the door. Her free hand trembled as she laid it over her mouth, her tired, worried eyes huge with apprehension. Her feet were rooted to the floor as she waited for Jacob, who seemed to be moving ever so slowly toward the door.

CHAPTER TWENTY-ONE

When Jacob opened the door, he saw the smiling faces of Dr. Patrick O'Brien and Captain Dane Kirkland. His heart was throbbing.

"Jacob," said Patrick, "we need to see Hannah. Is she asleep?"

"I'm right here, Patrick," said Hannah, as she and Glenda moved toward them.

The two men stepped in, and while Jacob was closing the door, Hannah left Glenda and rushed to them, her heart in her throat. "What is it? What's happened?"

She took a deep breath and held it, waiting to hear what they had to say.

"Hannah," said Patrick, "I told you if there was any change, I would come and tell you."

"Yes? Yes?" said Hannah, the pulse pounding in the sides of her neck. She felt Glenda move up beside her and put an arm around her waist.

Patrick's smile broadened as he said, "Hannah, just before 2:00 A.M., Mary Beth regained consciousness."

For a few seconds, Hannah couldn't move a muscle. Her eyes filled with tears, and finally her hands went to her mouth and she cried, "Oh, praise the Lord! Thank You, Jesus!"

Glenda was weeping too, as she tightened her hold on her best friend.

Jacob was using his handkerchief to dab at his tears once more.

"Let me explain, Hannah," said Patrick. "I've checked her vital signs and found them even more improved. This, along with her regaining consciousness, is cause for me to be optimistic. But she still has a ways to go before I can say for sure that she's out of danger. If there's more significant improvement in her vital signs in the next several hours, I'll be able to say the danger has passed. Do you understand?"

Hannah nodded, tears streaming down her face. "Yes. But she's better, and she's awake."

"Of course. And that sweet girl is asking for her mother."

"I'll get my coat," said Hannah, turning toward the wall where the family's wraps hung. She stopped suddenly, turned around, and set her eyes on the captain. "Dane Kirkland, I thought you were going home to get some rest."

Dane grinned shyly. "Well…I just couldn't do it. I had to be near Mary Beth. I talked to Colonel Bateman, and he gave me permission."

"But you need your sleep, and—"

"He was sleeping like a log in the office when I went in to tell him about Mary Beth waking up," said Patrick.

Hannah grinned at Dane. "Well, I'm glad to hear that."

Abruptly, three forms appeared, moving slowly and sleepy-eyed.

"Mama, we weren't sleeping very soundly, I guess," said Chris. "All three of us heard Dr. Patrick's voice out here. Patty Ruth came into our room to see if we were awake."

"Is Mary Beth all right, Dr. Patrick?" B. J. asked.

"She's much better. She's awake now."

"Oh!" squealed Patty Ruth. "I wanna go see her!"

"Me too!" chorused the brothers.

All three converged on their mother, hugging her and begging to go see their sister.

Patrick said, "Wait a minute, kids. Let me explain something here. Mary Beth is still very weak. Captain Kirkland and I are going to take your mother to see her, but she's not strong enough yet for more company. If she does better by morning, we'll see about you getting to see her later in the day. Do you understand what I'm saying?"

"I do," said Chris. "We sure don't want to cause Mary Beth a setback by too much company too soon."

"I understand," said Patty Ruth, "but I sure want to see her as soon as I can."

"You will, honey," said Glenda. "But right now, we need to let your mama go. Uncle Jacob and I will be here with you."

"I won't be gone long," Hannah said to her children. She then ran her gaze over the faces of the others. "I want to stop right here and thank the Lord for Mary Beth's improved condition."

The small group bowed their heads, and Hannah led in prayer, giving praise to the Lord for His mercy. When she finished praying, she said, "Patrick, I'm eager to go to Mary Beth, and we'll leave in just a moment, but there is more good news, and I just have to tell it."

All eyes were on Hannah as she stretched out a hand to Jacob, motioning for him to come to her. Hannah put an arm around the little man's bony shoulder and said, "I am superbly happy to announce that a little earlier tonight, Jacob received Jesus into his heart!"

Smiles broke out on the faces of the two men, and the eyes of the children widened.

"Really, Uncle Jacob?" gasped Patty Ruth.

"Really, honey. Your Uncle Jacob did what you said you wanted me to do. I asked Jesus to forgive me of my sin, and to come into my heart and save me."

The child dashed to him, and Hannah let go so Patty Ruth could hug him. The boys joined her, and there was a time of exultation and happy tears.

Jacob then took a few seconds to tell everybody what Mary Beth had said to him when she was witnessing to him in his quarters. To hear of her willing sacrifice of life to see Jacob saved touched everyone deeply.

"Patrick," said Hannah, "do you suppose Jacob could come with me and tell Mary Beth he got saved? It's going to make her so happy when she finds it out."

"I'd love for her to hear it, Hannah, but that might be too much excitement for her at this point. It would be best that you not even tell her about it."

"Oh, I wouldn't tell her under any circumstances. I want her to hear it from Jacob."

"Hopefully it can be real soon," Patrick said. "Mary Beth simply needs time to gain some strength."

As Dane was helping Hannah into her coat, Jacob said, "Hannah, I'll go along, stay in the office, and walk you back home."

Dane laid a hand on Jacob's shoulder. "It isn't necessary for you to do that. I'll be glad to escort her back here to the apartment. You really need to get some sleep, Jacob."

The little man grinned impishly. "Come on now, Captain. Is it my getting some sleep that you're concerned about, or is it that you want some time with this beautiful lady?"

Dane chuckled. "Well, to be honest, Mr. Kates, it's a bit of both!"

Hannah said, "I want you children to go back to bed now and get some sleep, so you'll be all rested up for seeing Mary Beth tomorrow."

"I'll see that they get back to bed," said Glenda.

Jacob sighed. "Well, I guess I'll go down to my quarters and get some sleep, since Captain Kirkland is so concerned about me."

Everybody laughed.

Hannah quickly planted a kiss on the cheek of each child, then hurried out the door with the captain and the doctor.

When Patrick and Hannah stepped into the back room at the clinic, Edie and Sundi were seated on chairs next to the table where Mary Beth lay. Doc was standing over the girl.

Both women left their chairs and hurried to embrace Hannah. Patrick went to the table to look at the patient, then beckoned Hannah to the table.

She moved cautiously, her heart in her throat. As she drew up to the table, she saw that Mary Beth's eyes were closed.

Doc smiled at Hannah, then patted Mary Beth's arm and said, "Open those peepers, sweetie, and see who's here!"

Mary Beth's eyes opened and a smile spread over her lips. "Mama!"

With her eyes misting, Hannah leaned down, cupped the girl's face in her hands, and kissed her cheek. "It's so good to see you awake! I love you, sweetheart."

"I love you too, Mama," Mary Beth said weakly.

Hannah looked at Doc. "Does she remember what happened to her?"

"I had to help her a bit, but it all finally came back to her."

"Mary Beth, there have been so many, many people praying for you," Hannah said.

She nodded. "Grandpa told me that."

"Your sister and brothers want to see you, but Dr. Patrick said they'll have to wait till you're stronger."

Mary Beth managed a thin smile. "Eddie too?"

"Yes. Eddie too. We haven't let your grandparents know yet. We'll tell them in the morning. I know they'll want to see you, too. And lots of other people, for that matter, but it'll be a while before your doctors allow that."

Mary Beth licked her lips. Her voice was frail as she said, "Mama, I asked Grandpa O'Brien about Bob Imler…if he's blaming himself for my being shot. Grandpa says he is. Mama, will you have Bob come and see me? I need to tell him it's okay. He did a very brave thing."

"I'll get word to Bob just as soon as your doctors tell me you can have visitors, honey. That is, after your sister and brothers get to see you. And your grandparents."

"Oh yes. I want to see them too, Mama. You will bring little Eddie, won't you?"

"Of course I will."

Mary Beth ran her dull gaze to the two other women. "Mama, it's been so good to have my teacher here with me since I woke up…and Grandma O'Brien too."

Edie and Sundi both smiled at the girl.

"Does…does Uncle Jacob know I'm awake?"

"Oh yes. He'll be here to see you as soon as the doctors say he can."

Mother and daughter talked to each other for a few more minutes, then Hannah said, "Sweetheart, I'll go now so you can rest. Dr. Patrick says you need a lot of rest. I'll be back early tomorrow afternoon."

"All right, Mama. Would you bend down so I can give you a kiss?"

When the soft kiss was planted on Hannah's cheek, she was about to explode with joy. She kissed her daughter, saying, "You rest now. I'll see you in a few hours."

Mary Beth nodded and gave her a weak smile.

Looking at the doctors, Hannah said, "Thank you for watching over Mary Beth. I will never be able to pay you sufficiently for what you're doing for her."

"I'll tell you right now," said Doc, "you're not paying us one red cent for what we're doing."

"That's for sure," spoke up Patrick. "And that's final."

Hannah shook her head. "We'll talk about it later."

"No, we won't," Doc said. "The subject will never be discussed again. And that's that. Now you get yourself home and jump in that bed real quick."

"I can be stubborn, too," Hannah said, jutting her jaw.

"Not as stubborn as two Irish doctors," Patrick said. "Good night, Mrs. Cooper. See you tomorrow about two o'clock."

"Yes, Doctor." Hannah noted that Mary Beth's eyes were already closed, and turned toward the door. Edie and Sundi escorted her to the office.

Both Edie and Sundi greeted Captain Kirkland in low voices. Edie said, "Captain, will you see that Hannah gets home right away, please? She's supposed to get some sleep immediately. Doctor's orders."

"Will do," said Dane, picking up Hannah's coat.

"Edie, Sundi, before I go, I have to tell you about Jacob."

Both looked at her quizzically.

Taking a deep breath, Hannah said in a low whisper, "Jacob got saved tonight!"

Sundi said, "Oh, that's good news! Why didn't you tell Mary Beth, Hannah?"

"Because your husband said it would be too much excitement for her tonight. Besides, Jacob wants to tell her himself."

"I can understand that," said Edie. "Praise God! As hard as that little girl has tried to get her Uncle Jacob saved, this is going to do a lot for her." Edie leaned close and whispered, "Is it all right if I tell Doc?"

Hannah smiled. "As long as it is out of Mary Beth's hearing."

"I sure wouldn't want to get in trouble with Patrick for letting the good news leak to Mary Beth prematurely!"

They laughed together, and Dane helped Hannah into her coat. "Come on, Mrs. Cooper," he said, putting a mock tone of authority in his voice. "You need to get some sleep. It will soon be morning."

They told Edie and Sundi good night, then moved out the door onto the boardwalk. When they had taken a few steps, Hannah tugged at the captain's arm pulling him to a stop. Squeezing the arm gently, she looked up into his eyes by the light of the street lamp nearby and said, "You'll never know how much it means to me that you stayed here tonight to be near Mary Beth."

"Hannah, I have fallen in love with the Cooper family, and I want to do everything I can for each of you." He paused. "And I—"

"Yes, Dane?"

"I…ah…need to get you home. Come on."

It was still dark and the moon had disappeared, but the stars lent their twinkling light to Dane and Hannah as they walked briskly toward the store. Hannah sighed, feeling as if a great weight had been lifted off her shoulders. She was almost afraid to feel so happy, but in her heart she kept praising the Lord for His goodness.

Soon they reached the store, passed to the alley, and climbed the stairs. When they drew up to the apartment door, Dane said, "You get in there and get to bed. I'll see you tomorrow."

She touched his arm. "God's so good. Hasn't it been a wonderful night?"

"It sure has."

"Thank you for being so kind to my family," she said, reaching for the doorknob.

"Ah…Hannah…before you go inside…"

"Yes?"

"Well, if I may…I'd like to see you often…and your wonderful children, too."

Hannah smiled. "I believe that can be arranged."

A wide smile captured his face. "Great! Thank you!"

"The pleasure will be ours, Captain Dane Kirkland."

"Not as much as mine, Hannah Marie Cooper."

Her brow furrowed. "And just how did you find out my middle name?"

"Oh, a little bird told me."

"A little bird?"

"Mm-hmm. A cute little redheaded bird."

"Patty Ruth told you my middle name?"

"Yes. I asked her, and she happily told me."

Hannah shook her head, smiling. "Good night, Captain."

"No, no!" he said, waving a finger. "Dane, remember?"

"Good night, Dane."

Hannah opened the door, and Dane waited until she was inside and the door was latched. She stepped to the window, pulled the curtain back, and watched until he disappeared down the stairs. When she turned around, Glenda was standing there smiling at her. "How's our girl doing?" she asked.

Unbuttoning her coat, Hannah said, "Well, she's quite weak from loss of blood, and she'll be a while recovering from the wound and the trauma. But Mary Beth is a trouper, as you well know."

"And she was awake and clear-minded so you could talk to her?"

"Oh yes."

"Thank God."

"I know in my heart that she'll be just fine in time. God still has work for her to do. She's such a faithful witness. I don't know how to thank the Lord for His mercy in bringing my child back to me, Glenda. All He can do is look into my happy heart and know how grateful I am."

"He can handle that. Our Lord is a great heart reader." Glenda smiled as she took the coat and hung it on its hook. "I've got some tea ready. You must be exhausted. Come on into the kitchen. I'll get a cup of tea in your tummy, then you can hit the sack, as the cowboys say."

Hannah sat down in her regular chair at the kitchen table. Glenda patted her shoulder saying, "You just relax, now. I'll get the tea."

Hannah eased down a bit on the chair, closed her eyes, and laid her head back. A calmness descended over her.

Glenda's back was toward Hannah while she poured the steaming tea into cups. When she set the teapot back on the stove and turned around, she saw that Hannah's eyes were closed. "You asleep?" she asked timidly.

Hannah opened her eyes, rubbed them, and said, "Almost. But I'll stay awake long enough to get that tea down. It smells wonderful."

Glenda set a cup in front of Hannah, then carried the other to the chair just across the table, and sat down. "Well, honey, before you go to sleep on me, let me give you some very good news. We've had a marvelous night, what with Jacob getting saved and Mary Beth regaining consciousness; but there is more good news."

"Don't keep me in suspense. Let's hear it!"

"Well, there's someone else your little Mary Beth has been very burdened for; someone she has been wanting very, very much to see come to the Lord. I know she would like to lead the whole world to the Lord, but can you think of somebody she led to the Lord a few months ago, whose father she witnessed to, but he didn't get saved?"

Hannah's eyes widened. "You mean Bob Imler? His...his father?"

"And his mother."

"You mean the Imlers got saved?"

"Yes! Pastor Kelly was here a few minutes ago. He wanted to know how Mary Beth was doing. Said he hadn't been able to get to sleep, so he was walking toward the clinic when he saw a light on up here. He thought he would see if he could find out here about Mary Beth, rather than disturb the O'Briens. I told him you were at the clinic with Mary Beth, that she had regained consciousness, and that Dr. Patrick said her vital signs had improved some more. Then he told me about the Imlers."

Face bright, Hannah said, "Well, go on!"

Glenda related the story to Hannah as Pastor Andy Kelly had told it to her.

Hannah was overjoyed at the news. "Oh, Glenda," she said, clapping her hands together, "Mary Beth is going to be so happy to hear about this!"

"Won't she ever! Pastor Kelly said that Bob wants to tell Mary Beth about his parents being saved as soon as the doctors will let him. Pastor said he would come here to the apartment in the morning to talk to you and see what you think about it."

"Well," said Hannah, "I'll have to go to the clinic early in the morning and talk to the doctors. Mary Beth is going to have quite a few visitors tomorrow as it is—that is, if they'll even let her have me, her siblings, her grandparents, and Jacob. I'll send Chris to the hotel first thing in the morning to tell my parents about her being awake. I certainly want Mary Beth to see Bob and learn about his parents, but we must also be careful not to wear her out. It may have to wait."

Hannah drained her cup, sighed, and said, "Right now, both of us better see if we can get a little sleep before the sun comes up."

Chapter Twenty-Two

Wednesday morning came with a clear sky, and slowly the sun painted the dawn horizon a vermilion hue, then lifted its flaming head over the edge of the world to send its bright beams across the rolling hills around Fort Bridger.

Hannah Cooper was a bit disoriented when Patty Ruth bounced on her bed, waking her from a light sleep. She opened her eyes and saw the brilliant rays of the sun coming through the windows. A rush of joy filled her heart when she remembered that Mary Beth had regained consciousness and was showing other signs of improvement.

Patty Ruth smothered her mother with hugs, saying, "Oh, boy, Mama! I get to see Mary Beth today!"

Hannah hugged her in return.

"Mama, the boys and me want to know if we can stay home from school today, even though we won't be goin' to see Mary Beth till this afternoon."

Hannah kissed her cheek. "It's the boys and I, Patty Ruth."

The six-year-old frowned. "Can't I go?"

Hannah chuckled. "I'm talking about your English grammar, sweet stuff. You should say, 'The boys and I want to know if we can stay home from school.'"

"Oh. Okay. But can we?"

"I was thinking about that very thing myself, last night.

I'm sure Mrs. O'Brien will understand why you're not in school. Go tell your brothers they don't have to go to school today."

As she spoke, Hannah's eyes ran to the crib a few feet away. It was empty. "Patty Ruth, where's Eddie?"

"Aunt Glenda is feedin' him breakfast."

"Oh my. I'd better get out of this bed."

Patty Ruth darted out the door. Hannah struggled to sit up on the edge of the bed. After getting only a couple of hours sleep, her head felt as if it were stuffed with cotton, but her deep-seated joy over Mary Beth's improvement gave her the exuberance she needed to start her day.

While Hannah was getting dressed, she smelled the aroma of bacon in the air. Glenda was doing more than her share.

Moments later, the Cooper family and Glenda Williams sat down to breakfast. They were almost too excited to eat, but since there had been no supper the evening before, they each managed to devour a sufficient amount.

When everyone had finished, Hannah said, "Let's clear the table before we have Scripture reading and prayer."

Glenda jumped to her feet. "You stay seated, Hannah. The kids and I will clear the table."

"Glenda, I'm not an invalid."

"No, but you are a very tired mother. Stay put. We'll have it done in no time."

When the table was cleared, Patty Ruth delivered her mother's Bible to her, and everyone sat back down.

Little Eddie had eaten his breakfast, but was sitting in his high chair, chewing on a piece of hardtack.

Flipping pages, Hannah said, "I'm going to read the Twenty-third Psalm first, then I have a couple other verses in the Psalms I want to read to you."

She read through the Twenty-third Psalm slowly, making comments on each verse, and allowing the others to comment as they chose. When that was done, she turned ahead a couple of pages and said, "Now, I want to read two verses to you from Psalm 27. Verses 13 and 14. We all need strength of heart and courage in this horrible thing that happened to our Mary Beth yesterday. She is still not out of danger. These verses tell us how to obtain that strength and courage. David says, 'I had fainted, unless I had believed to see the goodness of the LORD in the land of the living. Wait on the LORD: be of good courage, and he shall strengthen thine heart: wait, I say, on the LORD.'"

Hannah closed the Bible. "No comment is needed. Wait, I say, on the Lord."

A quiet amen was said by each one at the table, then Hannah asked Chris to pray.

When prayer time was over, Hannah said, "I've got to get to the clinic to see what the doctors think about Bob Imler coming to see Mary Beth today. Chris, I want you and B. J. to hurry now and tell your grandparents about Mary Beth. Tell them to come to the apartment for lunch, then we'll all go to the clinic together at two o'clock."

"I'll help Aunt Glenda do the dishes, Mama," said Patty Ruth.

"Thank you, honey."

Suddenly there was a knock at the door.

"I'll get it," Chris announced, and hurried to the door. When he opened it, he said, "Good morning, Uncle Adam, Aunt Theresa. Come in."

Hannah hurried to Adam and Theresa, who told her they had gone to the clinic at dawn to see about Mary Beth. Doc O'Brien would not allow them to see her, but had told them of her improvement, for which they were praising the Lord. They just wanted to see if Hannah and the rest of the family were all right.

Hannah assured them that she and the children were fine, and that they were going to see Mary Beth that afternoon. Adam assured her they would check on Mary Beth tomorrow, and hopefully would be allowed to see her by then. After hugs from the niece and nephews, Adam and Theresa left.

The boys then hurried off to give the good news about Mary Beth to their grandparents, and leaving Patty Ruth and Eddie with Glenda, Hannah made her way down the stairs to the store.

Jacob had just unlocked the front door when Hannah came in the back.

Heading toward her, he said, "Good morning, boss. Did you get any sleep at all?"

"A couple of hours, anyway."

"And Mary Beth was still awake when you got to the clinic?"

"Yes. I didn't stay very long, but what time we had was sweet."

"And her vital signs were still showing improvement?"

"Yes, praise the Lord. And how did God's new child sleep?"

"Very well. What a sweet peace He has given me."

"Wonderful. I'm on my way to the clinic to see if Bob Imler can come and see Mary Beth today. He's quite eager to do so."

"I know they're good friends."

"Yes, but there's more to it than that. You know that Mary Beth led Bob to Jesus."

"Oh yes. She was so happy when that happened."

"Well, last night the pastor led Bob's parents to the Lord, and Bob wants to tell Mary Beth about it."

"I hope he can do it real soon. Now what shall we do about the store while I'm seeing Mary Beth?"

"Oh! During breakfast, Glenda said she'd come down and watch the store while you come with us this afternoon to see Mary Beth."

"Good. I can hardly wait to tell her what's happened to me."

"We'll be going about two. If that changes when I talk to the doctors, I'll let you know."

"Would you mind stopping by on your way back to the apartment and let me know how she is this morning?"

"Be glad to. See you in a little while."

It was about half an hour before the clinic's opening time when Hannah arrived, but Edie was at her desk and let her in.

"Well, Miss Hannah," said Edie, "did you get some sleep?"

"About two hours."

"Well, maybe you can do better tonight."

"I'm sure I will. How's my girl this morning?"

"She was awake earlier. Can't say if she is now. But she's holding her own with her vital signs, though she's still quite weak."

"Is it all right if I see her?"

"Of course."

"And I need to talk to Doc or Patrick. Pastor led Bob Imler's parents to the Lord last night, and Bob is eager to tell Mary Beth as soon as possible. I've got to see if he can visit her today."

"I kind of doubt it, honey. I heard Doc and Patrick talking about visitors. I think they may want to give her more time to recuperate. I'm sure glad to hear about the Imlers, though."

Hannah nodded. "Well, if that's how the doctors feel, I don't want anything to slow down Mary Beth's progress."

"I need to stay here at the desk. You go on back."

When Hannah entered the back room, both doctors were at the medicine cabinet, getting ready for their day. They both greeted her and told her to check on her daughter. They would be with her in a few minutes.

Hannah set her eyes on Mary Beth and saw that she was awake. Moving up to the bed, she said, "Good morning, sweetheart."

Mary Beth smiled. "Good morning, Mama."

Noting her hair, Hannah said, "My, oh, my! Don't you look pretty!"

"Grandma O'Brien gave me a bath and fixed my hair."

Mary Beth's blond hair had been washed and brushed, then plaited into two long braids, hanging over her slender shoulders. Her head lay on a snowy white pillow. Her face was wan, but there was a hint of color in her cheeks. As Hannah studied her daughter closely, however, she could see in her eyes the pain she was trying valiantly to hide.

"You're hurting, honey. Is it the bullet wound?"

The girl nodded.

At that instant, Patrick drew up.

"She's having pain," said Hannah. "Can you give her something for it?"

"Dad already did. About ten minutes ago. It'll take another ten or fifteen minutes before it will start to take effect."

"I hate to see her hurting."

"I do too, but we can only give her laudanum every four hours, so the pain does come back before it's time for another dose."

"I'll be fine, Mama," said the girl.

"Hannah," said Patrick, "Dad and I have been talking about Mary Beth's having visitors. She's still so weak, we think it would be best that only you and her siblings see her today and tomorrow, too. Then by Friday, if she's gotten stronger, we'll let your parents, Jacob, and maybe one or two others see her. We just can't let her overdo."

"I understand. I was going to ask you if Bob Imler could see her today, but it'll just have to wait. Maybe Friday."

"Maybe Friday," nodded Patrick.

"I do want to see Bob so badly, Mama," said Mary Beth. "I've just got to tell him not to feel bad that I got shot."

"It'll just have to wait," said Patrick. "Main thing now, is to see that you get lots of rest with minimal interruption. Your mama and your brothers and sister can come and see you this afternoon, but that's all today."

"What about Pastor and Mrs. Kelly?" asked Mary Beth.

"Well, maybe they could look in on you for a couple minutes, but no one else."

Hannah took hold of her daughter's hand. "Dr. Patrick is doing what's best for you, honey."

"I know. I just want to see Grandma and Grandpa, Uncle Jacob, and Bob as soon as I can. And Captain Kirkland, too. Dr. Patrick told me about his staying in the office to be near me. I want to thank him."

"You'll get your chance," said Patrick. "It'll just be a couple of days, I think. We'll see how you fare today and tomorrow."

"I'll go now," Hannah said, bending down to kiss her forehead. "Chris, B. J., Patty Ruth, and Eddie will be with me when I come back this afternoon."

As Hannah was heading back down the street toward the store, she saw Pastor Andy Kelly coming toward her. When he drew up, he told her he had just been at the apartment and learned that she had gone to the clinic.

Hannah explained what Dr. Patrick had said about visitors, adding that he would allow the Kellys a couple minutes to look in on her if they wished, but no one else. Kelly was glad to hear this and told Hannah that he and Rebecca would pay Mary Beth a visit around noon. He would ride out to the Imler place immediately and let Bob know that it would be at least Friday before he could see Mary Beth.

Upon entering the store, Hannah greeted customers, answering their questions about Mary Beth. She took Jacob aside and told him what Dr. Patrick had said. Jacob was disappointed, but said his excitement about telling Mary Beth he had gotten saved would just have to endure until Friday.

At noon, the Singletons arrived, and were disappointed when they learned they wouldn't be allowed to visit their granddaughter until Friday, but assured Hannah they understood.

After lunch, the Singletons returned to the hotel, accompanied by Glenda, who needed to get home and see to things there.

At 1:45 that afternoon, Hannah and her children left the apartment and headed for the clinic. When they entered the office, Edie was there to greet them and told Hannah she had changed appointments with a few people so there wouldn't be any interference with what was about to take place. A mother and her small child were just coming out of the back room.

"Is Mary Beth awake, Edie?" asked Hannah.

"Oh yes. And she's so excited about seeing her sister and brothers. This will have to be one at a time. Hannah, you might want to go in first, so you can satisfy yourself that she's up to seeing the rest of this crew."

"All right. I'll just do that."

Edie took little Eddie while the children were getting out of their wraps. Hannah laid her coat on a chair and went into the back room.

Doc was just finishing with the stethoscope when Hannah drew up to the table. He smiled and said, "Heart is sounding very good."

"Praise the Lord," said Hannah.

Mary Beth raised her arm and Hannah bent down. They kissed each other's cheeks, then Mary Beth said, "Pastor and Mrs. Kelly were here to see me, Mama."

"He told me they would be."

"Pastor told me he has contacted every member of the church so they would know what happened to me and could pray for me."

"Bless his heart. He's a great pastor."

"Patrick's gone home for a few minutes," said Doc, "but I'll be right over here by the medicine cabinet, so the family can have their time with this little gal. Edie did tell you it should be one at a time?"

"Yes," said Hannah. "I guess it'll be two when B. J. comes in. He's planning on bringing Eddie with him."

Doc grinned. "That'll be all right."

Squeezing Mary Beth's hand, Hannah said, "These visits will have to be short, sweetheart. I'll go now so your sister and brothers can come in. I'll come in just for a minute before we leave."

Mary Beth watched her mother pass through the door into the office, then seconds later, she saw the little redhead come in. Patty Ruth wore a bright smile as she drew up to the table. "Hi, big sister," she said, looking around for something to climb on. She spotted a chair nearby and dragged it up to the table.

Doc turned around, smiled, and said, "Sorry, Patty Ruth. I should have thought about that."

Mounting the chair, Patty Ruth said, "It's all right, Grandpa. I'm up now." She then looked down at her sister and said, "Is it all right if I hug you?"

"As long as you're gentle," said Mary Beth, giving her a loving smile.

When she had hugged her sister, Patty Ruth said, "I'm so glad you're better. Mama says you still have a lot of gettin' better to do, but I know Jesus is gonna let us keep you."

Mary Beth smiled.

"Just think, Mary Beth!" said Patty Ruth. "You'll be here for your birthday next Wednesday! Just a week from today! I didn't think you would still be alive there for a little while yesterday, but Jesus wanted you to have your birthday with us, instead of in heaven."

B. J. and Eddie were next to visit Mary Beth, and though the visit was brief, B. J. had time to tell his sister how glad he was that she was doing better, and that even though they joked with each other and picked on each other a lot, it was all in fun. He loved her very much.

Mary Beth was able to kiss baby Eddie's cheek before B. J. had to take him away.

Chris's visit was much the same as B. J.'s, with serious words about how much he loved Mary Beth, even though he joked with her a lot.

Hannah returned for only a minute or so to tell her daughter she would come back that evening to check on her. She added, "A few minutes ago, Captain Kirkland came by the clinic to see how you're doing. He's anxious to see you, once the doctors say he can."

Another smile graced the girl's lips. "I really like him, Mama. He's such a nice man and so kind and thoughtful. It was so sweet of him to stay so long last night just to be near me."

"Yes. I thanked him as best as I could for that. Well, precious daughter, you're looking tired. I'll go now."

Hannah visited Mary Beth for a short time that evening, escorted to the clinic by the captain. On Thursday, the patient was showing more improvement in her vital signs, and though she was still weak, she enjoyed the visits from her mother and siblings that afternoon.

That evening, Dane Kirkland escorted Hannah to the clinic once more.

Both doctors were there, and after giving Hannah a few private moments with Mary Beth, both of them told her they wanted to talk to her in the office when she was through.

After kissing her daughter good night and telling her she would see her in the morning, Hannah went into the office, where the doctors were talking to Captain Kirkland.

Doc turned to her, put an arm around her shoulder, and said, "Hannah, Patrick and I want to give you some very good news. Since we both can't talk at once, I'll keep this arm around you while he does the talking."

Patrick's eyes misted as he said, "Hannah, I told you we needed some time before we could say that Mary Beth was out of danger. Well, we can make it official, now. She has improved marvelously in the past two days. Barring any unforeseen complications, which we pray will not arise, we can tell you that Mary Beth will live to see her fourteenth birthday."

Hannah broke down and cried with sweet relief, laying her head on Doc's shoulder.

When the weeping subsided, Dane told her how happy he was, saying he was looking forward to seeing Mary Beth. Hannah told him the girl had said on Wednesday that she was anxious to see him, too.

Patrick said, "I see no reason that your parents, Jacob, and Bob Imler can't see her tomorrow, Hannah, as well as your other children. And the captain here. Just so the visits are kept short."

"Wonderful," said Hannah. "I'll be right here to make sure nobody stays too long."

"Is it still two o'clock, like it had been planned for Wednesday?" Dane asked.

"Yes," said Patrick. "That'll give Mary Beth time to rest before the parade starts."

"Then I'll be here at two tomorrow afternoon."

Friday came with another clear day, and at two that afternoon, the small group gathered in the office. Again, Edie had rescheduled some appointments to give Mary Beth some privacy as she welcomed her guests.

Hannah went in first and was pleasantly surprised to find Mary Beth in a single bed that had been brought into the clinic. She was sitting up, propped against a mound of pillows, and smiling. Edie had fixed her hair once more, and there was a hint of rose in her cheeks.

Hannah bent down and kissed her, and got one in return. "So do you think you're up to a string of visits today?"

"Oh yes! I'm so anxious to see everybody. I don't even know for sure who's here, but I sure want to see them."

"Well, we'll start out with your sister and brothers. Grandpa and Grandma will be next, then I'll be in after them to see how you're holding up."

After Mary Beth's siblings had been in to see her—including Eddie—the Singletons went in together and had a sweet time with their granddaughter. They stayed only a few minutes, but long enough to share hugs and kisses with her. Hannah appeared again, and looked the girl over, asking if she was up to more company.

"Oh yes, Mama. Who else is out there?"

Hannah grinned. "First, let me say that your Uncle Adam and Aunt Theresa are wanting to come, but they are going to give it another day, since you're having so much company today."

"It will be nice to see them again. But who's out there?"

"I'll send the next one in. You'll see."

Mary Beth watched her mother go out the door, then smiled as she saw the captain come in, smiling broadly.

They had a sweet few minutes together, in which Mary Beth expressed her thanks for his watching over her so faithfully.

"Little lady, it was my privilege," said Dane. "You and your family have really become special to me. There isn't anything I wouldn't do for any one of you."

Mary Beth looked up at him, her eyes misty. "You have been such a strength to Mama."

"I'm glad. She has indeed been a strength to me. She will never know how much she helped me handle the death of my wife and little boy."

"Both of you have had to face a lot of the same heartaches. Maybe…maybe you can help each other rebuild those broken lives."

Dane nodded, then said, "Maybe we can. Well, I'd better make room for whoever is next. Thanks for letting me come in and see you."

"Thank you for coming in, Captain."

"I wouldn't have missed it for the world," he said, bending down. He planted a kiss on her cheek, then turned and headed for the door.

Hannah came in and gave her daughter the once-over again. "Honey, I can see that you're tiring from all of this. Maybe I should tell the others to come back tomorrow."

"No, Mama. Please. I'm up to it."

"Would you like to lie down and rest before seeing anyone else?"

"I am a little tired, but I'll be all right. It's been so good to see everyone so far. How many more are out there?"

"Two."

"I'll rest in a little while, I promise. If I could just have a drink of water, I'll be fine."

Hannah stepped to a nearby cart, poured a cup of water, and returned to the bed. She brushed an errant wisp of hair from Mary Beth's brow, then helped her sit up a little straighter. She held the cup to her lips and let her drain it.

"More?"

"No, thank you, Mama," she said, easing back against the pillows and giving her anxious mother a wan smile. "That's enough. Who else is waiting to see me?" she asked, grinning impishly. "I feel like a celebrity."

"Well, Miss Celebrity, this next guest has some wonderful

news for you. I'll send him in."

Mary Beth's eyes lit up when she saw Bob Imler. As he moved toward the bed, she smiled. "Bob! How nice of you to come!"

"Wild Indians couldn't keep me away any longer, Mary Beth," he said, drawing up beside the bed.

"Let's settle one thing real quick," she said. "I don't want you feeling guilty because I got shot when you were so brave as to try to overcome those outlaws."

"Yes, but—"

"No 'buts,' Bob. The subject is not to be discussed between us. You did a wonderful thing, and that's that."

"It sure helps to know you feel this way."

"Good. Mama told me you have some wonderful news for me. What is it?"

"Remember how you prayed for me as you witnessed to me, Mary Beth? And the Lord used you to show me I was lost and needed to be saved?"

"Yes."

"And remember how you witnessed to my pa when he came to your apartment and lit into you for making a religious fanatic out of me?"

"Of course I remember."

"And you told me that you would be praying that both my parents would be saved."

"Yes."

"Well, Mary Beth, your prayers have been answered!"

She straightened up. "You mean—"

"Yes! Pa and Mom got saved Tuesday night!"

"Oh, wonderful!" she said, tears filling her eyes.

Bob told Mary Beth the details, pointing out that it was her loving witness to his father and the way she put him in a corner with the Scriptures that brought him to the place where he wanted to be saved. When Mary Beth heard that Bob's parents were going to be baptized on Sunday, she wept for joy, asking if his parents would come to see her.

"We've already talked about it," said Bob, "and as soon as the doctors say you can have visitors on a regular basis, they'll be here."

"Wonderful! I'll look forward to seeing them."

"Well, Mary Beth," said Bob, "they told me I could only stay a few minutes, so I'd better be going."

He leaned down and ventured a kiss on her cheek.

"Thank you for coming, Bob," she said. "And thank you for the kiss."

Bob Imler's face crimsoned. "Uh...you're welcome." With that, he hurried across the room and out the door.

Hannah returned, bent over her daughter, and said, "How about that good news?"

"Wonderful news," said Mary Beth.

"Sweetheart, have we worn you out?"

"Oh no. I'm fine."

"You're sure?"

"A little tired, yes, but I'm all right."

"Good, because there's one more visitor who is very eager to see you."

Mary Beth smiled. "It's Uncle Jacob, isn't it?"

"It sure is."

"Oh, I knew he would come today! I just knew it!"

CHAPTER TWENTY-THREE

Jacob Kates was telling Captain Dane Kirkland, the Singletons, and Doc and Edie O'Brien how he came to see the truth of Jesus Christ being the Messiah, when Hannah came from the back room, her eyes bright with joy.

"Mary Beth is eagerly waiting to see you," she said to Jacob.

Jacob smiled from ear to ear. "She's not as eager to see me as I am to see her!"

Hannah turned to Doc. "Do you suppose it would be all right if there were two people in there with Mary Beth for this visit? I'd really like to see her face when Jacob tells her what happened to him."

Doc grinned. "I suppose it'd be all right, since this is her last visit for the afternoon. Go ahead."

As Hannah and Jacob headed for the back room door, Esther said, "I'd like to be a fly on the wall in there, myself!"

Mary Beth's eyes brightened when she saw her Uncle Jacob come through the door with her mother.

"Hello, Uncle Jacob! I knew you would come to see me today!"

Hannah eased back, letting Jacob go ahead of her.

"Hello yourself, sweet girl," Jacob said as he bent down

and kissed her cheek. "I was so glad when I learned that you were going to be all right."

Mary Beth took hold of his hand. "Dr. Patrick told me I almost went to heaven, Uncle Jacob. He said it was real close."

"I know," said Jacob, squeezing her hand gently, "then I wouldn't have gotten to see you until I get to heaven, myself."

Mary Beth's pale brow furrowed. "But…"

Jacob grinned. "But what?"

"You have to be saved to go to heaven."

Jacob's grin broadened, and a gleam glinted in his eye. "I know, Mary Beth. I got saved Tuesday night."

Mary Beth blinked and shook her head. "You—you—"

"I got saved Tuesday night. You know…the same day you got shot."

Mary Beth's mouth dropped open and her eyes stretched wide. "You did? You got saved?"

"I sure did, sweetheart. I asked Jesus to come into my heart and be my Saviour. Just like you told me I should do."

Mary Beth's almost colorless face split in a wide smile. "Oh, Uncle Jacob, how wonderful!"

Jacob bent down, and Mary Beth flung her arms around his neck, breaking into sobs of joy.

Hannah's eyes filled with tears as she looked on.

When Mary Beth's sobbing eased, she released Jacob from her grip. Standing over her and holding a hand again, he said, "All the things you and your mother have shown me from the Bible about Jesus being the true Messiah and Saviour, and about His death on the cross and His resurrection—they simply closed in on me. I went to your mother late Tuesday night and told her I wanted to be saved. She led me to Jesus. I'm going to be baptized Sunday."

Tears flowed down Mary Beth's cheeks, and her throat had become so tight, she couldn't speak.

While holding her hand, Jacob patted it with his free

hand, and as tears streamed down his own cheeks, he said, "Mary Beth, I want you to know what the Lord used most to bring me to the place that I would repent and open my heart to Him. Remember the night you came down to my quarters and showed me about Jesus' prophecy concerning the destruction of Jerusalem?"

She nodded, sniffing and blinking at tears.

"Do you recall what you said, when you were yearning for me to know how desperately you wanted me to be saved?"

Again, she could only nod.

"You told me if it meant giving up your life to see me get saved, you would do it." Jacob took a deep breath, swallowed hard, and said, "That's what the Lord used the most to break down my stubborn will and get me to turn to Him for salvation."

Mary Beth lifted her free arm to encircle his neck. As he bent down and let her tighten her hold on him, she choked briefly, then said, "Uncle Jacob, I really meant it. I would have given my life if it would've brought you to Jesus!"

Dr. Patrick came in and saw Mary Beth hugging her Uncle Jacob's neck. He looked at Hannah and smiled, then waited for the tender moment to pass.

"And I love you for that, Mary Beth," sobbed Jacob. "You'll never know what it meant to me."

"I just love you so much," said the girl, clinging to his neck.

"Sorry to interrupt, here," Patrick said, "but it's time for my patient to take her medicine. She needs her laudanum."

Jacob kissed Mary Beth's cheek and said, "Sweetheart, I'll go now, and let Dr. Patrick do his work. I'll be back very soon to see you again."

"Promise?"

"Promise."

"Tomorrow?"

"Tomorrow."

As Jacob stepped back, Hannah bent down, hugged her daughter, and said, "I'll see you this evening, Mary Beth."

"All right, Mama."

"In the meantime, you take your medicine, then rest good."

"I will. I love you, Mama."

"I love you too, sweet baby," said Hannah, kissing her forehead.

"Mama, we really do have a powerful God, don't we?"

"We sure do, honey. We sure do."

Mary Beth watched her mother and her Uncle Jacob pass through the door together, then smiled up at the doctor as he held the cup of laudanum in his hand.

As Hannah and Jacob moved into the office, Hannah looked around at her children and the others and said, "Let me tell you, we have one happy girl in there!"

Dane Kirkland said, "I believe she has one happy mother, too."

Hannah laughed. "You're right about that!"

She thanked Doc and Edie for all they had done for Mary Beth, then saying she would be back that evening after supper, she led the group out into the sunshine on the boardwalk.

As they stood there for a moment, Ben Singleton patted the captain's arm and said, "Thank you for caring so much about our daughter and our grandchildren."

"Yes, thank you, Captain," said Esther. "It means a lot to us that they have you to lean on."

Dane gave them a warm smile. "Somehow Hannah and these children are like family to me. It's been my joy to watch over them."

Ben chuckled. "I think you're like family to them, too."

"I'm glad," said Dane, his eyes bright. He turned to Hannah, who was standing with her children. "I'll stop by the apartment and check on you this evening."

"We'll look forward to it," Hannah said with a smile.

Dane had spotted Captain John Fordham and Lieutenant Dobie Carlin coming down the boardwalk together and headed toward them.

Just then, Hannah called, "Dane!"

He stopped and turned around.

"How about coming for supper?"

"I'll be there!"

"Six o'clock?"

He smiled. "Six o'clock it is."

Dane then turned around as his army friends drew up.

"How's Mary Beth?" asked Dobie.

"Doing quite well. She's pretty well out of danger, now."

Both men spoke their praise to the Lord, then Captain Fordham looked toward the street and said, "Look there, guys."

A slender, silver-haired man was riding into town on a gray horse.

"Who's that?" Dane asked.

"That's Judge Hankins."

"I guess those outlaws in the jail can start sweating now," Dobie said.

"Mama, this little guy is in need of a diaper change," B. J. said. "I'll hurry on home and take care of it."

"We'll go with him, Mama," said Chris. "I think you and Grandpa and Grandma want to talk a little more. Let's go, Patty Ruth."

"All right," said Patty Ruth. "You coming pretty soon, Mama?"

"I'll be home in a few minutes."

Hannah watched her children cross the street, then turned and looked up the boardwalk at the captain, who was still talking to Fordham and Carlin.

Ben tapped her shoulder. "Hannah..."

"Yes, Papa?"

"As I was saying, you need to consider moving back to Independence. You know...since Solomon is gone, and the move to Wyoming was really his dream. After all, Independence is really your home."

"But, Papa," Hannah said, her voice a bit strained, "Fort Bridger is home to the children and me now. How about this? Since you're retired, I think you and Mama should have a house built in Fort Bridger and move here."

Esther smiled. "Now that's a good idea, Ben."

Ben set his gaze on his wife. "Well, dear, I wouldn't mind that, since it would put us close to our daughter and grandchildren." Then he turned to Hannah. "But is there something important enough in Fort Bridger to hold you here?"

Hannah glanced over her shoulder and saw Dane with Captain Fordham and Lieutenant Carlin. He was looking at her, smiling.

She smiled back at him warmly and said, "Yes, Papa. There really is."

Multnomah Publishers

The publisher and author would love to hear your comments about this book. *Please contact us at:*
www.multnomah.net/damascusjourney

Faith on the Frontier:
AL & JOANNA LACY'S

𝓜AIL 𝓞RDER 𝓑RIDE 𝓢ERIES

Have You Read
AL LACY'S

ANGEL of MERCY SERIES